The PC Internet Tour Guide™

The PC Internet Tour Guide™
Cruising the Internet the Easy Way

Michael Fraase

VENTANA
PRESS

The PC Internet Tour Guide™: Cruising the Internet the Easy Way
Copyright © 1994 by Michael Fraase

Library of Congress Cataloging-in-Publication Data
Fraase, Michael.
    The PC Internet tour guide : cruising the Internet the easy way /
Michael Fraase. -- 1st ed.
      p.   cm.
    Includes bibliographical references and index.
    ISBN 1-56604-084-1
    1. Internet (Computer network) I. Title.
TK5105.875.I57F57 1993
004.6'7--dc20
                                93-41603
                                CIP

Book design: Karen Wysocki
Cover design and icons: John Nedwidek, emDesign
Technical review: Darren A. Rousseau
Editorial staff: Diana Merelman, Ruffin Prevost, Pam Richardson, Jessica Ryan
Production staff: Terri March, Midgard Productions, Marcia Webb
Proofreader: Mesa Somer

First Edition 9 8 7 6 5 4 3 2 1
Printed in the United States of America

Ventana Press, Inc.
P.O. Box 2468
Chapel Hill, NC 27515
919/942-0220
FAX 919/942-1140

Limits of Liability and Disclaimer of Warranty
The author and publisher of this book have used their best efforts in preparing the book and the programs contained in it. These efforts include the development, research and testing of the theories and programs to determine their effectiveness. The author and publisher make no warranty of any kind, expressed or implied, with regard to these programs or the documentation contained in this book.

The author and publisher shall not be liable in the event of incidental or consequential damages in connection with, or arising out of, the furnishing, performance or use of the programs, associated instructions and/or claims of productivity gains.

# Trademarks

Trademarked names appear throughout this book. Rather than list the names and entities that own the trademarks or insert a trademark symbol with each mention of the trademarked name, the publisher states that it is using the names only for editorial purposes and to the benefit of the trademark owner with no intention of infringing upon that trademark.

About the Author

Michael Fraase is the proprietor of Arts & Farces, a multifaceted communications and professional services business specializing in hypermedia production, technical writing, desktop/electronic publishing, general consulting and software interface design.

Fraase is the author of numerous books, including the three-volume *Macintosh Hypermedia* series (ScottForesman, 1990–1991), *Farallon's MediaTracks* (Business One Irwin, 1991), *Groupware for the Macintosh* (Business One Irwin, 1991), *Structured Publishing From the Desktop: Frame Technology's FrameMaker* (Business One Irwin, 1992), the 15-volume *Rapid Reference Series* (Business One Irwin, 1992–1993) and *The Mac Internet Tour Guide* (Ventana Press, 1993).

Michael Fraase, proprietor
Arts & Farces
2285 Stewart Avenue
Suite 1315
Saint Paul, MN 55116
mfraase@farces.com

Acknowledgments

While the task of writing is a solitary one, the act of creating a book isn't. Thanks to everyone at Ventana Press for again proving what I suspected: small publishers can make a Big Difference.

I didn't want to do this book; I'm a Mac user and was brought kicking and screaming into the world of MS-DOS. Thanks to Joe Woodman for seeing the potential in this project and for helping me see it as well.

Thanks especially to Elizabeth Woodman for her unseen editing hand in this book as well as in *The Mac Internet Tour Guide*.

Thanks to Pam Richardson for routing and scheduling everything.

Thanks to Diane Lennox for publicity and promotion.

Thanks to Fran Phillips and Jamie Jaeger for sales.

Thanks to Karen Wysocki for the interior page design and to Marcia Webb for managing a feverish production schedule.

Thanks to Midgard Productions for the desktop publishing.

Thanks to John Nedwidek, of emDesign for the cover design and icons. Everyone who's seen the cover has had the same reaction: "Wow! That's really neat…. I like it…." then a sideways glance and "Do you like it?" Anyone who can evoke that kind of reaction is doing something right.

Thanks to Dennis Fazio and Dave Bergum at Minnesota Regional Network (MRNet) for support and advice on all things Internet.

A big thanks to Ruffin Prevost, my editor. Writers' nightmares are populated with bad editors. Ruffin is the exception that proves the rule; he's a real writer's editor, and approached this project as a true collaboration. Ruffin made this a better book with a reasoned, even hand. The world would be a better place if there were more editors like Ruffin.

Finally, thanks again to my wife, Karen Caldwell Fraase, for putting up with inhumane deadline pressures with style and grace.

About the Images in this Book

The graphic images shown on the opening pages of each chapter of *The PC Internet Tour Guide* are from the OTIS ("The Operative Term is STIMULATE") Project. OTIS is an electronic art gallery containing hundreds of images and animations. According to OTIS Project founder, Ed Stastny, OTIS exists "to distribute original creative images over the world's computer networks for public perusal, scrutiny, and retransmission, and to facilitate communication, inspiration, critique, and to set the foundations for digital immortality."

According to Stastny, "The basic idea behind 'digital immortality' is that computer networks are here to stay and that anything interesting you deposit on them will be around for near-forever. The images of today will be the artifacts of an information-laded future. Perhaps the images will be converted into newer formats when the current formats become obsolete—perhaps only surviving on forgotten backup reels—but they'll be there, and someone will dig them up. Data-archeologists sifting through the cobwebs of an old storage room."

The OTIS Project is currently accessible by anonymous FTP at three sites:

- no-name-broadband.med.umich.edu in the /projects/otis/ directory
- sunsite.unc.edu in the /pub/multimedia/pictures/OTIS/ directory
- aql.gatech.edu in the /pub/OTIS/ directory

For more information about the OTIS Project, contact:

OTIS Project
Ed Stastny
P.O. Box 241113   ed@cwis.unomaha.edu
Omaha, NE 68124   ed@sunsite.unc.edu

A special thanks goes out to those OTIS artists who generously allowed us to reproduce their images. Thanks to: Ed Stastny (Information Web, Chapter 1; VR2, Chapter 5; ©1993 Ed Stastny, used with permission); Tom Nawara (Stigmata, Chapter 2; Eye See U, Chapter 8; ©1993 Tom Nawara, used with permission); Michael Maier (Future Culture, Chapter 3; ©1993 Michael Maier, used with permission); David Anjo (No Roof, Chapter 4; ©1993 David Anjo, used with permission); Barrett Ryker (Fractal Moon, Chapter 6; Castle Spirit, Chapter 7; ©1993 Barrett Ryker, used with permission).

Contents

Getting Connected 15

Network Infrastructure 39

Electronic Mail 53

Appendix A

# Introduction

These are the days of lasers in the jungle
Lasers in the jungle somewhere
Staccato signals of constant information…
—Paul Simon

Part of the experience of using a PC connected to other computers is a sense that there's a collection of actual places behind the screen—places you can't see, but know are in there. Or, rather, out there. This feeling really hit home for me when I saw a photo a friend used to replace his usual Macintosh desktop pattern. (This was before you could do similar tricks with PCs running Windows.) It showed his face and hands scrunched up against a window pane, creating the illusion of someone *out there* trying to get *in here*. If you've ever used your PC to connect to another computer—either by network or modem—you know this experience, and you know it's real. Tapping into the Internet not only confirms, but *validates*, this feeling.

These days it's hip to call this collection of not-quite-real places *cyberspace*. Cyberspace is a term created by William Gibson in his novel, *Neuromancer*, to represent a universe sustained by a vast network of computers and telecommunications lines.

> People jacked in so they could hustle. Put the trodes on and they were out there, all the data in the world stacked up like one big neon city, so you could cruise around and have a kind of grip on it, visually anyway, because if you didn't, it was too complicated, trying to find your way to a particular piece of data you needed.
> —William Gibson from *Neuromancer*

But cyberspace isn't some wild future dream; it's here now. John Perry Barlow—sometimes Wyoming cattle rancher and sometimes lyricist for the Grateful Dead—describes cyberspace as where you are when you are on the telephone. Think about that for a minute—and then realize that cyberspace is also where your bank accounts, credit history and tax records are. And in the near future, cyberspace is also likely to be where you earn a good portion of your income.

This book is about the Internet—a vast computer network of many component networks. Think of it as a web. Think of it as the first *really real* cyberspace.

For too many years the Internet has been the playground of propeller-heads and spooks, inaccessible to mere mortals. But lately, the Internet has changed, becoming a critical tool for millions of computer users. Powerful but simple software tools have made the Net accessible to practically anyone. And that's what this book is all about: making the Internet as friendly and familiar as everything else you do with your PC.

Explosive Growth

The past few years have seen the Internet expand at an astonishing rate. Individuals and businesses are rushing to the Internet in droves for a good reason: it's an invaluable resource for anyone who works with information. Its power and potential are practically limitless. Just a few of the most popular features of the Internet include:

▨ **Electronic mail**. Send electronic mail (e-mail) to virtually any networked computer user. Internet e-mail reaches its destination—practically anywhere on the planet—in a matter of minutes.

▨ **Network news**. Participate in a wide variety of electronic discussion groups on just about any topic you can think of. There are literally thousands of in-depth discussions on topics ranging from the essential to the arcane. Molecular biology, politics, comic books, the stock market, computers and practically anything else you can think of are all covered in the Internet's network news.

▨ **File transfer**. Transfer any kind of file between your computer and any other computer on the Internet. The Internet boasts the largest collection of MS-DOS software and shareware in the world, and its libraries are growing at an unprecedented rate every minute of every day.

▨ **Information browsing**. You can browse through a never-ending collection of information resources available throughout the Internet. Weather reports, electronic information databases and electronic journals (and much more) are available—free to anyone with access to the Internet.

Who Can Use The PC Internet Tour Guide?

If you use a PC and already have Internet access, or if you're interested in obtaining Internet access in the future, this book is for you. If you subscribe to one of the commercial information services (such as CompuServe or America Online), you can use this book for exchanging electronic mail with Internet users, subscribing to mailing lists and retrieving files available on the Internet by electronic mail.

This *Tour Guide* is written for Internet newcomers. No knowledge of the Internet is assumed (although experienced Internet users are sure to find plenty of interest here as well). I do assume, however, that you're comfortable finding your way around a PC. You should be able to copy files from a floppy to your hard drive, launch application programs, work with AUTOEXEC.BAT files and connect peripherals to your PC. If you haven't yet mastered these simple skills, don't despair. A couple of hours with your PC manuals (or a beginning PC tutorial) will bring you up to speed.

Although the *Tour Guide* will help you navigate the Internet and lead you through its vast resources, regardless of what hardware or software you have, you'll need a few things in order to get the most out of this book:

- An IBM PC or compatible with at least 640kb of RAM.

- An Internet account (or an account on one of the commercial information services if you want to exchange electronic mail with Internet users).

- An appropriate network connection. To make the most of the tools and techniques discussed in this book, you should have a SLIP or PPP connection or direct connection to the Internet. If you have a dial-up connection, you will find many of the tips and resources useful, but you won't be able to make full use of the companion software.

- The floppy disk that comes with this book.

If some of this sounds Greek to you, don't despair. Information on joining the Internet can be found throughout these pages, with specifics in Chapter 2, "Getting Connected."

The PC Internet Tour Guide will not only show you the most fascinating and helpful places on the Internet, it will also give you the tools and techniques you need to navigate the vast landscape of information out there. The software on the enclosed companion disk will bring new power and simplicity to everything you do on the Internet. Best of all, every detail of configuring and using the companion software is discussed in detail throughout the book—using real-world examples to show you how to get the most out of your time on the Net. Here's a brief look at what you'll find inside the *Tour Guide*:

What's Inside

Chapter 1: **What is the Internet?** (And Why Should I Use It?) covers network benefits for the average user and provides a general overview of the Internet for beginners. It also includes information about the history, growth and future of the Internet.

Chapter 2: **Getting Connected** (The Big Plug-In) provides information for all different types of users about how to physically connect to the Internet. If you work for a mid-sized or large organization, you may want to talk with your system administrator; you may already have an Internet account and not even know it. If you're with a smaller firm, or simply an individual looking to "plug in," this chapter also covers the basics of the various kinds of Internet connections.

Chapter 3: **Networking Infrastructure** (Electronic Alphabet Soup) offers a background on how the Internet is organized, what you need to know about networking protocols and the parts of an Internet address. We'll also go over some basic information about being a good Internet citizen. This chapter is a must-read before venturing out into the Net— it will make future chapters easier to understand.

Chapter 4: **Electronic Mail** (The Pony Express Goes Digital) covers everything you need to know about sending, receiving and replying to electronic mail (e-mail). You'll learn how to send e-mail from the Internet to virtually any other networked computer. You'll also learn how to use Minuet (an invaluable e-mail program included on the companion disk). Finally, you'll also learn how to find addresses, participate in mailing lists, and send and receive attached files with your e-mail messages.

Chapter 5: **Network News & Newsgroups** (Broadsheets of the Broadband) offers information on reading, posting and replying to the tens of thousands of news articles available via the Internet. This chapter shows you how to quickly and effectively browse, track and search newsgroups and articles using Trumpet (a program you'll download as part of a step-by-step tutorial). A brief discussion of posting etiquette and a general overview of available newsgroups are also provided.

Chapter 6: **Transferring Files** (The Mother Downlode) provides complete instructions for using the File Transfer Protocol (FTP) for downloading and uploading files on any of the thousands of publicly accessible file archives on the Net. We'll also cover the basics of computer viruses and how to use the popular SCAN antivirus shareware program.

Chapter 7: **Using Gopher** (Burrowing for Information) covers the details of using the powerful and user-friendly Gopher software to browse information resources and download files on any Gopher server on the Internet. Information on creating and sharing Gopher bookmarks (electronic crumb trails through vast amounts of information) is also included.

Chapter 8: **Other Internet Resources** (Geez, what is all this stuff?) offers information on various Internet resources, both human and electronic. Just as the Internet promises something for everyone, so will this eclectic chapter. The Electronic Frontier Foundation (EFF) and Internet Society, for instance, are bountiful organizations that provide a wealth of information for Internet users at any level of expertise. This chapter also includes information about relatively "minor" or esoteric Internet services that sometimes get overlooked, including time- and money-saving gems like: knowbots, Netfind, Network Information Centers, Finger, the Internet Business Pages, Archie, RFCs, FAQs and the World Wide Web (WWW). This chapter also features an overview of dozens of other fascinating information sources.

A complete glossary, bibliography and index are also included in the last sections of the book.

But perhaps the best thing about *The PC Internet Tour Guide* is that you can't get lost or left behind—just follow along at your own pace. Everything is covered in simple, step-by-step detail. Even if you've never used the Internet before, you'll find the software and instructions in this *Tour Guide* as easy to use as all your other favorite DOS applications.

Everything you need to connect to the Internet—via SLIP or direct Internet access—is included on the disk that comes with this book. Minuet is an integrated program that provides Internet electronic mail, file transfer, network news, Gopher, TELNET and directory services. UMSLIP is a program that allows you to establish a SLIP connection to the Net with a modem over ordinary telephone lines.

And to keep the trip interesting, our tour will take frequent sidetrips to visit some of the most fascinating people, places and resources throughout the Internet. Keep an eye out for these "scenic route sidebars"—they'll feature people profiles, file reviews, resources listings and fun and intriguing examples of the kinds of information you'll find (by chance or design) as you cruise the Internet (for more details on sidebars, see Chapter 1, page 3).

So forget what you've heard about how complicated and frustrating the Internet can be. With the right software and a few pointers from a pro, it's a lot easier than you think—in fact, it's actually fun. Hop aboard, our tour is about to begin!

Michael Fraase
Saint Paul, Minnesota
September 1993

CHAPTER 1

WHAT IS THE INTERNET?
And Why Should I Use It?

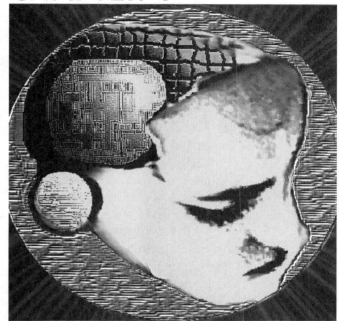

Imagine downloading Dante's *Inferno* from a computer in Massachusetts or California, just as quickly as if you were copying the file from a floppy disk. Imagine corresponding with anyone on almost a billion different computers, anywhere in the world, as easily as typing a letter with a word processor. Imagine reading the latest news practically as soon as it's written, or cruising through a web of connected computer networks and information resources so vast that no one knows for sure how big it is, or how many people it reaches.

Need to know what the weather is like for your trip to New England this weekend? No problem—weather reports and even weather maps are only a few mouse clicks away. Want to find out who wrote a particular book or article? You don't even have to leave your chair to browse the holdings of the Library of Congress. This isn't a scenario from some commercial for a futuristic telephone company or a guess at what television will be like in the year 2050. This is a snapshot of the Internet as it exists *right now*.

It's Easier Than You Think

Forget everything you've heard about how complicated it is to use the Internet. Tools with a DOS interface are available for just about every Internet service. You don't need to know any arcane UNIX commands or have an office next-door to a mainframe computer. The myth is still there, but it's all smoke and no fire. Oh, sure, you can still plod around the Net the hard way, pecking out abbreviated gibberish on your keyboard like so much secret code. But there's a much easier and more powerful way to cruise the Internet—one that will make your time online more fun and more productive—and that's what this book and its companion software tools are all about.

I grew up in cities when I was a kid, and my cousins all grew up on farms in the country. Whenever I went to visit, they would tease me because I didn't know much about driving a tractor, saddling a horse or tossing a cowpie. I couldn't tease them about not knowing how to play stickball or dodge traffic because I was on their turf—my city experiences weren't relevant. It's sort of like that on the Internet, but the turf is common to everyone. If the UNIX fans and command-line aficionados want to pump water by hand, that's fine. Since your PC is capable of using a host of powerful software tools to make navigating the Net a breeze, you can just smile at the water-pumpers politely while you turn on your PC faucet.

The main reason my country cousins teased me was because I wasn't familiar with their turf. I didn't have a tour guide or a map of the territory. The same is true for new Internet users. It's a daunting task to navigate new terrain without a guide to point out the landmarks.

This book is a tour guide to the Internet, designed to provide you with the tools and information you need to effectively navigate its vast information resources. You'll also find step-by-step tutorials for using a wide array of DOS software tools that help you effectively communicate with people and travel to both the "cities" and the "rural areas" that make up this vast information resource. In fact, many of these tools are included on *The PC Internet Tour Guide Companion Disk.*

Finding Your Way Around

Also included in our *Tour Guide* are what information designers and cartographers humbly call *wayfinding elements*, little signs that help you find locations of interest. Being a computer user, you'll know them simply as icons. Look for these four icons for interesting landmarks and tidbits of information.

People profiles are snapshots of how real people use the Internet. These are the true stories of real people, not techno-nerds. With luck, these vignettes will stimulate you to use the Internet in ways you may have never thought of. Look for them to provide insight about the general workings of the Internet, not necessarily relevant to the surrounding text.

Software reviews are brief overviews of some of the best public domain, freeware and shareware software programs available on the Internet. Because space is limited, only the best or most interesting software is mentioned. The archive location and pathname for each program is also provided. All of the programs mentioned can be downloaded to your computer using FTP. (For information on FTP, see Chapter 6, "Transferring Files.")

Hot spots and cool resources are short descriptions of both the most popular and the more offbeat information resources available on the Internet. Complete connection information is provided. These resources usually require you to use a specific software program or Internet client for access. Refer to the appropriate chapter for more information on using the right software tool for the job. Any passwords required to access these resources are provided in the sidebar.

Found text excerpts are brief passages of network news exchanges, electronic mailing list information, amusing conversations, general tips and tricks, and other information morsels that may not fit within the context of a chapter, but are interesting nonetheless.

Cruising the Easy Way

Neal Cassady was one of the most tenacious drivers of his generation. He'd think nothing of hopping in a Buick and driving Jack Kerouac coast to coast—stopping only for gas—with just a hip flask and a pack of smokes. Cassady was a pretty lousy guide though, especially when he was trundling along in the big Merry Prankster bus, Further, on one of Ken Kesey's intrepid trips.

This book is a tour guide of the Internet, but my pace is a little less frantic than Cassady's (then again, I'm still alive). Since getting there is half the fun, we'll be making frequent stops to wander the nooks and crannies of cyberspace. And the great thing about this bus trip is that, although I'm driving, you can take things at your own pace. If you're anxious to get moving, you can bail out and catch up with the group at the next stop. If you're a slow starter, you can slow things down to a more leisurely pace. So, before we leave the station, let's take a couple minutes to check the map and itinerary for a quick overview of where we're headed and what we'll see.

A Sense of Place

People often describe the Internet as a worldwide network of computer networks. That's as good a description as anything I can come up with, but the experience of using the Internet—*being in the Net*—is something completely different. For instance, when I login to the simple local area network in my office, I'm pretty certain of what I'll find there; it doesn't really feel like a place. Instead it's sort of like insipid American hotel chains. There's hardly ever anything different—never a surprise—the same bedspreads, brown Formica, loud air conditioner and view of the interstate.

But when I login to the Internet, it feels like a real place, just as real as the bar on the corner or the deli down the street. There's always something new to explore, and usually an interesting message or two in my e-mail box. And you can no more explore the entire Internet than you could visit every country on the globe. Things change too quickly and dramatically for you to ever become bored.

In this chapter, we'll take a look at what the Internet is, what kinds of information it contains, and how you can use that information to your advantage. We'll also explore a little of the history of the Internet, and speculate about what the future might hold for network users. But best of all, we'll take a look at the places, people and things you'll discover on your tour through the Net.

If you're already familiar with the Internet and how it works, or if you're just anxious to get connected and start exploring, you may want to skip ahead to Chapter 2, "Getting Connected."

Internet Benefits for the Average User

The Internet is much more than a network of networks. It's also much more than a huge repository of information. The Internet is a virtual community, existing only ephemerally in physical reality. While all this philosophical mumbo jumbo is a great mental exercise—something interesting to think about while you're waiting in the dentist's office or the airport—it probably doesn't have much impact on your daily life.

But the Internet provides several very real benefits that can have an enormous impact on your daily life:

- **Electronic mail**. You can use the Internet to send electronic mail (e-mail) to virtually any networked computer user on the planet. Traditional post office mail ("snail mail" or "the paper net" to e-mail users) may take several days to reach its destination. Internet e-mail can be delivered anywhere on the planet in a matter of minutes, or at most, a few hours. I used e-mail to correspond with my editor (who is also on the Internet), sending chapters back and forth during the entire writing cycle of this book. When the manuscript was finished, I used e-mail to correspond with the publisher's marketing and publicity staff—and they weren't even on the Internet.

- **Network news**. You can participate in a wide variety of electronic discussion groups on just about any topic imaginable, from investment strategies to molecular biology, from comic books to politics. If you can think of a topic that isn't already represented by a *newsgroup*, you can start your own. As of the fall of 1993, there were more than 4,000 active newsgroups accessible through the Internet. That number continues to grow steadily, and there are hundreds of additional commercial newsgroups that are available for a fee. As I was writing this book, Microsoft announced its intent to open a publicly accessible FTP server. This bit of news, accompanied by discussion and analysis, was posted to several network newsgroups and electronic mailing lists within a few minutes of its announcement—days ahead of the trade press. Similarly, when the Clinton administration voiced its support for the Clipper encryption chip, lively and informative discussions on all sides of the issue were taking place in various newsgroups and mailing lists within minutes of the announcement.

■ **File transfer**. You can use the Internet's standard protocols to transfer computer files between your PC and just about any other computer on the Internet. It doesn't matter where the other computer is located, how it's attached to the network or even if it uses the same operating system as yours. You can just as easily download a file from a UNIX-based mainframe in Tokyo as you can copy it from another PC in the next room.

■ **Information browsing**. You can use specialized software tools to browse through an almost limitless collection of information resources. Everything from weather reports and electronic journals to university and government databases is available. Shortly after I began work on this book, for example, the Clinton administration made its plan to reinvent government available on the Internet. And that's just the beginning of what the Internet has to offer. As you explore, you'll discover people, places and other resources that will become invaluable to you. Because of its size, depth and diversity, the Internet can truly be all things to all people. But if you're new to the Net, you may be still wondering exactly what it *is*. The answer is at the same time simple and complicated. And the Internet changes so quickly, it's become something of a moving target—like a lemon seed on your kitchen counter—just when you think you have it in your grasp, it slips away.

A General Overview of the Internet

If you're a technophobe and don't much care about how things work, feel free to skip this section. It contains information about the plumbing of the Internet, and you can always read it later.

The Internet is a collection of various computer networks, linked together and communicating by a common protocol known as TCP/IP (Transmission Control Protocol/Internet Protocol). Because every computer on the Internet agrees to communicate using this protocol, it doesn't matter what kinds of computers you travel to, or even what operating system they are running.

In order for your PC to communicate with other computers using TCP/IP, you must have the appropriate TCP/IP software installed and properly configured. This process is discussed in more detail in the next chapter.

Although most of the computers that are connected to the Internet run some form of UNIX (the software that controls the computers), as a DOS user, you don't need to know one whit about UNIX. Though it probably wouldn't kill you to know a little UNIX, it's important to understand that, for the purposes of basic Internet activity, you don't need to know anything about UNIX—especially if you follow the advice and step-by-step instructions in this book.

The Internet is often defined as that group of computer networks that cooperatively form a seamless network using TCP/IP. But what about those computer systems that don't use TCP/IP but appear to be part of the Internet? For example, I can send electronic mail and even file enclosures from my Internet account to any user on MCI Mail. Yet MCI Mail's computers technically aren't on the Internet. MCI Mail maintains a *gateway* that's used to transfer electronic mail between their computers and the Internet. So, if you have an MCI Mail account, you can be reached from the Internet even though you don't have a computer on the Internet.

Internet Governance

Consensual anarchy best describes the governance of the Internet. While the individual networks that make up the Internet are likely to have executive officers, there's no such person running the entire Internet. The closest thing to an absolute governing authority is the Internet Society. The Internet Society is a group of volunteers whose charter is to promote the exchange of information using Internet technology. The Internet Society appoints a subgroup, the Internet Architecture Board, that authorizes standards and allocates and keeps track of Internet resources (such as unique computer addresses). Another volunteer group, the Internet Engineering Task Force, handles acute operational and technical problems.

If you've ever driven in Paris, you'll understand this notion of consensual anarchy. The French have traffic lights, but they don't pay much attention to them. The traffic sort of develops a rhythm of its own without regard to the traffic lights. Drivers take account of the weather, the time of day, the number of vehicles, but not the traffic lights. If you come to a dead stop at a red light in Paris, people will honk their horns and shout silly sounding French epithets at you. It's hard for an American mind to grasp a situation where there's a sense of everyone doing the right thing without external rules or order. But that's the way it is with the Internet. There are only two "rules" for life on the Internet, and they're unwritten:

- Don't waste bandwidth.

- Don't do anything that threatens the Net.

You can do just about anything you like on the Internet, so long as you keep these two guidelines in mind. Would that the rest of life were as easy.

Each member network maintains its own Network Operations Center. These centers communicate with each other and arrive at a consensus on how to facilitate communications and resolve problems.

Since the Internet doesn't really exist in physical reality, there's nowhere to send a check for access. Each of the component networks that make up the Internet pays for its own operations. I send payment for my organization's connection to a regional network, which in turn pays a national provider for its connection. In theory, everyone on the Internet pays for his or her share, and in practice, this actually works amazingly well.

A Brief History of the Internet

The Internet began in the early 1970s as a U.S. Defense Department network called ARPAnet. The ARPAnet was originally implemented to support military research about how to build networks that could withstand partial outages and still function properly.

This network design approach assumed that the network itself was unreliable—a very realistic approach in hindsight, bomb attacks notwithstanding. Because the original ARPAnet model called for all communication to occur between two computers directly, any segment of the network could suffer an outage and the communication would still take place using any available alternative route across the network. The *computers* on the network—rather than the *network* itself—were responsible for correctly addressing and verifying communications. In network lingo, this is called *peer-to-peer* networking.

All that was needed for two computers to communicate on the ARPAnet was a message enclosed in a standard envelope—called an Internet Protocol (IP) packet—with a correct "address" for the destination computer.

In the early 1980s, Ethernet-based local area networks were developed. Most of the workstations that made up a local area network (LAN) in the early 1980s ran the UNIX operating system. The UNIX operating system came with IP networking capabilities built-in. Organizations using these workstations wanted to connect their LANs to the ARPAnet, rather than connecting to one large timesharing computer at each site. Since all of the networks were speaking IP, the benefits of enabling users on one network to communicate with those on any other network became obvious.

In the late 1980s, the National Science Foundation (NSF) created five regional supercomputer centers, making the resources of the world's fastest computers available for academic research. Because the supercomputer centers were so expensive, only five could be created and the resources were to be shared. A communications problem became immediately apparent: researchers and administrators at the different supercomputer sites needed to connect their centers together and also had to provide access for their clients. The ARPAnet seemed to be the solution to the communications problem, but it was abandoned, mostly because of bureaucratic problems.

The NSF built its own network—NSFNET— based on the ARPAnet's IP technology, with connections running at 56,000 bits per second (56 kbps) over special telephone lines. This kind of connection was capable of sending about two pages per second to be transferred across the network—slow by today's standards. Because these special telephone lines were expensive (the telephone companies charge for these lines by the mile) the NSF decided to create regional networks, allowing sites to connect to their nearest neighbor, in daisy chain fashion. Each daisy chain was connected to one of the regional supercomputer centers, and the centers themselves were linked together. This strategy allowed any computer to communicate with any other computer by passing messages up and down the daisy chain.

This strategy was successful—too successful, actually, and the network quickly became overloaded when the researchers discovered that the network was also useful for sharing resources not directly related to the supercomputer centers. In 1987, Merit Network Inc. received a contract to maintain and upgrade the network. Merit, in conjunction with IBM and MCI, ran Michigan's educational network. The original NSF network was replaced with telephone lines that were 20 times faster, and quicker computers were also installed. The network was subsequently opened to most academic researchers, government employees and contractors. Access was extended to international research organizations in countries that were allies of the United States.

In the early 1990s the network was opened up to a few large commercial sites, and international Internet access has also started expanding rapidly.

Today, the Internet is a collection of high-speed networks composed of the national backbone network provided by the National Science Foundation and a hierarchy of more than 5,000 attached regional, state, federal agency, campus and corporate networks. Links to networks in Canada, Europe, Japan, Australia, Central America and South America are in place. There are more than 750,000 computers and workstations of various sizes connected to the Internet with millions of users. Even the U.S. research station in Antartica has an Internet connection.

The Future of the Internet

The Internet is growing at a rate of about 10 percent per month as more colleges, universities and businesses come online. As of April 1992, observers estimated the total Internet population at somewhere between 7 million and 14 million people. The future of the Internet lies in three key areas: *commercialization, privatization* and *bandwidth.*

Commercialization

Lots of large multinational corporations have been on the Internet for years, although their access has been limited to research and engineering departments.

Corporations have recently discovered how expensive running multiple networks can be and have begun to look for ways to consolidate their separate networks. Many have discovered that the Internet is at least part of the answer to their problems. In 1992, many of the restrictions on commercial use of the Net began to change. In fact, there are already more commercial sites on the Internet than educational and research sites combined.

Privatization

Internet proponents have always wanted the various telephone companies—or other commercial organizations—to provide Internet connections. They claim you should be able to order an Internet connection just like you order call waiting or a second line for your telephone service. The telephone companies haven't jumped on this idea right away, but the recent corporate interest in the Internet has not gone unheeded, and this attitude is (slowly) changing.

But before the Internet can be fully privatized, users must find a method for funding the connections that are already in place. As soon as enough small businesses and individuals—the driving force of our economy—decide that connection to the Internet is an important asset, privatization of the Internet will occur very quickly.

One of the short-term changes likely to be brought about by commercialization and privatization is that transactions will become commonplace on the Internet. You will soon be able to order and pay for software and information via e-mail. More important, people will actually begin to make their livings in cyberspace.

Bandwidth

Bandwidth is the range of transmission frequencies a network can use. What this means is that as bandwidth increases (which it will dramatically in the next few years), you can transfer *more* information *faster*.

Increasing available bandwidth will not necessarily change the way many people currently use the Internet, but it will improve certain aspects of the way we use it:

- Electronic mail will be richer in media type and benefit from faster delivery.
- File transfers will take much less time—a mere fraction of their current rate.
- Electronic publications—telepublications—will be richer in media type and benefit from faster delivery.
- Telecommuting (working from home via phone, fax and modem) will be more enjoyable and effective.
- Remote collaboration will become easier, more rewarding and more effective.

In short, the way we use and work with information will change drastically. More than ever before, information will take on new value and urgency, while at the same time becoming more accessible and available.

Moving On

This chapter has introduced you to the basic aspects of the Internet as well as its history and future. By now you're probably ready to get connected and see for yourself what the Internet is all about. Don't worry, we'll get there. But first, you should know how to establish an Internet account and learn a little bit about the mechanics of the Net. The next chapter explains how to establish your actual account on the Internet.

The road ahead is long and winding, and it's not without its pitfalls. But if you stick with the group and follow instructions, you're guaranteed to enjoy every second of the journey. Let's get started!

CHAPTER 2

GETTING CONNECTED
The Big Plug-In

Before actually
starting our tour of the Internet, we'll spend this chapter covering the
details of how to get connected. If you already have an Internet connection, you can probably skip all this and go straight to Chapter 3, "Network Infrastructure," where you'll learn about how the places and
pathways of the Internet are constructed and connected. Getting connected to the Internet traditionally has been either exceptionally easy or
almost impossible. If you're with a university, government agency or
corporation that already has computers connected to the Internet—or
"on the Net," as veteran netters say—your task is remarkably easy:
sweet-talk the folks in your computer support department to create an
account for you. It will take them less than 15 minutes, but they'll
probably tell you it will take anywhere from a few hours to a few
weeks. Don't argue; bite your tongue, smile pleasantly, thank them for
their time and efforts, and count your blessings—you are one of the
lucky few. If you're not part of an organization that's already on the
Net, don't worry; it's not nearly as hard to get connected as it was just a
few years ago.

Where to Sign Up

Because the Internet is not a single computer system—it's not even centrally managed—there is literally no "where" to sign up. For years it was nearly impossible to get connected to the Internet. Most people talked to a friend of a friend or found someone inside an organization who could provide them with a news and mail *feed*, sending packets of electronic mail and a limited number of newsgroups.

PGP v2.2 encryption software.

Encryption is an important way to assure privacy and authentication of e-mail messages. PGP v2.2 uses the non-NSA approved IDEA cipher patented in Switzerland.

You can download the current version of PGP by FTP at soda.berkeley.edu in the /pub/ directory.

In those days, when "real people" could only wheedle their way onto the Internet, there was always a feeling of dealing with an "information black market." People passed around secret tips and covert instructions for bluffing their way into getting an account on the sly. Invariably, these instructions were to approach a sympathetic librarian in the musty basement of the local university computer center and imply that you were either a student or on the faculty. (The feeling was always one of begging for an audience with a scribe in the Holy Roman catacomb.) If luck was with you, your account would be activated later that day, and you were off to explore the nether regions of the net, hoping nothing would go wrong and you wouldn't be found out.

These days, it's much easier. The following four sections provide general instructions about who to befriend and what arcane terms to utter so you'll sound like a seasoned expert. You'll be able to obtain your very own Internet connection, regardless of what type of user you are—academic, government, business or individual.

University Users

If you're a university user—faculty, staff or student—you're in luck. Chances are, your college or university is already directly connected to the Internet. Contact anyone in the computing center and ask them for—or perhaps tell them you *must have*—access to the Net. After you've been shuttled to the right person, he or she will probably ask you a series of questions like the ones shown in Table 2-1. Note that these questions are general in nature and the responses are merely examples, so your mileage will surely vary depending on your situation. But since half the game of getting the kind of Internet connection you want is just knowing what to ask for, the table shows you how to ask for the most and best of everything. If you sound like you know what you're talking about, most people will assume that you do. Don't worry about what it means; that's all explained later.

Table 2-1: University users Internet information.

They'll Ask:	Your Response:
Do you want a full or partial connection?	I need a connection to both my department's local area network, the campus wide area network and the Internet.
What kind of computer do you have?	I have a '486-based PC with 8mb of RAM running DOS 6.0.
Do you want a dedicated, SLIP/PPP, UUCP or dial-in connection?	Preferably both a dedicated and a SLIP/PPP connection. I have a second PC in my homeoffice, and I'd like to have a PPP or SLIP connection to the network.
Do you have an Ethernet card for your dedicated connection?	No, please install and configure one.
What speed modem do you need for your home office connection?	I need a V.32bis/V.42/V.42bis modem and the appropriate software to make the network connection.
Do you want a PPP or a SLIP connection?	I'd prefer a PPP connection.
What do you want for your username?	I'd like my username to be jsmith, which is my first initial and last name with no punctuation.

After all that, the odds are in your favor that you'll get at least some of what you asked for; and at this point you'll probably be scheduled to have your office computer network connection upgraded. Your account should be activated in a day or two. You will probably be given a packet of software, an instruction manual and the name, telephone number and e-mail address of your network administrator (often known as a "net ghod"). Most important, you'll probably get the telephone number of the campus help desk for any problems you have while using your Internet connection. That's it—you're now an Internet citizen.

Today's baseball schedule.
You can get today's schedule for any major league baseball team by TELNET to culine.colorado.edu port 862. Press the Return key for today's schedules. You'll be prompted to enter a team. Here are sample schedules for the Minnesota Twins and the Chicago Cubs:

MLB schedule for Minnesota on Wednesday, 5/12...

Minnesota at California

MLB schedule for Cubs on Wednesday, 5/12...

Los Angeles at Chicago

Government Users

If you work for a government agency, it's likely your agency is already connected to the Internet. Begin by asking your supervisor (or the appropriate computer techie) if your office has an Internet connection. He or she may not know, but will probably know someone who can help. The person responsible for maintaining Internet accounts within your agency may or may not be affiliated with your local office.

In any case, finding the right person to help set up your connection is probably the hardest part. The questions—and your responses—will likely be very similar to the ones shown in Table 2-1. It's not likely that you'll be able to request a dial-in connection—government agencies are fairly stingy with that type of connection, which is usually reserved for work-at-home types or people who travel extensively. But who knows, maybe you'll get lucky.

You'll probably have duplicate requisition forms to fill out, you may have to demonstrate that you have a direct need for an Internet account (a little creativity goes a long way here), and it will probably take you several attempts to fill out all the forms properly.

When your forms are correct and complete and your access has been authorized, someone will come and wire your computer for the network connection. This person will install a network card if necessary and provide you with software and an instruction manual. Here's an important tip: try to get the installer to test the connection for you. The installation person will also give you the name, telephone number and e-mail address of your local network administrator. You probably won't be provided with a help desk telephone number (but you can always call the nearest university help desk and try to sound professorial). You'll also be instructed where to report network problems. Once that's done, you're all set.

Business Users

Many large businesses—especially those involved with the computer industry—are old-timers when it comes to the Internet. Here you may find one person (or even a whole department) in charge of maintaining Internet connections. These are the people you want to seek out: ask your supervisor or refer to your corporate employee manual or inter-office directory. If you've been using a local area network within your department, ask the person who comes to fix your computer when it breaks or when the network goes down. (Odds are, they'll be so happy to hear from someone who isn't reporting a problem, they'll be happy to hook you up to the Net.)

The procedure for acquiring an Internet connection within most businesses usually falls somewhere between the looseness of a university connection and the structure of a government connection. You may be able to get a dial-in connection, depending on your organization and its corporate culture. But as a starting point, you should be able to use the responses from Table 2-1.

If the company you work for isn't on the Internet, you may have to look into opening an individual account on your own and seek reimbursement from the company (for more information on this approach, see "Individual Users" beginning on page 20). Alternatively, you may be able to generate enough interest within your workgroup or department to have management look into connecting existing local and wide area networks to the Internet.

Flame wars, affirmative action and babies (oh my!).

People love to carry out heated debates via the electronic messages they can post throughout the Internet. Here's a great "net.story" from Mikki Barry:

"In 1991, a huge flame war (a heated debate carried out via electronic messages) erupted over affirmative action in the soc.women newsgroup. The flames were exchanged for many months, tensions getting higher and higher. Not being one to let anyone else have the 'last word,' I helped fuel this war with my obviously eloquent articles, made increasingly virile through the evil hormones prevalent through late pregnancy. However, nobody on the net knew I was pregnant, since I was at work until the day I went into labor.

"Just as the flame war reached it's peak, however, I had the strange feeling that I wasn't going to be able to participate for awhile. So I posted a message saying, in effect, 'Sorry, I can't respond to this thread anymore. I have to go have a baby now.' Morgan Elizabeth Baumann was born later that night."

The procedure for establishing an Internet account varies widely from business to business. Some firms create an account for all new employees, while others offer accounts only to "critical" employees. In most medium and large businesses, there will be a help desk (or at least an MIS specialist) available if you have any questions or problems with your Internet account.

Individual Users

Unlike universities and large companies, individuals and small business users rarely need a full-time connection and are well served with only a dial-in connection. With a *dial-in* connection, you use your PC and a modem to dial another computer or server where your Internet account is stationed. This is less convenient (but usually cheaper) than a standard connection, where your computer is always connected directly to the Internet. For more information on the advantages and disadvantages of a dial-in connection, see "Types of Connections" beginning on page 21.

Individuals and small businesses typically have the hardest time establishing an Internet account. Until recently, the Internet has been geared for users within large organizations communicating only with users inside other large organizations. Thankfully, this is changing rapidly, and now it's fairly common to find individuals and small businesses with full Internet access.

The main difference in individuals and small businesses using the Internet is that *you (or your business) have to foot the complete bill for your account*. Needless to say, this affects the kind of connection and level of service you select. But Internet access is not nearly as expensive as it used to be and is now usually well within the means of most small businesses.

Take a quick look at the next two sections, "Types of Connections" and "Resource Requirements," before you jump in and order the most extensive Internet connection offered by your service provider. You run the risk of buying a fully loaded Cadillac with power windows, sunroof and Corinthian leather interior when a more sensible Saturn or even a VW microbus will do.

Types of Connections

This book assumes that your Internet connection is a "full" connection—one that includes electronic mail, TELNET, FTP, network news and all the other network niceties. "Partial" connections with only some of the features of a full connection are also available from some institutions and service providers, but they are not powerful enough to be of much use to the dedicated Internet cybernaut. With that understanding, there are only two types of individual or small business connections you need concern yourself with: a dedicated connection and a SLIP (Serial Line Internet Protocol) or PPP (Point-to-Point Protocol) connection.

Dedicated Connection

If you have a dedicated Internet connection, your computer—or the local area network to which your PC is connected—is directly connected to the Internet. These connections are most common for users within universities, government agencies and large corporations; they're usually too expensive for individuals and small businesses.

Dedicated connections offer three distinct advantages over SLIP or PPP connections:

- You can set up an FTP server, allowing anyone else on the Internet to access your files when it is most convenient for them (be careful, this can also be seen as a disadvantage in some organizations).

- You don't have to connect to the network each time you want to use it—you're always connected. Whenever you go, there you are.

- Your file transfers (and any other work you do on the Internet) will be accomplished much faster.

When you contract for a dedicated Internet connection, your service provider will lease a dedicated telephone line at the speed you specify and will install a *router* at your site. The faster the telephone line you specify, the more you'll pay.

The only disadvantage to a dedicated connection is that it's expensive; but like most everything else, you get what you pay for. If you need convenient, constant access or lightning-fast file transfer and data throughput, you won't be happy with anything less than a dedicated connection. But that performance comes at a great cost. As of 1993, a dedicated Internet connection would cost most small businesses between $15,000 and $20,000 for the first year and about $5,000 to $10,000 each subsequent year. Organizations with more than 50 employees pay fees tied more directly to their usage rates, but the average per-employee cost is as much or more than for small businesses.

SLIP & PPP Connection

Luckily, access to the Internet needn't cost several thousands of dollars. Using a modem, you can get most of the benefits of a dedicated connection at only a fraction of the cost. SLIP and PPP allow you to establish an Internet connection over standard telephone lines via high-speed modems. If you have a SLIP or PPP Internet connection, your PC is also directly connected to the Internet—*but only while the SLIP or PPP link is active.*

Although SLIP is currently the more common protocol, PPP will probably surpass SLIP in the near future. PPP offers more features and better throughput during interactive sessions where small bits of information are passed in both directions. Additionally, PPP is a recognized Internet standard for transferring IP information over serial lines (SLIP isn't). If you're given a choice, you're better off to go with a PPP connection—it's the up-and-coming standard.

Fractint 18.2.

Fractint is an attractive, easy-to-use, fractal generator. The program allows you to create varied iterations of graphic images based on the concepts of fractal mathematics. You can download it by FTP from oak.oakland.edu in the /pub/msdos/graphics/ directory. The filename is FRAIN182.ZIP.

UMSLIP is available as freeware by anonymous FTP at boombox.micro.umn.edu in the /pub/slipdial/ directory. It's also on the companion disk that came with this book. (For information on using FTP, see "Using FTP to Transfer Files" beginning on page 151.)

UMSLIP is a complete SLIP and modem dialing program that sets your modem, dials into a SLIP server and automatically performs the SLIP login process.

SLIP or PPP connections lack many of the features of a dedicated connection:

- Because you're using a modem rather than a direct network connection, getting files from here to there (and back again) takes significantly longer over a SLIP or PPP connection than with a dedicated connection.

- You cannot offer a reliable, constant FTP archive, so other users can't directly access your files at any time.

- Your connection to the Internet is active only while the modem connection is active; when you hang up the modem, you are no longer on the Internet.

- The connection isn't fast enough to support more than two or three users.

- You have to pay for at least one high-speed modem.

The biggest advantages to a SLIP or PPP connection is that you pay much lower connection costs. And unlike a less-powerful dial-in connection, you are actually on the Internet while the connection is active. With the exception of offering a full-time FTP archive (something most individuals and small businesses would have limited use for anyway), you can do anything on the Internet with a SLIP or PPP connection that you can do with a dedicated connection at a literal fraction of the cost.

As of summer 1993, an individual commercial user can get SLIP or PPP access for a one-time startup fee of about $150 and monthly charges of about $65 for 80 hours of service. If you use more than 80 hours of connect time per month, you can expect to pay about $2 per hour for each additional hour. SLIP or PPP access is usually the best alternative for individuals and is the method I use to connect myself and my very small business to the Internet.

Other Types of Connections

You can dial in to gain access to the Internet if you have an account on a computer that has a dedicated connection to the Internet (a university mainframe, for instance). Dial-in access to another computer is not as useful, powerful or easy to use as a SLIP or PPP connection, but it's much easier (and usually cheaper—sometimes free) to set up. Unfortunately for PC users, dial-in access methods most often require you to use the archaic UNIX commands to traverse the Internet. And your dial-in connection may be limited to what Internet services you can use.

UUCP (UNIX-to-UNIX Copy Protocol) can also be considered as an alternative type of connection. Every UNIX system supports UUCP as a method of moving information across standard telephone lines. You can usually find a service provider or an existing UUCP site that will allow you to use UUCP to transfer Internet mail and network news to your PC—via a modem—but you won't really be "connected" to the Internet.

While this *Tour Guide* is geared for users with dedicated or SLIP/PPP connections, if you only have limited dial-in access, you'll still find much of the information on electronic mail, network news and other Internet resources highly useful.

Service Providers

The following table shows contact information for some of the major service providers in the United States.

Table 2-2: Internet service providers in the United States.

Service Provider	Region	Connections Offered
Advanced Networks and Services (ANS) 1875 Campus Commons Drive Reston, VA 22091 800/456-8267 info@ans.net	World	High-speed dedicated connections
BARRNET Pine Hall, Room 115 Stanford, CA 94305 415/723-3104 gd.why@forsythe.stanford.edu	San Francisco, Calif.	Dedicated connections; SLIP/PPP
CERFnet P.O. Box 85608 San Diego, CA 92186 800/876-2373 or 619/455-3900 help@cerf.net	Southern Calif.	Low- and medium-speed dedicated connections; SLIP/PPP
CICNET 2901 Hubbard Drive ITI Building, Pod A Ann Arbor, MI 48105 313/998-6103 info@cic.net	Midwest	Medium- and high-speed dedicated connections

Service Provider	Region	Connections Offered
Colorado Supernet Colorado School of Mines 1500 Illinois Street Golden, CO 80401 800/748-0800 info@csn.org	National	Low- and medium-speed dedicated connections; SLIP/PPP
CONCERT P.O. Box 12889 3021 Cornwallis Road Research Triangle Park, NC 27709 919/248-1999 jrr@concert.net	North Carolina	Medium-speed dedicated connections; SLIP/PPP
Express Access Digital Express Group 6006 Greenbelt Road, Suite 228 Greenbelt, MD 20770 301/220-2020 info@access.digex.net	Mid-Atlantic, California, Pennsylvania, Minnesota, Georgia, Illinois	Low- to high-speed dedicated connections, SLIP/PPP
JVNCnet Global Enterprise Services 3 Independence Way Princeton, NJ 08540 609/897-7300 market@jvnc.net	National	Low- and medium-speed dedicated connections; SLIP
Merit 2200 Bonisteel Boulevard Ann Arbor, MI 48109 313/764-9430 jogden@merit.edu	Michigan	Low- and high-speed dedicated connections; SLIP/PPP
MIDnet 29 WSEC University of Nebraska Lincoln, NE 68588 402/472-8971 dmf@westie.unl.edu	Lower Midwest	Low- and medium-speed dedicated connections
Minnesota Regional Network (MRNet) 511 11th Avenue South, Box 212 Minneapolis, MN 55415 612/342-2570 info@mr.net	Minnesota	Low- and medium-speed dedicated connections; SLIP

Service Provider	Region	Connections Offered
MSEN 628 Brooks Street Ann Arbor, MI 48103 313/998-4562 info@msen.com	Michigan	Low- and medium-speed dedicated connections; SLIP/PPP
BBN Systems and Technologies (NEARnet) 10 Moulton Street Cambridge, MA 02138 617/873-8730 nearnet-join@nic.near.net	New England	Low- to high-speed dedicated connections; SLIP/PPP
NETCOM On-Line Communication Services 4000 Moorpark Avenue Suite 209 San Jose, CA 95117 408/554-8649 info@netcom.com	National	Low- and medium-speed dedicated connections; SLIP/PPP
netIllinois Bradley University 1501 West Bradley Avenue Peoria, IL 61625 309/677-3100 joel@bradley.edu	Illinois	Low- and medium-speed dedicated connections
NorthWestNet 15400 SE 30th Place Suite 202 Bellevue, WA 98007 206/562-3000 info@nwnet.net	Pacific Northwest, Northern Plains, Alaska	Low- and medium-speed dedicated connections
NYSERNet 200 Elwood Davis Road Suite 103 Liverpool, NY 13088-6147 315/453-2912 luckett@nysernet.org	New York State; National	Low- and medium-speed dedicated connections; SLIP/PPP
OARnet 1224 Kinnear Road Columbus, OH 43212 614/292-9248 alison@oar.net	Ohio	Low- and medium-speed dedicated connections; SLIP/PPP

Service Provider	Region	Connections Offered
Performance Systems International (PSI) 11800 Sunrise Valley Drive, Suite 1100 Reston, VA 22019 703/620-6651 info@psi.com	World	Low- and medium-speed dedicated connections; SLIP/PPP
PREPnet 305 South Craig, 2nd Floor Pittsburgh, PA 15213 412/268-7870 twb+@andrew.cmu.edu	Pennsylvania	Low- and medium-speed dedicated connections; SLIP/PPP
PSCnet 4400 Fifth Avenue Pittsburgh, PA 15213 412/268-4960 hastings@psc.edu	National	Low- to high-speed dedicated connections
Sprint International 13221 Woodland Park Road Herndon, VA 22071 703/904-2156 mkiser@icm1.icp.net	World	Low- and medium-speed dedicated connections
SURAnet 8400 Baltimore Boulevard, Ste. 101 College Park, MD 20740 301/982-4600 info@sura.net	Southeast	Medium- and high-speed dedicated connections
THEnet Texas Higher Education NIC c/o UT System-Office of Telecommunication Services Service Building 319 Austin, TX 78712 512/471-2400 info@nic.the.net	Texas	Low- and medium-speed dedicated connections; SLIP
UUNET 3110 Fairview Park Drive, Suite 570 Falls Church, VA 22042 703/204-8000 info@uunet.uu.net	World	Low- and medium-speed dedicated connections; SLIP/PPP

Service Provider	Region	Connections Offered
VERnet Academic Computing Center, Gilmer Hall University of Virginia Charlottesville, VA 22903 804/924-0616 info@ver.net	Virginia	Low- and medium-speed dedicated connections
VNET Internet Access, Inc. 229 E. 8th Street Charlotte, NC 28202 704/374-0779 info@char.vnet.net	World	Low- to high-speed dedicated connections; SLIP/PPP
Westnet 601 South Howes, 6th Floor South Fort Collins, CO 80523 303/491-7260 pburns@yuma.acns.colostate.edu	West	Low- and medium-speed dedicated connections
WiscNet 1210 West Dayton Street Madison, WI 53706 608/262-8874 dorl@macc.wisc.edu	Wisconsin	Low- and medium-speed dedicated connections; SLIP/PPP

Resource Requirements

Hang on, you're almost there! Now that you know about the different types of available connections, and assuming you have an appropriate network connection, and your account has been activated, let's explore exactly what hardware and software resources are required to connect to the Internet.

IBM PC or Compatible

You'll need a PC of course. Almost any PC will do, although you'll be hard-pressed if your computer doesn't have a hard disk drive and at least 2mb of RAM. As in all things related to computers, you can never have too much hard drive space or memory.

Library of Congress Information System (LOCIS).

It's a great spectator sport to watch Congress in action, and you can do it if you have an IBM 3270-compatible terminal emulator. Telnet to locis.loc.gov and browse through the legislation that has been introduced.

Sometimes it's rather alarming:

OFFICIAL TITLE(S):

AS INTRODUCED: (DATA FURNISHED BY THE HOUSE)

A concurrent resolution stating that Congress supports the suspension, with respect to the leadership of Iraq, of the prohibition of Executive Order 12333 on assassinations until Iraq has complied fully with all United Nations Security Council resolutions concerning the withdrawal of Iraqi military forces from Kuwait.

COMMITTEE(S) OF REFERRAL: House Foreign Affairs

SUBCOMMITTEE(S) OF REFERRAL:

Hsc International Security and Scientific Affairs Hsc Europe and the Middle East

COSPONSOR:

Rep. Holloway

Rep. Solomon

Rep. Paxon

Rep. Inhofe

Rep. Santorum

Rep. Barton

Rep. Rohrabacher

Rep. Spence

Rep. Ravenel

Network Interface Card or Modem

You'll also need a way of connecting to the Internet: either a high-speed modem or a network interface card. If you're with a large organization, someone will probably install and configure your network card hardware for you. If you're on your own, simply refer to the instructions that came with the card.

If you plan to access the Internet by SLIP or PPP, use at least a V.32 (9600 baud) modem, although I'd highly recommend a V.32bis/V.42bis (14,400 baud) modem, assuming your service provider supports the higher speed (and most do).

Buying a modem is simple in theory but difficult in practice: purchase the modem supporting the fastest *standard* modulation protocol and the best error correction and data compression you can afford.

SLIP or PPP

If you're connecting to the Internet with either SLIP or PPP, you'll need the appropriate LAP (Link Access Protocol) driver. In most cases, your service provider or network administrator will configure and install this software for you. *If you have a dedicated Internet connection, you do not need either of these drivers*; you can skip the rest of this section and continue with "TCP/IP" (located below).

The University of Minnesota's SLIP program, UMSLIP, is available by anonymous FTP at boombox.micro.umn.edu in the /pub/slipdial/ directory. UMSLIP is also packaged as a component of the University of Minnesota's SLIPdial software, which is available in the same FTP archive. (For information on using FTP, see "Downloading Files With Minuet" beginning on page 152.)

TCP/IP

If you enjoy a direct connection to the Internet, you'll also need to install and properly configure TCP/IP, the software that allows your PC to communicate with other computers on the Net. If you're dying to know the technicalities of it all, this software enables your PC to use Transmission Control Protocol/Internet Protocol (TCP/IP) to communicate with available devices on the Internet.

If you're using UMSLIP to connect to the Internet, the translation capabilities are built into the SLIP software. There is no need to install or configure TCP/IP software for a SLIP connection on a PC.

Alice in Wonderland.

The complete text of *Alice in Wonderland* has been made available by Project Gutenberg. Project Gutenberg was formed to encourage the creation and distribution of electronic text.

You can download the complete text of this and other works by FTP at mrcnext.cso.uiuc.edu in the /etext/directory.

Client Application Software

Unless you're part of a large organization, getting a network connection and an account on the Internet is only half the battle. You'll also need some client application software (or software that lets you navigate and take advantage of the Internet). This can be something of a chicken-and-the-egg situation, since no such software is built into DOS or provided with your PC when you buy it. If you need a special program to transfer other software programs to your PC (*and you do*), how do you download a program that you need the program to download?

The PC Internet Tour Guide Companion Disk is the best place to start. The disk is packed with powerful programs and utilities for both *establishing* and *using* your Internet connection. The basic software needed for e-mail, directory services, network news, file transfers, Gopher and remote login is provided on the disk that comes with this book. In the next two sections, I'll discuss how to install and configure UMSLIP and Minuet. UMSLIP is the software that you use to establish your connection to the Internet, with a modem, over an ordinary telephone line. Minuet is an integrated program that provides an easy-to-use graphical interface for navigating the six major Internet services: e-mail, file transfer, network news, Gopher, TELNET and directory services. But this is just the beginning. Once you've installed and configured the companion software, I'll cover in step-by-step detail how to use all the powerful features of the companion software. Best of all, this *Tour Guide* also covers the high points of finding and using tons of other hot software available on the Internet.

Installing UMSLIP & Minuet

Installing the University of Minnesota's UMSLIP and Minuet software packages are straightforward and very simple. The SLIP software allows you to route Internet information over a standard telephone line with a modem. The Minuet—Minnesota Internet User's Essential Tools—software provides all the basic client services you need to access the Internet in a single program.

If you enjoy a direct connection to the Internet, there's no need for you to install UMSLIP; you can skip ahead to the "Installing Minuet" section below.

Installing UMSLIP

The University of Minnesota's UMSLIP software allows you to establish a high-speed remote connection to the Internet over the phone lines using only your PC and a modem. (Remember, if you have a direct Internet connection, skip to the next section; there's no need for you to install SLIP software.) To install UMSLIP:

1. At the command prompt, enter **mkdir c:\slip** and press **Enter** to create a directory, named \SLIP, at the root level of your hard disk. This book assumes that your hard disk is the C: drive.

2. Insert *The PC Internet Tour Guide* disk in your floppy drive. This book assumes that your floppy drive is the A: drive.

3. Enter **copy a:\sliparc.exe c:\slip\sliparc.exe** and press **Enter**. The self-extracting archive containing the SLIP software will be copied from the floppy disk to your hard drive's C:\SLIP directory.

4. Enter **cd c:\slip** and press **Enter**. The current directory will change to the C:\SLIP directory as reflected by the prompt.

5. Enter **sliparc** and press **Enter**. The contents of the self-extracting archive will be expanded within the C:\SLIP directory and the status of each extracted file will be displayed on the screen.

6. Optionally, enter **del sliparc.exe** and press **Enter** to delete the no-longer-needed self-extracting archive.

7. Add the C:\SLIP directory to the appropriate PATH statement in your AUTOEXEC.BAT file (**PATH = C:\SLIP**).

8. Reboot your computer.

Installing Minuet

The University of Minnesota's Minuet software is a powerful integrated package of tools for exploiting the full potential of the Internet. Using Minuet, you can send and read mail, download files, read news and perform a host of other crucial Net tasks. To install Minuet:

1. At the command prompt, enter **mkdir c:\minuet** and press **Enter** to create a directory, named \MINUET, at the root level of your hard disk. This book assumes that your hard disk is the C: drive.

2. Insert *The PC Internet Tour Guide Companion Disk* in your floppy drive. This book assumes that your floppy drive is the A: drive.

3. Enter **copy a:\minuarc.exe c:\minuet\minuarc.exe** and press **Enter**. The self-extracting archive containing the Minuet software will be copied from the floppy disk to your hard drive's C:\MINUET directory.

4. Enter **cd c:\minuet** and press **Enter**. The current directory will change to the C:\MINUET directory as reflected by the prompt.

5. Enter **minuarc** and press **Enter**. The contents of the self-extracting archive will be expanded within the C:\MINUET directory and the status of each extracted file will be displayed on the screen.

6. Optionally, enter **del minuarc.exe** and press **Enter** to delete the no-longer-needed self-extracting archive.

7. Add the C:\MINUET directory to the appropriate PATH statement in your AUTOEXEC.BAT file (**PATH = C:\MINUET**).

8. Reboot your computer.

Detailed instructions for configuring and using certain features of the Minuet program are provided throughout the *Tour Guide*. Chapter 4, "Electronic Mail," Chapter 5, "Network News," and Chapter 6, "Transferring Files," all discuss configuring and using Minuet's tools for those particular tasks.

Configuring UMSLIP

If you enjoy a direct connection to the Internet, there's no need for you to install UMSLIP; you can skip ahead to the next section.

To configure the University of Minnesota's UMSLIP software:

1. At the command prompt, enter **slip setup** and press **Enter**. The UMSLIP Transition Log window appears, as shown in Figure 2-1.

The PC Internet Tour Guide

Figure 2-1: UMSLIP
Transaction Log
window.

Figure 2-1: UMSLIP
Transaction Log
window.

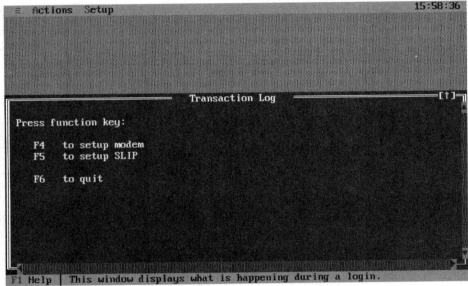

2. Press **F4**. The Modem Settings dialog box appears, as shown in
Figure 2-2.

Figure 2-2: UMSLIP
Modem Settings
dialog box.

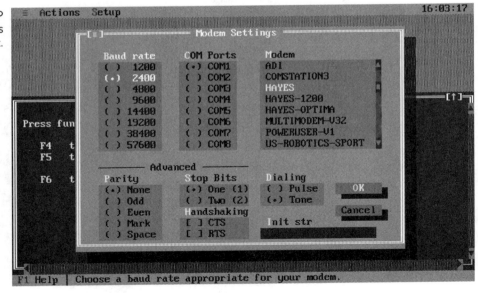

3. Use the **Up** and **Down arrow** keys to select the appropriate baud rate for your modem and press **Tab**.

4. Use the **Up** and **Down arrow** keys to select the COM port to which your modem is attached and press **Tab.**

5. Use the **Up** and **Down arrow** keys to select the type of modem you have and press **Tab.**

6. Use the **Up** and **Down arrow** keys to select the appropriate parity for your modem and press **Tab**. This setting is almost always None.

7. Use the **Up** and **Down arrow** keys to select the appropriate number of stop bits for your modem and press **Tab**. This setting is almost always One (1).

8. If you're using a high-speed modem, press the **Spacebar** to select CTS Handshaking and press the **Down arrow** key.

   ▪ If you're using a low-speed modem, and don't wish to enable hardware handshaking, tab through the Handshaking panel to the Dialing panel.

9. If you're using a high-speed modem, press the **Spacebar** to select RTS Handshaking and press **Tab**.

10. Use the **Up** and **Down arrow** keys to select the appropriate dialing method for your modem and press **Tab.**

11. Enter any additional modem initialization string that may be necessary for your modem or SLIP server and press **Tab**.

    ▪ For example, to force a V.32bis connection with a Hayes modem, enter **S37=11N0** in the Init str field.

12. Press **Enter** to save your modem settings to disk.

13. Press **F5**. The UMSLIP Setup dialog box appears, as shown in Figure 2-3.

Figure 2-3: UMSLIP
Setup dialog box.

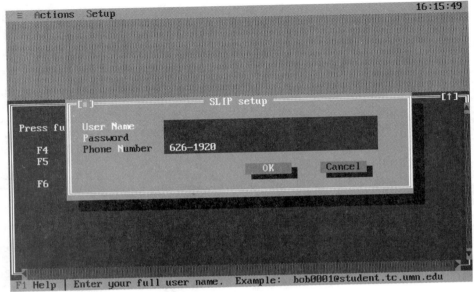

14. Enter your user name—in the format username@domain.top-domain—in the User Name field and press **Tab**.

15. Enter your account password in the Password field and press **Tab**.

16. Enter the telephone number for your SLIP server in the Phone Number field and press **Enter**. Your UMSLIP settings will be saved to disk.

17. Press **F6**. The UMSLIP Transaction Log window will be dismissed and the command prompt will be displayed.

That's it. You've successfully configured your UMSLIP connection. Don't despair if you're still trying to figure out the difference between TCP, FTP and UUCP. The important thing to keep in mind is that you've laid the foundation for exploring the Internet with a set of powerful tools, which we'll cover one at a time in upcoming chapters.

Making the Leap

OK, you've got your account established, you've got your network connection or modem configured, you've got SLIP or TCP/IP installed and configured, and you've got the software that came with this book loaded. Congratulations! You're finally ready to make the leap and make your first Internet connection.

If you enjoy a dedicated Internet connection, simply launch the client software program you want to use.

If you use a PPP or SLIP Internet connection, you will have to establish a modem connection to the network before you can launch any of the client software programs you may want to use. For information on how to establish a modem connection with your PPP or SLIP driver, refer to the documentation that came with the software or talk to your service provider or network administrator who should give you a customized settings document to use with your PPP or SLIP driver to establish your Internet connection.

Moving On

Now you know how to get an Internet account—who to talk to and what to ask for—and a little bit about what you need to actually establish the connection.

As the bus pulls out of the station, go ahead and stretch your legs as we get up to speed; that was a long time to spend in the terminal waiting for our old bus to be gassed up and made roadworthy. But the weather ahead looks favorable—feels like we even have a bit of a tail wind.

If you're anxious to get on the road and take a quick sidetrip on your own, feel free to skip ahead to Chapter 4, "Electronic Mail," where you'll learn how to send e-mail, search for addresses and even subscribe to mailing lists. Or, you can jump to Chapter 6, "Transferring Files," and download some software. But if you want to stay with the main group, we're heading for Chapter 3, where we'll learn what we need to know about the terrain and the natives we're likely to encounter.

NETWORK INFRASTRUCTURE
Electronic Alphabet Soup

As the bus wends its way along the back-roads route (I hate the interstates—they all look the same—so this tour will follow the roads less traveled), now might be a good time to talk about the customs of the people you'll be meeting and the places you'll be visiting as we continue to explore the Internet.

I know you're eager to begin prowling the Internet, but reading this brief chapter before resuming our tour will pay off down the road. This chapter covers what absolute beginners need to know about how the Internet works. One of the most crucial aspects of navigating and using the Internet is understanding the complex and sometimes confusing addressing schemes used throughout the Net. It's important to know how Internet addresses work, not only for sending e-mail, but for locating and using the vast resources available throughout the Net. This chapter explores all you need to know about network addresses to find your way to any resource on the Internet.

We'll also cover what it means to be a good Internet citizen.

An Information Democracy

The Internet's strongest single organizing principle is the democratization of information. As open and untamed as the Wild West, the Internet has no formal organization.

What organization there is can be thought of as a sort of "consensual information anarchy"; a network of networks connected by everything from standard telephone lines to high-speed, dedicated, leased lines to fiber-optic links. Think of each component network as a fiefdom with its own organizational structure.

When someone talks about being "on" the Internet, their computer is connected to one of the interconnected networks that make up the Internet. Computers on the Internet talk to each other by passing notes to each other—just like we all did when we were in grade school. Only the computers on the Internet are a lot more particular about the whole process, as I'll explain shortly.

The Internet has only two practical organizing principles:

1. It serves to democratize information. Your network communications are handled in exactly the same manner, whether you are the chief executive of a Fortune 100 corporation or a junior high student.

2. Every computer on the Internet agrees to follow the same protocol—to speak a common language: TCP/IP, which is short for Transmission Control Protocol/Internet Protocol.

The Oakland archive.

The Oak Software Repository is provided as a service of Oakland University of Rochester, Michigan, and has become one of the best MS-DOS software archives on the Internet. Just about any public domain, freeware or shareware software for computers running MS-DOS is available here. The archive is accessible with Gopher, so use that whenever you can. Point your Gopher at gopher.acs.oakland.edu port 70. Alternatively, all files are available by anonymous FTP at oak.oakland.edu. A text file containing abstracts of all available files is available in the pub/msdos/filedocs/ directory.

The Internet Rosetta Stone

To understand how your communications on the Internet are handled, you have to know a little bit about TCP/IP, the network's common language. Rather than bore you with unnecessary details, I'll only discuss the main points of TCP/IP. You need to know a good bit about TCP/IP to *administer* an Internet connection, but not to *use* one.

As I mentioned earlier, computers on the Internet talk to each other by passing notes, just like we did in grade school. Unfortunately, the Internet's component networks—and the computers that use the Net to communicate—aren't as intelligent as grade-schoolers. Grade-school kids can decipher just about any kind of note, folded any which way. Computers on the Internet are like a picky penmanship teacher; they require the message to be in a very specific language, and the note has to be folded just so. If the Internet note doesn't comply with the TCP/IP standard, it gets tossed faster than a school love poem intercepted by a lunchroom monitor.

So, if you want to communicate on the Internet, the software you use has to pass properly worded, carefully formatted notes. You can't just shout across the lunchroom, *"Hey! Augie! Pass me those peas!"* You have to use the proper decorum. You have to quietly pass your message in a note to your neighbor closest to Augie.

Transmission Control Protocol (TCP)

The Transmission Control Protocol (TCP)—the first piece of the protocol puzzle—controls the information you want to send across the Internet and separates it into smaller pieces that are easily managed. This allows you to send virtually any type of information, from text and graphics to sounds and video, or even actual shareware and software programs. And that information can range in size from a brief e-mail message to the complete works of William Shakespeare.

As TCP separates your information into manageable chunks, it numbers each piece, so the receiving end can put the pieces back together again in the proper order. As soon as each piece of information is received at the destination, TCP verifies it. If some pieces of your information are missing or garbled, TCP requests the originator to re-send the missing or garbled pieces. When TCP has assembled all the information in the correct order, it sends it to the software program using its services. But remember, all this is going on at several thousands of bits per second (bps), even if you're working over a modem, so the whole process is transparent to you.

Going back to Augie in the lunchroom, Augie would number each pea before putting them in a bowl and then pass you the bowl. You'd then take the bowl and eat each pea in numerical sequence. If you found a squished or missing pea, you'd pass a note back to Augie asking for a specific replacement pea. Hey now, I've seen stranger things in a lunchroom.

Internet Protocol (IP)

When you mail a paper message to a friend via the U.S. Postal Service, you seal your message in an envelope containing both a destination and return address. When you drop your message in the mailbox, a mail carrier transports the message to a local post office, where your message is combined with others bound for the same general destination. The messages are then loaded on trucks and planes and shipped off to their destinations. Once there, the sorting process is reversed, and your message is delivered.

Messages sent on the Internet (and everything you do on the Internet is basically a message) work in roughly the same way, thanks to the Internet Protocol (IP). The networks that make up the Internet are connected by special-purpose computers, called *routers*. These routers are the network equivalent of post offices; they determine how to route the information traffic on the Internet. Each router need only know what different connections are available and which is the best next destination to get a message closer to its final destination. The routers are physically linked by Ethernet networks and telephone lines—the network equivalents of the Postal Service's trucks and planes.

The Internet Protocol manages each message's addressing, working just like an addressed envelope for your paper mail.

Once again returning to the lunchroom metaphor—and I promise this is the last time—think of the Internet Protocol (IP) as the lunchroom monitor. The monitor makes sure the bowl of peas Augie passes down the line gets routed most efficiently among all the schoolmates between the two of you, including the class bully, until it finally reaches you.

Travel advisories.

The State Department of the United States provides foreign travel advisories by FTP from world.std.com in the /obi/US.StateDept/Travel/ directory. I've always wanted to go to Belize; let's check out the travel advisory:

Belize—Consular Information Sheet—December 15, 1992

Embassy Location: The U.S. Embassy in Belize is located at the intersection of Gabourel Lane and Hutson Street in Belize City; telephone (501-2) 77161.

Country Description: Belize is a developing country. Its tourism facilities vary in quality.

Entry Requirements: A passport, a return/onward ticket and sufficient funds are required for travel to Belize. U.S. citizens who stay less than three months do not need visas. However, for visits exceeding one month, travelers must obtain permits from the immigration authorities in Belize. For further information, the traveler can contact the Embassy of Belize at 2535 Massachusetts Avenue N.W., Washington, D.C. 20008, tel: (202) 332-9636, or the Belize Mission to the U.N. in New York.

Medical Facilities: Medical care is limited. Doctors and hospitals often expect immediate cash payment for health services.

Crime Information: Petty crime, including pickpocketing and mugging, occurs. Visitors who walk alone on city streets, especially at night, or travel alone to a remote tourist site, are particularly at risk.

Drug Penalties: Penalties for possession and trafficking in drugs are strict, and convicted offenders can expect jail sentences and fines.

Where.Is.That.Thing@On.the.Net?

While messages sent across the Internet may travel in a fashion similar to regular letters, the Internet addressing system looks nothing like a street address. Many beginners are intimidated by the complex and seemingly arcane—or apparently random—way Internet sites are named, or addressed. But a closer look at the process reveals a method to the madness, and learning that method will help you avoid plenty of confusion, panic and frustration.

Each computer on the Internet has two unique addresses:

- IP address like 134.84.101.48 (always four numbers—each less than 256—separated by periods).

- Domain name like deeper.farces.com (always at least two words—or numbers—separated by periods).

All you really have to know is the domain name (the nonnumeric one) of any computer on the Internet you want to communicate with. The Internet addressing schemes were designed so that people only had to use the domain name address, while the computers would use the IP address.

Each person on the Internet has his or her own unique address: username@domain.top-domain. My Internet address, for example, is mfraase@farces.com. My machine name address is deeper.farces.com or moriarity.farces.com ("deeper" is the name of my Macintosh; "moriarity" is the name of my PC, both of which connect to the Net via SLIP). An example of this domain name address and its structure is shown in Figure 3-1.

Figure 3-1:
Example domain
name address and
structure.

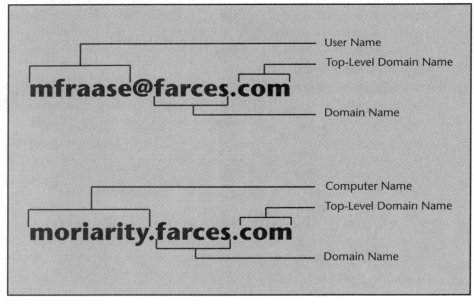

'Zine scene.
Lots of electronic 'zines are available at the Electronic Frontier Foundation's Gopher server and FTP archive. *Athene, CORE, Quanta, Unplastic News* and *ScreamBaby* are all available. Point your Gopher at gopher.eff.org port 70. Alternatively, you can FTP to ftp.eff.org and browse through the /pub/journals/ directory.

Domain name addresses have special pronunciation rules:

- mfraase@farces.com is pronounced "em-frazy at farces dot com"
- moriarity.farces.com is pronounced "moriarity dot farces dot com"
- deeper.farces.com is pronounced "deeper dot farces dot com"

User names aren't always a first initial followed by the last name, as mine is. Sometimes they're a first and last name separated by an underscore, like Ida_Jones@idacorp.com. Others may be almost indecipherable, like mx121bc@cowcollege.edu. If you get a chance to choose your own user name, remember that people who send you e-mail will have to remember it. So pick something that's meaningful to other people as well as yourself.

Similarly, domain names aren't always a recognizable company or organization name. Domain names can be virtually anything, so long as they're unique, and they don't always refer to a specific business or other organization.

Generally, you can refer to computers on the Internet with either their IP address or their domain name address (although it's usually much easier to remember a domain name address), and you always refer to people with their domain name address.

Have Your .Org Call My .Gov About that .Com

The last portion of a domain name address is called the top-level domain. It provides a clue about the computer or the person you're addressing. Top-level domain names are standardized throughout the Internet, as shown in Table 3-1.

Table 3-1: U.S. top-level domain names.

Domain	Represents
com	Businesses and commercial organizations
edu	Educational institutions
gov	Government institutions
mil	Military organizations
net	Network resources
org	Other (usually non-profit) organizations

All Internet sites outside of the United States are identified by a unique two-character top-level domain name, as shown by the examples in Table 3-2.

Table 3-2:
International top-
level domain
names.

Domain	Represents
au	Australia
at	Austria
bz	Belize
ca	Canada
dk	Denmark
fi	Finland
fr	France
de	Germany
it	Italy
jp	Japan
no	Norway

The top-level domain name for the United States is "us," although it's not used very often. Some Internet users identify themselves by their geographic location in their domain names. For example, the domain name username@well.sf.ca.us indicates a user on the Whole Earth 'Lectronic Link (WELL) located in San Francisco, California, United States.

Finger.
Finger is a command you can execute from your keyboard during any TELNET (remote login) session to a UNIX-based host. Type **finger** and the name of the user or machine you want information about. For example, the command finger @riverside.mr.net would return information about the computer named riverside at the mr.net host.

Here are a few tips to help you deal with this alphabet soup of Internet domain-name addresses:

- The example addresses used in this chapter are very simple. My editor's Internet address, for example, is ruffin@gibbs.oit.unc.edu. Ruffin's account is on a computer named Gibbs (gibbs) in the Office of Information and Technology (oit) at the University of North Carolina (unc), an educational facility (edu).

- The computer networks on the Internet aren't very picky about case-sensitivity. For instance, mFraase@Farces.COM, Mfraase@farces.Com, MFRAASE@FARCES.COM will all reach me just as efficiently. Consequently, most veteran netters stick to just lowercase letters when typing addresses because it's the easiest option.

- Make sure to write down important e-mail addresses. I can't tell you the number of times I thought I could remember an e-mail address only to have forgotten it by the time I needed it. Keep a hard-copy record of your e-mail address book. You never know when it might be accidentally deleted from the computer that maintains your account.

POPmail.

POPmail, freeware from the University of Minnesota, is one of the best Internet e-mail programs available. You can always download the latest release of the program and its associated documentation by FTP from boombox.micro.umn.edu in the /pub/pc/popmail/ directory.

When in Rome... Don't Tie Up the Phone Lines

If your friend Augie invites you to dinner, you have to know more than just how to get to his house. You also need to know things like which water glass is yours (is it the one on the left or the one on the right) and which fork to use for the salad. Before you set out on your Internet explorations, take a moment to review a few tips that may keep you from alienating anyone or making a fool out of yourself right away. We all make fools of ourselves on the Net at one time or another; here's hoping you can delay your fool debut for a while.

Acceptable Use Policies

Although the acceptable use policies of the various networks that make up the Internet are rapidly changing, we'll all probably have to deal with them at least until the mid-1990s. Instead of reprinting all of the different acceptable use policies, I'll just go over the main points.

To some extent, your category of Internet connection determines how you can use the Internet. If you're classified as an educational, research or noncommercial user, your Internet activities must be restricted to the purpose of research, education, charitable activities, government affairs, individual professional development or public service. If you're classified as a commercial user, your Internet activities are unrestricted (except, of course, for activities that are specified as unacceptable). Research and educational network traffic is routed over connections subsidized by taxpayers; commercial network traffic is routed over private connections. You don't have to worry about how your network traffic is routed; that's the responsibility of your service provider.

Most service providers specify these uses as unacceptable:

- Distribution of unsolicited advertising.
- Transmission of anything that causes disruption of service to others.
- Propagation of computer worms or viruses.
- Use of the network to make unauthorized entry to any resource.

In addition, most service providers require you to abide by some general common-sense usage guidelines:

- Respect the privacy of other users.
- Usage must be consistent with common ethical practice and community standards.
- Respect copyright and licenses of programs, information and documents.

Trumpet.
Trumpet is a network news reader for PCs that employs an easy-to-use interface. It uses the NNTP protocol and allows you to follow message threads within the various newsgroups. The program is available by FTP from ftp.utas.edu.au in the /pc/trumpet/ directory.

Finally, some service providers may require you to comply with the NSFNET Backbone Services Acceptable Use Policy. Ask your service provider or network administrator if your Internet activity is affected by this policy.

And if your idea of a good time is to wade through pages of legalese, you can always retrieve the complete documents from various archives on the Internet. For more information on how and where to get these documents, refer to "Using FTP to Transfer Files" in Chapter 6, "Transferring Files."

Security Issues

With the rapid growth of the Internet, computer security becomes a more serious issue each year, especially when you're sharing resources across the Net. While your Internet connection is active, your computer—and perhaps more important, any other resources attached to your computer via a local area network—are all on the Internet. It is your responsibility to protect your own system.

You also have a responsibility to be a good Internet citizen. You have been granted access to a worldwide resource and should respect the privacy and property of others.

If we, as Internet inhabitants, don't manage our own security wisely, it's likely that some less-than-benevolent government agency will take it upon itself to manage things for us.

FTP.

FTP is an Internet acronym for File Transfer Protocol, and it's used to upload and download files on the Net. The best MS-DOS-based FTP client currently available comes with the freeware NCSA TELNET package. The program's integrated online help system makes it easy to navigate the otherwise intimidating process of moving files across the Net. You can always download the latest release of the software and its associated documentation by FTP from oak.oakland.edu in the /pub/msdos/ncsatelnet/ directory. Additionally, the NCSA TELNET package is distributed as part of the University of Minnesota's SLIPdial (available as freeware by anonymous FTP at boombox.micro.umn.edu in the /pub/slipdial/ directory).

First Names are Lousy Passwords

Your login password is your security key and is the most likely way someone will gain unauthorized access to your Internet account. Guard your password with care, don't write it down, don't allow others to use it and change it often.

A good password:

■ Is made up of at least six characters that do not form a word.

■ Includes both upper- and lowercase letters and numerals.

■ Is easily remembered but something no one can guess.

If you think your Internet account is being hacked—or if you suspect that your computer has been broken into—talk to your network administrator or service provider immediately.

Gopher.
Gopher lets you burrow through information resources using a series of easy-to-navigate menus that appear on your screen. You can use Gopher to navigate huge dataspaces with just a few key presses. The current version of Gopher is always available by FTP (or Gopher) from boombox.micro.umn.edu in the /pub/gopher/PC_client/ directory.

Usage Courtesy

Everything you do on the Internet has potential ramifications beyond the Net. The unwritten rule underlying all Internet activity is simple: *The Internet is a good thing and it must be protected.* While unwritten, this rule is enforced with impartial severity. If you screw up badly enough, you can expect to lose your access privileges. While there are no etiquette handbooks or Internet finishing schools, the same common sense and social grace you use in the real world will generally be enough to get you through most potentially sticky Internet situations.

While some of the tips and advice in this section may mean little to you now, they'll become second nature once you get your Internet legs:

■ **Anonymous FTP isn't.** Always use your e-mail address as your login password when accessing remote FTP servers as an anonymous user. (See Chapter 6, "Transferring Files," for more information on accessing FTP sites.) You can always make up a phony e-mail address when you visit far-flung spots on the Net, but don't bother. Cookie-crumb trails will lead back to your site, if not directly to you.

■ **Leave your ethnocentricity at the door**. Many juicy Internet resources reside in foreign countries. Be careful with the cultural references you use.

■ **Don't tie up popular sites at busy times**. Be aware that shared resources on the Internet may actually be in use by real people trying to do real work. Try to access the busiest resources during off-peak hours whenever possible (unless, of course, you're a real person doing real work). Be sensitive to time zones; think about what time it is where you're *going* rather than where you *are*. Try to find alternative routes to the busiest and most popular resources. Many popular archives have less crowded "mirror" sites elsewhere on the Net. Learn where they are and use them when possible.

■ **Try to find the closest source for what you need**. Don't FTP or Gopher to Finland for a file you know is available one or two hops away from your local site.

■ **Don't use remote resources when you can use local ones**. Don't use archive space clear across the world for your personal files just because you can't afford a bigger hard drive.

■ **Log off properly**. Make sure you leave all resources in the same condition and state in which you found them. If you log off improperly, you may leave certain tasks or processes running in the background of the host machine, causing problems for other users or worse, network administrators.

Keep in mind that nothing on the Internet is really free. Somebody is paying for it. And if everyone takes a "free ride" on the most popular and expensive Net resources, it won't be long before those same resources are protected, restricted or closed to public access.

You'll find more Internet etiquette advice in the chapters that deal with specific network services.

Moving On

Now you know how the Internet works and how computers and people are identified. You've also looked at how to best get along with your fellow Internet inhabitants. The next chapter guides you through the wonders of using electronic mail on the Internet. We'll cover how to use some of the most powerful tools available for sending, receiving, reading and sorting electronic mail and how to communicate via e-mail with people who aren't even on the Internet.

ELECTRONIC MAIL
The Pony Express Goes Digital

Our tour bus has been making pretty good time, sticking to the back roads. But we've been rolling along for some time now, and some of you may want to send a message to your friends and family back home, just to let them know you're having a great time. So let's take a look at how to use electronic mail to communicate privately with individuals and small groups on the Internet.

With the exception of gestures, e-mail is arguably the most efficient means of communication yet devised by humans. Because it uses recycled phosphors on your computer screen, e-mail is ecological—nary a tree and very little energy is used to create, deliver and read e-mail messages. You can choose to read your e-mail whenever it's most convenient for you, not when it's convenient for someone else. You can scan an electronic in-box full of e-mail faster than you can open a single paper mail envelope. You can easily forward, store or reply to e-mail messages with the touch of a button. Sending messages to dozens of people is a snap with the multiple-addressing capabilities of e-mail. And there are a host of other features that make e-mail one of the most powerful and convenient ways to communicate.

But lots of people never get the most from their e-mail systems because they have to wrestle with arcane and obscure commands and abbreviations, just to send a simple message. There are a host of powerful tools available for PCs that provide an easy-to-use interface for the Internet's electronic mail services. After all, electronic mail is only effective if you actually use it, and who wants to put up with a UNIX-based e-mail program with practically no features or options, when simple, PC-specific alternatives are available? E-mail is an incredibly powerful form of communication, and there are plenty of Internet users who do little on the Net besides send mail. Consequently, we'll be spending more time discussing e-mail than any other topic in the course of our tour. So before we get started, let's pull off to the side of the road and take a look at the map of what we'll be covering in this chapter:

- What is E-Mail & How Does it Work?
- E-Mail Etiquette & Courtesy
- How to Send E-Mail Anywhere
- Quick Guide to Using Minuet (included on companion disk)
- Finding Addresses
- Electronic Mailing Lists
- E-Mail & Attached Files

We've got a long road ahead, so buckle up and let's get started!

What Is E-Mail & How Does it Work?

Most people who have never used e-mail have trouble understanding why it's touted over regular mail, fax or even phone conversations. It takes anywhere from a few seconds to a few minutes to deliver an e-mail message (complete with attached files) anywhere in the world. A postal delivery usually takes several days to reach its destination, and the telephone system is immediate, but both parties have to be on the phone at the same time. Fax was the rage in the '80s because it was fairly easy to use and didn't require a computer. But this chapter shows why so many people prefer e-mail to phone, fax or paper mail.

You can use e-mail to:

- **Send text-based messages to any other Internet user**. You can also send messages to users on commercial electronic mail and information services. Soon you'll be able to send messages that contain fully formatted text, pictures, sound and even video—*between different types of computers and operating systems.*

- **Attach computer files to text messages**. You can send binary files—complete software programs or fully formatted files—to any other Internet user and users on most of the commercial electronic mail and information services. (Why send a static, dead document via fax when you can work with a live one via e-mail?)

- **Send messages and files to multiple recipients**. Where telephones tend to be useful for one-to-one communications, e-mail is useful for both one-to-one and one-to-many communications.

- **Reply to or forward messages you receive**. You can quickly and easily dash off a reply to a message, or forward it to other users around the world.

- **Subscribe to electronic mailing lists**. You can add your name to any of thousands of mailing lists whose topics range from PC hardware and software to political debates and discussions.

- **Communicate with mail list servers**. By sending e-mail queries to special addresses, you can query list servers that automatically respond to special commands by returning to you specific information, documents or other files.

Electronic mail is different from other Internet services in one important way—the sending and the receiving computers need not be able to connect directly with each other. You create e-mail messages on your computer and send them to a *mail server*. The mail server determines the best route to reach the recipient and passes the e-mail to the next closest mail server. The e-mail is passed through any number of mail servers and is eventually delivered to the final recipient's mail server. This is called a *store-and-forward* service, and it happens much faster than it took you to read about the process.

Smithsonian Institution photograph archive.
The Smithsonian Institution has begun to archive electronic versions of its photographs and art collections. The archive is accessible by FTP at photo1.si.edu in the directory /pub/images/. Unfortunately, this machine has a poor network connection. Daily updates are mirrored at the University of North Carolina and accessible by FTP at sunsite.unc.edu in the /pub/multimedia/pictures/smithsonian/ directory.

Like the phone system and the Postal Service, e-mail isn't infallible. Occasionally, an e-mail message doesn't reach its intended destination. Any e-mail that does not reach its recipient is returned to the sender as undeliverable mail. This is called a *bounced* e-mail message. Reasons for bounced mail include (in order of likelihood):

- **User unknown** (incorrect address in the username portion of the address).

- **Host unknown** (incorrect address in the domain or top-domain portions of the address).

- **Network unreachable** (gateway limitations or problems with the network backbone).

- **Connection timed out** (software problem on the destination mail server).

- **Connection refused** (problem with the destination mail server).

The important point here is, if your e-mail message is undeliverable—for whatever reason—it will be bounced back to you. Many first-time e-mail users waste countless hours worrying if their messages are delivered, often following e-mail transmissions with faxes and phone calls to the effect of "Did you get my e-mail?" As a general rule, assume that your e-mail efforts are successful rather than figuring they don't work at all.

E-Mail Etiquette & Courtesy

Electronic mail eliminates a lot of subtle impediments to effective communication. Judgments based on appearance, voice or social position are impossible in electronic communications. E-mail's asynchronous nature—the ability to deal with a message when it's most convenient for all parties involved—is truly a boon to communications among individuals and groups.

One of the most amazing things about e-mail is the immediacy of its delivery. When you click that **Send** button, your message is delivered in seconds. This is a great advantage in most cases, but can work as a disadvantage if you have a short fuse. Unlike a letter, which may sit on a desk for hours or days before being mailed, electronic communications are usually dashed off as soon as they're completed. If you've been using e-mail for a while, you'll notice that a lot of the messages you receive (and perhaps a few you've written) shouldn't have been sent. It pays to ponder the ramifications of an e-mail message before launching it into the electronic ether—once it's gone out, there's no way to get it back.

The price you pay for e-mail's convenience and speed is a fairly high potential for misunderstanding. The best way to avoid e-mail misinterpretations and mixed signals is to follow three simple, common-sense rules of etiquette and courtesy.

1. *Don't send anything via e-mail that you wouldn't want to read in your hometown newspaper.* Invariably, that juicy e-mail message is read by the one person who was never meant to read it. There are lots of stories about the politics of e-mail, and until the law catches up with the technology, you're better off playing it safe. Assume your e-mail messages are available to anyone who wants to read them. Some companies even have a policy making e-mail the property of the company, not the individual correspondents. In early 1993, the Georgia Institute of Technology announced that it would no longer consider e-mail delivered to any of its systems on the Internet to be private. Already, landmark legal cases about trade secrets, corporate espionage and e-mail are filtering through the courts. E-mail *should* enjoy all the rights and securities of paper mail, but don't make the mistake of assuming that it *does*.

2. *Facial expressions and body language don't fit through the narrow bandwidth of e-mail.* Statements that you intend as pithy may come across as condescending or sarcastic. Some people approach e-mail as conversational; others don't. Some people never take e-mail personally, others always do. Unless you're close friends with an e-mail recipient, never expect that he or she will understand your sense of humor, wry wit or playful repartee.

3. *You can't control when your message will be delivered, so assume it will arrive at the worst possible time.* Be careful with your wording. What may seem funny or cute today may be inappropriate or rude when e-mail is read tomorrow. Just because e-mail is delivered at warp speed doesn't mean it's read at the same rate. Lots of people get more e-mail than they can keep up with; keep that in mind as you compose your missive. If you only read three e-mail messages a day, you'll probably remember them all for a few days. But people who receive dozens of messages need reminders (or forwarded messages) to help clue them in to the context of previous correspondence.

Auto-Advice From EmilyPost.

If you think you get some perplexing junk paper mail, consider receiving this automated e-mail message:

Dear Net-Mail User [o **EweR-635-78-2267-3 aSp**]:

Your mailbox has just been rifled by EmilyPost, an autonomous courtesy-worm chain program released in October 2036 by an anonymous group of net subscribers in western Alaska. [**ref: sequestered confession 592864 -2376298.98634, deposited with Bank Leumi 10/ 23/36:20:34:21. Expiration-disclosure 10 years.**] Under the civil disobedience sections of the Charter of Rio, we accept in advance the fines and penalties that will come due when our confession is released in 2046. However we feel that's a small price to pay for the message brought to you by EmilyPost.

In brief, dear friend, you are not a very polite person. EmilyPost's syntax analysis subroutines show that a very high fraction of your net exchanges are heated, vituperative, even obscene.

Of course you enjoy free speech. But EmilyPost has been designed by people who are concerned about the recent trend toward excessive nastiness in some parts of the net. EmilyPost homes in on folks like you and begins by asking them to please consider the advantages of politeness.

For one thing, your credibility ratings would rise. (EmilyPost has checked your favorite bulletin boards, and finds your ratings aren't high at all. Nobody is listening to you, sir!) Moreover, consider that courtesy can foster calm reason, turning shrill antagonism into useful debate and even consensus.

We suggest introducing an automatic delay to your mail system. Communications are so fast these days, people seldom stop and think. Some net users act like mental patients who shout out anything that comes to mind, rather than as functioning citizens with the human gift of tact.

If you wish, you may use one of the public-domain delay programs included in this version of EmilyPost, free of charge.

Of course, should you insist on continuing as before, disseminating nastiness in all directions, we have equipped EmilyPost with other options you'll soon find out about....

—From David Brin's *Earth* (Bantam, 1990).

E-Mail Privacy

If I took a paper letter from your mailbox, opened it and read it, I'd be guilty of a federal offense. If I did the same thing by intercepting or retrieving your e-mail, chances are I would not be committing a crime.

Electronic communications are not given the same protection as first class mail. As the rapid rate of change outpaces the social and legal conventions that govern how we use technology, we continue to suppose that we have freedoms and rights that simply do not exist. For example, in the past, wiretapping had to be physically carried out. A spook had to be near the person under surveillance. A tape recorder had to be in the immediate vicinity of persons recorded. With advancements in telephone switching technology, this is no longer the case. Anyone can now easily eavesdrop on conversations simply by sending the proper signal tones down the telephone wire—from anywhere.

In 1986, President Ronald Reagan signed into law the Electronic Communications Privacy Act (ECPA). The act is designed to expand the scope of telecommunications covered under the protection of the 1968 federal wiretapping laws. The ECPA protects electronic mail, cellular telephones, pagers and electronic data transmission. It also requires government agencies to obtain a court order before intercepting electronic communications.

The ECPA, as currently written, has two main goals:

1. Protecting all electronic communications systems, including e-mail, from outside intrusion.

2. Protecting the privacy of certain messages transmitted over public-service e-mail systems.

The ECPA makes it a federal crime to intercept certain electronic communications, but makes a distinction between public and internal electronic communications systems. Most important, electronic mail messages transmitted within internal e-mail systems that are used solely for interoffice communications are not subject to the privacy provisions of the ECPA. That means that a company can read such messages without invading the privacy of employees. Electronic mail messages transmitted within internal e-mail systems that allow outside access can be read by a company if either the sender or receiver grants permission. Reading electronic mail messages exchanged over public e-mail systems by anyone other than the sender and receiver is a felony under the ECPA. To make matters more confusing, it's not clear whether the Internet is considered a public e-mail system under the ECPA.

If this all seems a little vague and you're wondering how it relates to you as an e-mail user, a recent poll conducted by *Macworld* magazine might bring the issue into clearer focus. In its July 1993 issue, *Macworld* published the results of a nationwide poll of top corporate managers from 301 businesses of varying sizes. The poll found that 21 percent of respondents have "engaged in searches of employee computer files, voice mail, electronic mail or other networking communications." The figure was even higher—30 percent—among large companies.

E-Mail Horror Stories.

Linda Ellerbee's infamous Associated Press e-mail incident didn't so much involve eavesdropping or invasion of privacy as it did the simple misrouting of electronic communications. Ellerbee, so the story goes, sent a note to a friend through the Associated Press e-mail system. The note included some very nasty comments about her boss and the Dallas city council, as well as other Texas luminaries. An accident in the network caused the message to be distributed to every AP outlet in four states. Ellerbee lost her job over the incident, and the potential for legal action by everyone involved—including Ellerbee, her boss and the AP—was gigantic.

In the summer of 1990, the members of the city council of Colorado Springs became outraged when they discovered the mayor was secretly intercepting and reading their private e-mail messages.

In August of 1990, Alana Shoars, a network administrator in charge of electronic mail at Epson America Inc., filed a lawsuit against the company. Shoars' lawsuit alleged that her supervisor, Robert Hillseth, manager of data communications for Epson America Inc., had intercepted her MCI Mail messages on a regular basis as they were passing through the company's network gateway. Shoars claims that when she complained about Hillseth's activities, he fired her. Shoars filed an individual suit for wrongful termination and also filed a class action suit with 2,500 other current and former Epson employees asking for unspecified damages of up to $3,000 per violation. That's $3,000 for each message that was intercepted. The class action suit was filed as an invasion of privacy under Section 631 of the California Penal Code.

Secret Service Director John Simpson admitted in a letter to California State Representative Don Edwards that the U.S. government has been intercepting private e-mail and surreptitiously monitoring computer bulletin boards in order to track the activities of suspected hackers.

While there are various techniques for encrypting or otherwise protecting e-mail messages, they are not always practical or convenient, and no system is completely foolproof. So until specific laws are passed and sweeping policy changes are enacted by government and business alike, the lesson here is clear: assume that your e-mail messages are being read by people other than their intended recipients.

How to Send E-Mail Anywhere

You can do anything with e-mail that you can do with postal mail, except mail physical objects. With an Internet account you can even send e-mail to people who have accounts on one of the commercial electronic mail or information services like MCI Mail or CompuServe.

Addressing e-mail on the Internet is standardized and simple, despite how arcane or inscrutable some Internet addresses may seem. Everyone's Internet e-mail address, as explained in "Where.Is.That.Thing@On.the.Net?" on page 43, is formatted the same: **username@domain.top-domain**.

To send e-mail to someone on the Internet, just address the message to their Internet address.

The next six sections detail how to send and receive mail from most of the common commercial information services that provide an *e-mail gateway* to the Internet.

An e-mail gateway is software or hardware that connects networks that use different protocols. In effect, it translates between the protocols so that computers on the connected networks can exchange data. Be careful with the size of the files you send by e-mail. Most of the e-mail gateways provided by the commercial information services like CompuServe and America Online have severe file-size limitations, as indicated in Table 4-1.

E-mail addresses are not case-sensitive, and most people don't care how you capitalize their name or domain name, as long as their e-mail gets to them.

Internet to UUCP & Back

UUCP, the UNIX-to-UNIX Copy Protocol, is a protocol used by UNIX workstations to communicate with each other over telephone lines. UUCP is also commonly referred to as a network, because e-mail and files can be sent to any UUCP-capable computer by specifying which intermediate computers the e-mail must pass through to reach the final recipient. Since many UUCP sites are switching over to full domain name registration, you might first check to see if your recipient has a standard Internet domain name address.

To send e-mail to a UUCP user, use the format:

user@host.uucp

or

user%host.uucp@gateway

For example, to send e-mail to Peter Piper (whose user ID is ppiper) at his Megacorp (megacorp.uucp) host, use the format:

ppiper@megacorp.uucp

Alternatively, if Megacorp uses the Performance Systems International (PSI) gateway to receive e-mail (check with Peter or his assistant if you aren't sure), use the address format:

ppiper%megacorp.uucp@uu.psi.com

Sometimes UUCP users will provide you with what's called a *bang-path address*. Bang-path addresses are easily spotted because they contain exclamation marks (!):

...!uunet!megacorp!ppiper

The exclamation marks are pronounced as "bang." The above address would be pronounced as "from bang uunet bang megacorp bang ppiper."

You can always convert bang-path addresses to this format:

user%host.uucp@gateway

UUCP users with access to an e-mail gateway send e-mail messages to colleagues on the Internet using the standard domain name addressing:

user@domain.top-domain

For example, UUCP users with access to a gateway address e-mail to my Internet address as:

mfraase@farces.com

UUCP users without access to a gateway must route Internet e-mail using whatever paths are appropriate to reach a computer that is connected to the Internet.

"Dear Sysadmin, Punish your user for what he said!"

In mid-April 1993, Carl Kadie asked a variety of system administrators how they respond to the above request from Internet users. The responses were very interesting:

Ten respondents explained the value of free expression or replied that punishing users wasn't their job.

Seven respondents told the accused to "cool it" (or else).

Four respondents said the situation has never come up.

Two respondents said they judge the article and punish the user if the posting is found to violate policy.

One respondent removed the entire newsgroup in which the article was posted.

One respondent told the complainer "we'll handle it," but didn't do anything to follow up.

One respondent passed the complaint up the chain of command.

Internet to CompuServe & Back

CompuServe is a commercial information service that opened an e-mail gateway to the Internet in July 1989. CompuServe subscribers are assigned a unique identification number as a user name, in the format:

71234,5678

To send e-mail to a CompuServe subscriber, use the format:

useridentification.number@compuserve.com

For example, to send e-mail to Peter Piper (whose CompuServe ID number is 71234,5678) use the address format:

71234.5678@compuserve.com

Note that the comma in the recipient's user identification number is translated to a period.

You should also remember that there is a 50,000-character limit on e-mail messages that pass through CompuServe's Internet gateway.

CompuServe subscribers send e-mail to the Internet using the format:

>Internet:user@domain.top-domain

For example, CompuServe subscribers address e-mail to my Internet address as:

>Internet:mfraase@farces.com

Internet to MCI Mail & Back

MCI Mail is a commercial electronic mail service that has offered an experimental Internet gateway since the late 1980s; the gateway is no longer considered experimental. MCI Mail subscribers are assigned a unique MCI ID number, an MCI ID name and a full user name, in the following respective formats:

557-4126
mfraase
Michael Fraase

To send e-mail to an MCI Mail subscriber, use any of the three following formats:

idnumber@mcimail.com
idname@mcimail.com
full_user_name@mcimail.com

For example, to send e-mail to any of the above three MCI Mail address formats, use the three following formats respectively:

5574126@mcimail.com
mfraase@mcimail.com
michael_fraase@mcimail.com

Note that when you use the idnumber@mcimail.com format, the dash separating the numbers is eliminated. Also, spaces—like those between first and last names—are translated to the underscore (_) character.

There is no limit on the size of e-mail messages that pass through the MCI Mail Internet gateway.

MCI Mail subscribers send e-mail to the Internet with the following steps:

1. At the **Command**: prompt, type **create** and press **Enter**.

2. At the **TO**: prompt, type the full name of the recipient followed by **(EMS)** and press **Enter**.

3. At the **EMS**: prompt, type **Internet** and press **Enter**.

4. At the **MBX**: prompt, type the recipient's Internet domain name address in the format **user@domain.top-domain** and press **Enter**.

For example, MCI Mail subscribers address e-mail to my Internet address as follows:

1. At the **Command**: prompt, type **create** and press **Enter**.
2. At the **TO**: prompt, type **Michael Fraase (EMS)** and press **Enter**.
3. At the **EMS**: Prompt, type **Internet** and press **Enter**.
4. At the **MBX**: Prompt, type **mfraase@farces.com** and press **Enter**.

Internet to America Online & Back

America Online is a commercial information service that maintains an e-mail gateway to the Internet. Each America Online subscriber has a unique "screen name" as a user name, which is at least three and no more than ten characters long.

To send e-mail to an America Online subscriber, use the format:

screenname@aol.com

For example, to send e-mail to Peter Piper (PetePiper) use the address format:

petepiper@aol.com

Note that there is a 27,000-character limit on e-mail messages that pass through America Online's Internet gateway.

America Online subscribers send e-mail to the Internet using the standard domain name addressing:

user@domain.top-domain

For example, America Online subscribers address e-mail to my Internet address as:

mfraase@farces.com

Internet to AT&T Mail & Back

AT&T Mail is a commercial electronic mail service that opened an e-mail gateway to the Internet in June 1990. Each AT&T Mail subscriber is assigned a unique user name.

To send e-mail to an AT&T Mail subscriber, use the format:

username@attmail.com

For example, to send e-mail to Peter Piper (ppiper) use the address format:

ppiper@attmail.com

AT&T Mail subscribers send e-mail to the Internet using the standard domain name addressing:

user@domain.top-domain

For example, AT&T Mail subscribers address e-mail to my Internet address as:

mfraase@farces.com

"Dear Sysadmin, Punish your user for what he said!" Revisited.

In mid-April 1993, Carl Kadie asked a variety of system administrators how they respond to the above request from Internet users. Here's one of the responses he received:

"I believe you need a short lesson in the operation of free speech. I have no particular opinions on the subject of this newsgroup, but I took the trouble to read some of the 'belligerent and harassing' postings of which you speak, and, frankly, they weren't."

"It seems to me that your attempt to characterize them as such stems from a desire to stifle ideas with which you disagree. I have no intention of cooperating with you in this. The remedy for speech with which you disagree is more speech, not a silencing (the rather low signal-to-noise ratio on USENET notwithstanding)."

"If these postings offend you, I suggest you find out how 'kill files' work, rather than wasting the time of overworked system administrators who aren't being underpaid to deal with this sort of childishness."

Cross-Network E-Mail Addressing Quick Reference

The addressing information presented in the previous six sections is distilled for quick reference in Table 4-1.

Table 4-1: Cross-network e-mail addressing at a glance.

Service	From Internet	To Internet
UUCP	user@host.uucp user%host.uucp@gateway ...!gateway!host!user	user@domain.top-domain[1]
CompuServe	user.number@compuserve.com[2]	>Internet:user@domain.topdomain
MCI Mail	idnumber@mcimail.com[3] idname@mcimail.com full_user_name@mcimail.com	TO: recipient's full name (EMS) EMS: Internet MBX: user@domain.top-domain
America Online	screenname@aol.com[4]	user@domain.top-domain
AT&T Mail	username@attmail.com	user@domain.top-domain

1. Requires access to a gateway.
2. The comma in the recipient's user identification number is translated to a period. There is a 50,000-character limit on e-mail messages that pass through CompuServe's Internet gateway.
3. The dash separating the numbers is eliminated.
4. There is a 27,000-character limit on e-mail messages that pass through America Online's Internet gateway.

Quick Guide to Using Minuet E-Mail

Minuet E-Mail is an electronic mail program for the PC that is fully compatible with the POP3 mail server offered by most Internet service providers. (If you're not sure whether Minuet E-Mail is compatible with your mail server, ask your network administrator.) Minuet E-Mail was written by associates of the University of Minnesota's Computer and Information Services Microcomputer Center and is based on the University's POPmail product.

The current release of the freeware Minuet is provided on *The PC Internet Tour Guide's Companion Disk*. The Minuet program is packaged in a self-extracting archive file on the disk and is automatically decompressed and properly installed as part of the installation process described in Chapter 2, "Getting Connected."

Minuet is distributed via the expressed written permission of the University of Minnesota's Computer and Information Services Microcomputer Center. It's a shareware product, and you are free to distribute it to others so long as the program is distributed in its entirety. For more information, please see the ReadMe documents that accompany Minuet on the companion disk. If you are a commercial user, Minuet is provided to you for evaluation purposes only. If you continue to use the program after the evaluation period, you are required to pay the $50 shareware fee to the Regents of the University of Minnesota.

Configuring Minuet E-Mail

Minuet E-Mail must be properly configured before you can begin using it to send e-mail. To use Minuet E-Mail, you must have an account on a computer that runs a POP3 (Post Office Protocol version 3) mail server. Use the sequences in this section to configure the Minuet software.

Note: This section assumes that you have installed the Minuet program as part of the installation process outlined in Chapter 2. If you have manually installed Minuet, you'll have to add the appropriate path statement to your AUTOEXEC.BAT file if you want to launch the program from any directory. The rest of this chapter assumes that Minuet is installed in the C:\Minuet directory.

Use these steps to configure your personal information in Minuet.

1. Launch the Minuet program by typing **minuet** at the prompt. The INBOX Viewer appears.

2. Press **Alt-S** to display the Setup menu.

3. From the Setup menu, select the User... command. The Setup Personal Information dialog box appears, as shown in Figure 4-1.

Figure 4-1: Minuet
Setup Personal
Information
dialog box.

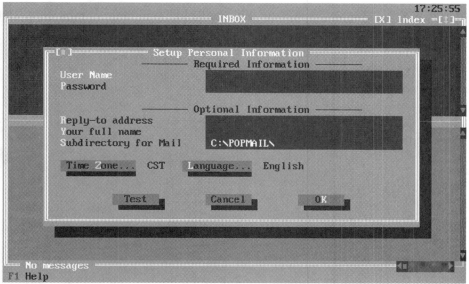

4. Enter your user name in the User Name field and press **Tab**. Enter only your user name on the host computer, not your entire e-mail address.

5. Enter your password in the Password field and press **Tab**.

6. Optionally, enter your e-mail address in the Reply-to address field, using the format: user@domain.top-domain, and press **Tab**.

7. Optionally, enter your full name in the Your full name field and press **Tab**.

8. Optionally, enter a complete pathname for your e-mail files in the Subdirectory for Mail field and press **Alt-Z**.

9. With the **Up** and **Down arrow** keys, select your time zone from the scrolling list and press **Enter**.

10. If necessary, press **Alt-L**, select a language to use with Minuet from the scrolling list and press **Enter**.

11. Press **Enter** to save your settings and dismiss the Setup Personal Information dialog box.

Use these steps to configure your server connection information in Minuet.

1. With Minuet running, press **Alt-S** to display the Setup menu.

2. From the Setup menu, select the Servers… command. The Setup Servers dialog box appears, as shown in Figure 4-2.

Figure 4-2: Minuet Setup Servers dialog box.

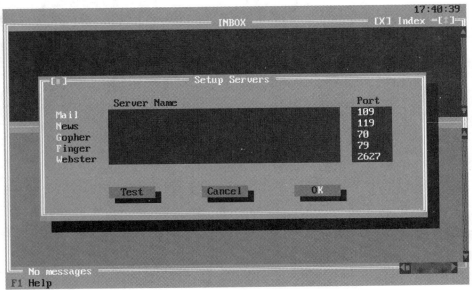

3. Enter the domain address for your mail server in the Mail field—using the domain.top-domain format—and press **Tab** twice.

   ■ This step (and steps 4–7 that follow) require that you know the domain addresses for various servers that are specific to your connection. If you don't know these addresses, ask your network administrator or Internet service provider. In addition, you'll need to know the port numbers for the various servers, although the default port settings are almost always correct. Again, ask your network administrator or Internet service provider if you're not sure. *This sequence assumes that the default port settings are correct for your connection.* Whatever the case is in your situation, it might be a good idea to make a written record of the various domain addresses and port settings so that, should you have to reinstall the software for some reason, you can do so quickly and easily.

4. Enter the domain address for your network news server in the News field—using the domain.top-domain format—and press **Tab** twice.

5. Enter the domain address for your Gopher server in the Gopher field—using the domain.top-domain format—and press **Tab** twice.

6. Enter the domain address for your finger server in the Finger field—using the domain.top-domain format—and press **Tab** twice.

7. Enter the domain address for your dictionary server in the Webster field—using the domain.top-domain format—and press **Tab**.

8. Press **Alt-K** to save the configuration settings to disk.

TeX.

It's pronounced "tech," and if you're an academician you probably already know about it. TeX is a very specialized typesetting software program. It's notoriously difficult to learn, and painful to use, but for some things—like typesetting mathematical equations—it's indispensable. Several versions of TeX, sample files and utilities are available by anonymous FTP at oak.oakland.edu in the /pub/msdos/tex/ directory.

Use these steps to configure your network connection information in Minuet.

1. With Minuet running, press **Alt-S** to display the Setup menu.

2. From the Setup menu, select the Network… command. The Setup Network dialog box appears, as shown in Figure 4-3.

Figure 4-3: Minuet
Setup Network
dialog box.

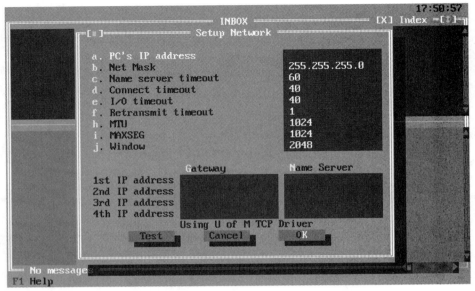

3. If you have a direct connection to the Internet, enter your assigned IP address in the PC's IP address field and press **Tab**.

▨ Be careful! Don't make up an address in this field. Nothing will raise the ire of your network administrator or Internet service provider more than if you enter an invalid IP address in this field.

▨ If you have a SLIP connection to the Internet, leave this field empty.

4. Enter the network mask in the Net Mask field and press **Tab**.

▨ This step (and the remaining steps that follow in this sequence) require that you know various values that are specific to your connection. If you don't know these values, ask your network administrator or Internet service provider. *This sequence assumes that the default port settings are correct for your connection.* Again, consider keeping a written record of these settings so you can easily reconfigure the software should you ever need to reinstall it.

5. Press **Tab** seven times. The cursor should be positioned in the field for the first gateway IP address.

6. Enter the IP address for your gateway server in the 1st Gateway IP address field and press **Tab**.

   ▪ Most connections will require only a single gateway server address. If your connection requires more, or if more are available for your use, enter them in the remaining Gateway IP address fields, pressing **Tab** after each entry. If your connection requires only one gateway server address, press **Tab** three times to move the cursor to the 1st Name Server IP address field.

7. With the cursor in the 1st Name Server IP address field, enter the IP address for your connection's domain name server and press **Tab**.

   ▪ Most connections will require only a single domain name server address. If your connection requires more, or if more are available to you, enter them in the remaining Name Server IP address fields, pressing **Tab** after each entry.

8. Press **Alt-K** to save the configuration settings to disk.

There are several other convenient features Minuet offers that you might want to take advantage of. Or, you can begin using the program to compose and send e-mail messages. If you want to begin using Minuet without configuring it for your own personal preferences, you can skip the rest of this section and advance to "Using Minuet E-Mail" on page 76.

Follow these steps to further customize Minuet to your own personal preferences.

1. Press **Alt-S** to display the Setup menu.

2. From the Setup menu, select the Preferences… command. The Preferences dialog box appears, as shown in Figure 4-4.

Figure 4-4: Minuet
Preferences
dialog box.

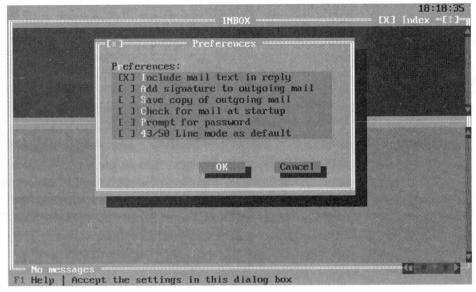

3. Press **Alt-I** to include the text of the original e-mail messages when you reply to them.

   ▨ Note that you can toggle the state of any of the available options in the Minuet Preferences dialog box with the appropriate **Alt**-key combination. You can also repeatedly press **Tab** to highlight an option and press the **Spacebar** to toggle its state.

4. Press **Alt-A** to include your *signature* in all outgoing e-mail messages.

   ▨ A signature is a three- or four-line text file containing your contact information. An example is shown in Figure 4-5. (For more on signatures, see the sidebar on page 129.)

5. Press **Alt-S** to save a copy of all outgoing e-mail messages. All outgoing messages will be saved in the SENTMAIL folder.

6. Press **Alt-C** to automatically check for new e-mail each time you launch Minuet.

7. Press **Alt-P** to prompt you for your e-mail account password each time you send or retrieve e-mail.

8. Press **Alt-4** to launch Minuet with the highest resolution mode allowed by your computer's video display.

9. Press **Alt-K** to save your settings to disk and dismiss the Minuet Preferences dialog box.

Define a *signature* (a three- or four-line text file containing your contact information) for your outgoing e-mail with these steps.

1. Press **Alt-S** to display the Setup menu.

2. From the Setup menu, select the Signature… command. The Signature dialog box appears, as shown in the example in Figure 4-5.

Figure 4-5: Example Minuet Signature dialog box.

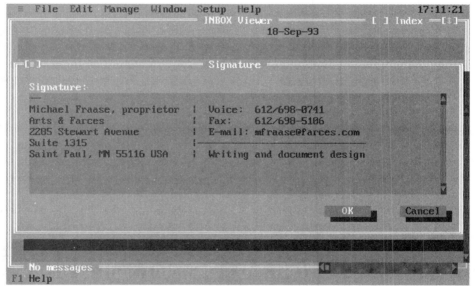

3. Enter your signature information in the dialog box.

4. Press **Alt-K** to save your signature file to disk and dismiss the Signature dialog box.

For more information on signatures, see the sidebar in Chapter 5 on page 129.

You have now completely configured Minuet and are ready to use it to send and receive e-mail, read and post network news, upload and download files, browse information resources and login to remote computers.

Internet/NREN Business Journal.
The *Internet/NREN Business Journal* is a new hardcopy newsletter from Michael Strangelove. Internet/Bitnet/NREN topics will include case studies of business ventures, legislation news, advertising strategy and ethics, net-based public relations, university-industry activity, resource directories and emerging opportunities. Bimonthly plus six annual special supplements, $75– $149. For information contact 441495@acadvm1.uottawa.ca

Using Minuet E-Mail

Minuet contains a full-featured e-mail program comparable to many commercial products. You can download complete documentation —in Microsoft Word and ASCII text formats—from the boombox.micro.umn.edu in the /pub/pc/popmail-3.2.2/manuals/ directory.

Retrieving & Reading E-Mail With Minuet

Use these steps to login to your mail server and automatically retrieve any waiting e-mail.

1. Establish your connection to the Internet, if necessary. If you're using UMSLIP, type **slip dial** at the command prompt, and the connection will be automatically established.

   ▨ If you are using other SLIP or PPP software, follow the directions provided by your network administrator or service provider to establish the connection.

   ▨ If you enjoy a direct connection to the Internet, there is no need to establish a connection.

2. Launch Minuet by typing **minuet** at the command prompt.

   ▨ If you have configured Minuet to automatically check for mail, the program will automatically login to the server and download any e-mail addressed to you. The rest of this section assumes that you will be checking for e-mail manually. In either case, the INBOX Viewer will appear.

3. Press **F3** to retrieve your e-mail from the e-mail server you specified during the configuration process. The User Information dialog box will be displayed, as shown in Figure 4-6.

Figure 4-6: Minuet
User Information
dialog box.

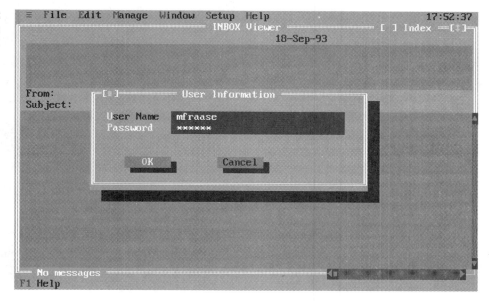

4. Enter your e-mail password and press **Enter**. The Progress dialog box appears, providing feedback about the status of your e-mail retrieval.

   ▧ If your password is rejected you'll have to press **F3** and then reenter your password in the User Information dialog box.

   ▧ If there is a problem connecting to the mail server, a dialog box will inform you of the problem. Try pressing **F3** again; if Minuet still has problems establishing a connection, see your network administrator.

   ▧ If you have no e-mail waiting on the server, the Progress window will disappear, and Minuet will return to its previous state. If you have waiting e-mail, it will be downloaded and the process will be updated in the Progress dialog box. When all your waiting e-mail has been retrieved, you will be notified (based on the configuration settings you specified), and the first new message will automatically be displayed, as shown in Figure 4-7.

Figure 4-7: Minuet
INBOX Viewer.

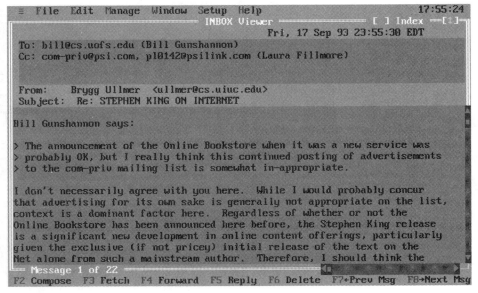

```
≡  File  Edit  Manage  Window  Setup  Help                    17:55:24
═══════════════════════════════ INBOX Viewer ═══════════════════ [ ] Index ══[ ]═
                                             Fri, 17 Sep 93 23:55:30 EDT
To: bill@cs.uofs.edu (Bill Gunshannon)
Cc: com-priv@psi.com, p10142@psilink.com (Laura Fillmore)


From:    Brygg Ullmer  <ullmer@cs.uiuc.edu>
Subject:  Re: STEPHEN KING ON INTERNET

Bill Gunshannon says:

> The announcement of the Online Bookstore when it was a new service was
> probably OK, but I really think this continued posting of advertisements
> to the com-priv mailing list is somewhat in-appropriate.

I don't necessarily agree with you here.  While I would probably concur
that advertising for its own sake is generally not appropriate on the list,
context is a dominant factor here.  Regardless of whether or not the
Online Bookstore has been announced here before, the Stephen King release
is a significant new development in online content offerings, particularly
given the exclusive (if not pricey) initial release of the text on the
Net alone from such a mainstream author.  Therefore, I should think the
═ Message 1 of 22 ═══════════════════════════════════◁▯                    ▶
F2 Compose  F3 Fetch  F4 Forward  F5 Reply  F6 Delete  F7←Prev Msg  F8→Next Msg
```

5. Press **F5** to reply to the current message (see "Replying to E-Mail Messages With Minuet" on page 81 for more information).

6. Press **F6** to delete the current message and advance to the next message.

   ▪ Messages that you delete are moved to the TRASH folder; they are not removed from your hard disk until you use the Empty Trash command.

7. Press **F8** to advance to the next message without deleting the current message.

E-mail messages are stored in the In mail folder until they are deleted or transferred to another mail folder. See "Managing E-Mail With Minuet" on page 82 for more information.

Creating & Sending an E-Mail Message With Minuet

Use these steps to create and send an e-mail message with Minuet.

1. Establish your connection to the Internet, if necessary. If you're using UMSLIP, type **slip dial** at the command prompt, and the connection will be automatically established.

- If you are using other SLIP or PPP software, follow the directions provided by your network administrator or service provider to establish the connection.

- If you enjoy a direct connection to the Internet, there is no need to establish a connection.

2. Launch Minuet by typing **minuet** at the command prompt.

- If you have configured Minuet to automatically check for mail, the program will automatically login to the server and download any e-mail addressed to you. In either case, the INBOX Viewer will appear.

3. Press **F2**. The Minuet Composer appears, as shown in Figure 4-8.

Figure 4-8: Minuet Composer.

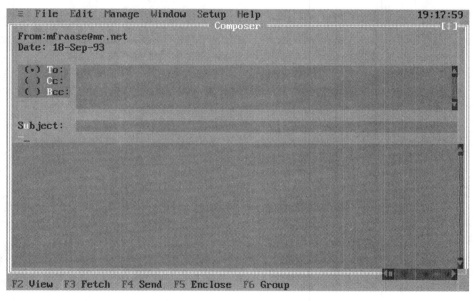

4. Enter the e-mail address of the recipient in the To: field and press **Tab**.

5. Enter the e-mail address of any recipients to whom you want to send a courtesy copy in the Cc: field and press **Tab**. **Tab** through the field if you don't want to include any courtesy copies.

- Courtesy copies (known as *carbon copies* in the snail-mail business world) are copies of your message sent to third parties *with* a notification to the addressee.

6. Enter the e-mail address of any recipients to whom you want to send a blind courtesy copy in the Bcc: field and press **Tab**. **Tab** through the field if you don't want to include any blind courtesy copies.

   ▧ Blind courtesy copies are copies of your message sent to third parties *without* a notification to the addressee.

7. Enter a short subject for the message in the Subject: field and press **Tab**.

Blind Courtesy Copies.

Courtesy copies used to be called carbon copies. But since we don't use carbon paper anymore, they're now called courtesy copies by the high-tech, in-the-know crowd. They're useful for distributing identical messages to a number of people.

Most people don't consider *blind* courtesy copies very nice, because they're secretive. They're generally used by someone who is either trying to cover a mistake or by someone who has something to hide. Privacy is a good thing. Secrecy isn't.

Blind courtesy copies are useful for very large mailing lists because sending letters using the blind courtesy copy addressing feature prevents the names of all the recipients from appearing in the message header and overwhelming the actual message.

The distribution list for the electronic updates for this book is handled with blind courtesy copies. I could be altruistic and say that I do it that way to keep the header short, but that would not be completely true. If I used courtesy copies instead of blind courtesy copies, anyone on the list would have access to the entire list. That's not a good thing for your privacy. Nor is it a good thing for my bank account. I'm not sure how to balance the tension between privacy and secrecy. Let me know if you've figured it out.

8. Enter the body of your message. You can type or paste text into this field.

9. Press **F4**. Your message will be sent to the mail server.

Replying to E-Mail Messages With Minuet

Replying to an e-mail message is similar to creating a new message. Here's how to do it:

1. Navigate to the message to which you want to reply.

2. Press **F5**. The original message will be opened in the Minuet Composer, with a ">" preceding each line, as shown in Figure 4-9.

Figure 4-9:
Replying to an
e-mail message
with Minuet.

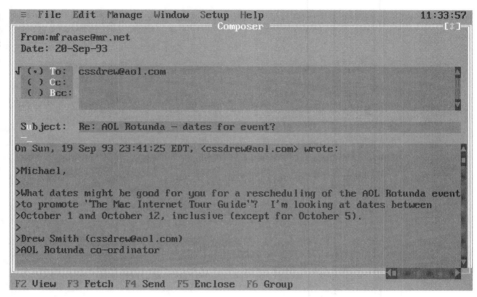

Internet Quoting Conventions.

The ">" that precedes each line of a message is the Internet convention for quoted text. There are several variations, but ">" is the most common.

Second-hand quotes—quoted replies to quotes—are shown with a ">>" preceding each line.

This can soon get ridiculous. I've seen heated *flame wars* (vitriolic online debates) erupt into five or six levels of ">"s. It's not a pretty sight, and it's impossible to figure out who said what to whom.

A good rule of thumb when replying to e-mail or responding to a message posting is to quote only material that is necessary to further the understanding of the letter or message thread. Don't, for instance, quote a 300-line message in its entirety and add only "I agree" at the end.

The PC Internet Tour Guide

3. Enter the body of your message. You can type or paste text into this area.

4. Press **F4**. Your message will be sent to the mail server you specified when you configured Minuet. A dialog box is displayed informing you of the status of the message sending process.

Managing E-Mail With Minuet

Minuet lets you organize your incoming e-mail by creating new mail folders for storing and moving messages. Minuet defaults to routing all incoming e-mail to a single mail folder named INBOX. In Minuet, a "mail folder" is a collection of e-mail messages.

To create new mail folders:

1. Launch Minuet by typing **minuet** at the command prompt.

   ▪ If you have configured Minuet to automatically check for mail, the program will automatically login to the server and download any e-mail addressed to you. In either case, the INBOX Viewer will appear.

2. Press **Alt-M** to display the Manage menu.

3. From the Manage menu, select the Go to folder... command. The Go to folder dialog box appears, as shown in Figure 4-10.

Figure 4-10: Minuet Go to folder dialog box.

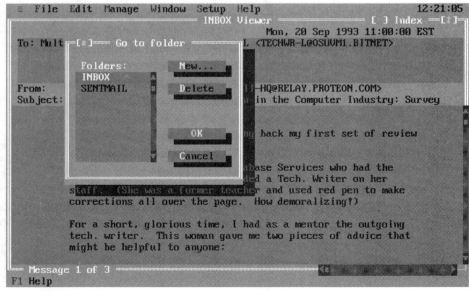

▓ The scrolling list in the left panel of the dialog box contains a list of available mail folders. Two mail folders—INBOX and SENTMAIL—were automatically created when you installed Minuet.

4. Move to any available mail folder by using the **Up** and **Down arrow** keys to select the mail folder and pressing **Enter**.

5. Create a new mail folder by pressing **Alt-N**. The New folder dialog box appears, as shown in Figure 4-11.

Figure 4-11: Minuet New folder dialog box.

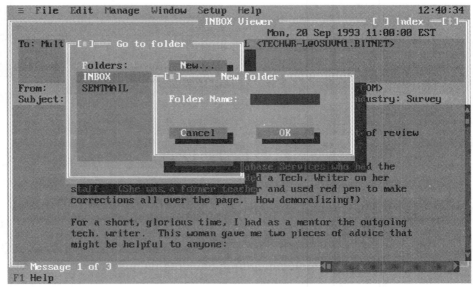

6. Enter a name for the new mail folder and press **Enter** to create it. A new mail folder will be created with the name you specified, as shown in the example in Figure 4-12.

Figure 4-12: Minuet
Go to folder
dialog box with
new mail folder.

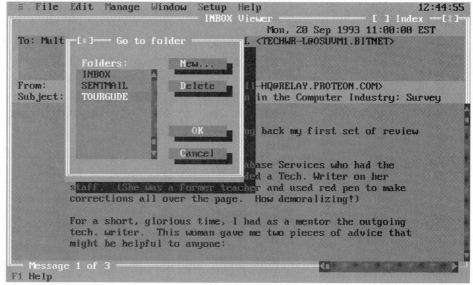

7. Repeat steps 5–6 to create any additional mail folders you may need.

To delete any unneeded mail folders:

1. Launch Minuet by typing **minuet** at the command prompt.

   ▣ If you have configured Minuet to automatically check for mail, the program will automatically login to the server and download any e-mail addressed to you. In either case, the INBOX Viewer will appear.

2. Press **Alt-M** to display the Manage menu.

3. From the Manage menu, select the Go to folder… command. The Go to folder dialog box appears, as shown in Figure 4-10.

4. Select the mail folder you want to delete by using the **Up** and **Down arrow** keys.

5. Press **Alt-D**. A Confirm dialog box will appear asking if you're sure you want to delete the selected mail folder *and its contents*, as shown in Figure 4-13.

Figure 4-13: Minuet
Confirm delete
mail folder
dialog box.

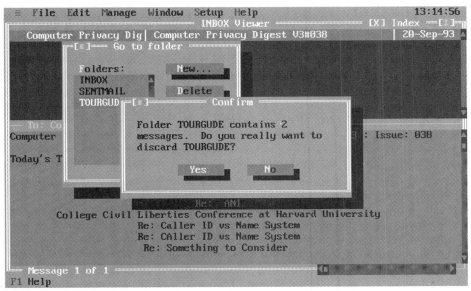

6. Press **Enter**. The selected mail folder *and its contents* will be deleted.

Mailbox Strategies.

You can create mail folders for any number of filing and organization strategies. Some people like to create folders for each month or week, filing their messages by date. Others like to create a folder for each person they regularly correspond with, organizing messages based on contact.

The strategy that works best for me is to create mail folders for various topics or projects I'm working on. When new e-mail messages come in, I sort them by content. Many e-mail programs have intelligent *filters* that can be used to automatically sort incoming e-mail based on a wide range of criteria, including sender, addressee or even the site from which the message was sent.

To move e-mail messages between your mail folders:

1. Launch Minuet by typing **minuet** at the command prompt.

   ▓ If you have configured Minuet to automatically check for mail, the program will automatically login to the server and download any e-mail addressed to you. In either case, the INBOX Viewer will appear.

2. Press **F7** and/or **F8** to navigate to the e-mail message you wish to move from your INBOX to another mail folder.

   ▓ Alternatively, you can use the Go to folder… command on the Manage menu to open a mail folder other than your INBOX.

3. Press **Alt-M** to display the Manage menu.

4. From the Manage menu, select the Move this message command. The Move msgs. to folder dialog box appears, as shown in Figure 4-14.

Figure 4-14: Minuet Move msgs. to folder dialog box.

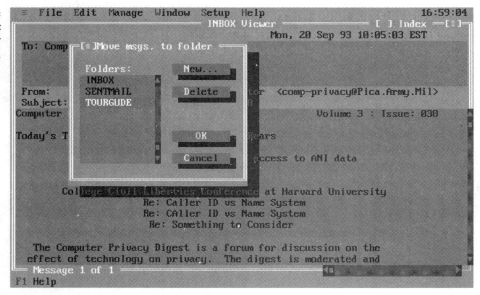

5. Use the **Up** and **Down arrow** keys to select the mail folder into which you want to move the current e-mail message.

6. Press **Enter**. The current e-mail message will be moved to the mail folder you selected.

7. Repeat steps 2–6 for each additional message you want to move. Alternatively, you can navigate to the message you wish to move and press **Alt-T**, bypassing the Manage menu.

E-mail is easier to manage if you can see and work with a listing of messages, rather than a single entire message itself. To display and navigate an index of messages in Minuet:

1. Press **Alt-I**. The Minuet display changes to show an index of e-mail messages for the current mail folder in the top portion of the screen, as shown in Figure 4-15.

Figure 4-15: Minuet e-mail message index.

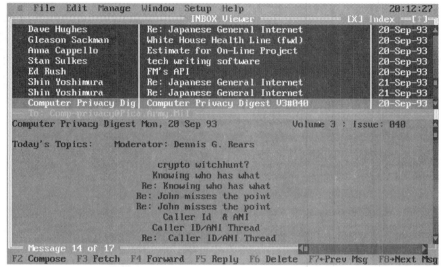

2. Press **Alt-M** to display the Manage menu.

3. From the Manage menu, select the Sort folder… command. The Sort Mail Folder dialog box appears, as shown in Figure 4-16.

Figure 4-16: Minuet Sort Mail Folder dialog box.

4. Select the key on which you want the messages sorted: arrival time, message subject or sender.

5. Press **Enter**. The messages in the mail folder will be sorted on the criterion you specified.

6. Use the **Up** and **Down arrow** keys to navigate to the index line of the first message you want to work with.

7. Press **Alt-M** to display the Manage menu.

8. From the Manage menu, select the Mark this message command. A check mark appears next to the marked message.

9. Repeat steps 6–8 for additional messages with which you want to work.

10. Press **Alt-M** to display the Manage menu.

11. From the Manage menu, select the operation you want to perform on the group of marked messages:

   ▪ Select the Move marked messages command to move the group of messages to another mail folder.

   ▪ Select the Trash marked messages command to move the group of messages to the TRASH mail folder.

   ▪ Select the Copy marked messages command to copy the group of messages to another mail folder.

You can search for text contained within the e-mail messages stored in a mail folder with these steps.

1. Press **Alt-M** to display the Manage menu.

2. From the Manage menu, select the Mark messages with… command. The Mark messages containing dialog box appears, as shown in Figure 4-17.

Figure 4-17:
Minuet Mark
messages
containing
dialog box.

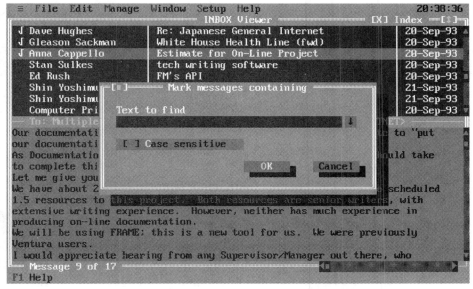

3. Enter the text you want to search for in the field.

4. Press **Enter**. Messages that contain the text you specified will be marked in the message index.

5. Press **Alt-M** to display the Manage menu.

6. From the Manage menu, select the operation you want to perform on the group of marked messages:

   ▪ Select the Move marked messages command to move the group of messages to another mail folder.

   ▪ Select the Trash marked messages command to move the group of messages to the TRASH mail folder.

   ▪ Select the Copy marked messages command to copy the group of messages to another mail folder.

E-mail messages are stored in the INBOX mail folder until they are deleted or transferred to another mail folder. To delete existing e-mail from any of your mail folders:

1. Launch Minuet by typing **minuet** at the command prompt.

   ▪ If you have configured Minuet to automatically check for mail, the program will automatically login to the server and download any e-mail addressed to you. In either case, the INBOX Viewer will appear.

2. Press **F7** and/or **F8** to navigate to the e-mail message you wish to delete.

   ▓ Alternatively, you can use the Index toggle command (**Alt-I**) to display an index of available messages.

3. Press **Alt-M** to display the Manage menu.

4. From the Manage menu, select the Trash this message command. A Confirm dialog box appears asking if you really want to move this message to the Trash, as shown in Figure 4-18.

Figure 4-18: Minuet Confirm delete message dialog box.

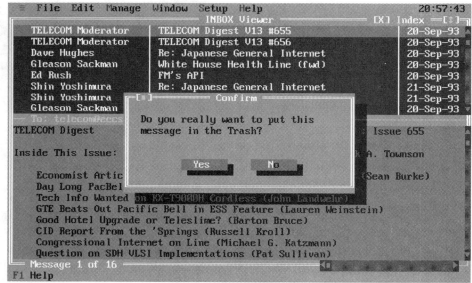

   ▓ As with transferring messages, you can select a range of messages by using the Mark this message command.

5. Press **Enter**. The message (or group of marked messages) is moved to the TRASH mail folder.

   ▓ "Deleted" messages aren't actually erased; they're simply moved to a special TRASH mail folder. Any message that has been "deleted" can be recovered by moving it out of the TRASH mail folder before the Empty trash command is chosen.

6. Press **Alt-M** to display the Manage menu.

7. From the Manage menu, select the Empty trash command. A Confirm dialog box appears, asking you if you're sure you want to discard the Trash.

8. Press **Enter**. The messages contained in the TRASH mail folder will be deleted from your hard disk.

Compressing space and time.

Ralph Brandi uses the Internet to compress space and time and to meet people that he would otherwise never encounter. Here is his story of how he uses the Internet:

"The net demolishes the barriers of time and location. If you've got some kind of fairly obscure interest, you can be pretty sure there is someone else on the net who shares it. The fact that they don't live in your neighborhood doesn't prevent you from carrying on an extended conversation. They can even live on the other side of the world and you don't have to worry about waking them up.

The best thing about the net that I've encountered in my 6 or so years connected has nothing to do with computers: it's the people. By communicating with people I share interests with, I've made a number of good friends.

I had a net.friend from New Zealand visit me for a week last year after a couple of years of corresponding over the net. I had a great time showing him New York City and the east coast, and he brought some books and records for me from New Zealand that I couldn't find for love nor money here in the U.S. I'm going to be visiting him in London, where he lives now, this summer.

Some months ago, I was receiving a couple of low-powered radio stations from Australia on my shortwave radio. I had been trying to receive these stations literally for years, and they're highly sought-after targets among shortwave listeners. I posted a note to the rec.radio.shortwave newsgroup. The following morning I had e-mail from a couple of people in Boston who had followed up on that tip and been rewarded with their first receptions of the stations. I later met them at a convention of shortwave enthusiasts, and had a very enjoyable lunch with them and some of their friends.

The common thread here is the interactions with *people*, not computers."

Ph Servers.

The Ph protocol was developed by Steve Dorner—author of the Eudora e-mail program—while he was at the Urbana-Champaign campus of the University of Illinois. Ph provides a way to look up e-mail addresses for colleagues and associates, usually at a single location.

In order for you to use the Ph lookup capabilities of an e-mail program, your mail server must also have a Ph server installed and properly configured.

Unfortunately, Ph servers are provided only for single locations—a large corporate site or a university, for example. Ph is useful only if you know the organization with which the person you want to contact is affiliated.

There are other methods—some relatively simple, others mind-numbingly sophisticated—to find e-mail addresses, and a few are covered elsewhere in this book. But the easiest way to find out someone's e-mail address is to call him or her on the telephone and ask. Sometimes the simplest methods are the best.

Finding Addresses

If you work within a large corporation or university, finding the e-mail addresses of your colleagues is usually simple enough because your site will probably have a Ph server. For more information on the Ph protocol and Ph servers, see the Ph Servers sidebar above. The problem is that the Ph server will probably only have addresses for people at your site or within your organization, which doesn't help you if you're trying to send e-mail to someone across the country or around the world.

The easiest way to find the e-mail address of someone is to call him or her on the telephone and ask for the e-mail address. It's a low-tech solution to a high-tech problem. Because of security and privacy concerns, and because there is no unifying standard for e-mail directories on disparate systems, there is no central directory for Internet e-mail addresses.

But even though no central Internet directory exists, there are a few tools you can use to try to find e-mail addresses.

Qedit.

Qedit is a high-quality text editor that allows you to use the UNIX grep command to search for patterns of text across multiple files. The program is both powerful and easy to use and has become a mainstay on most MS-DOS users' computers. Qedit is so popular, it has its own directory at the largest MS-DOS file archive on the Internet. The program is available by FTP from oak.oakland.edu in the /pub/msdos/qedit/ directory.

Using Finger

Finger is a command that looks at the user login file on a UNIX system. Since most computers on the Internet run some variation of UNIX, Finger is probably the best place to start.

Minuet includes a built-in Finger interface that's very easy to use:

1. Establish your connection to the Internet, if necessary. If you're using UMSLIP, type **slip dial** at the command prompt, and the connection will be automatically established.

   ▤ If you are using other SLIP or PPP software, follow the directions provided by your network administrator or service provider to establish the connection.

   ▤ If you enjoy a direct connection to the Internet, there is no need to establish a connection.

2. Launch Minuet by typing **minuet** at the command prompt. The INBOX Viewer appears.

3. Press **Alt-Space.** The System menu appears.

4. From the System menu, select the Finger command. The Global Address Book dialog box appears, as shown in Figure 4-19.

Figure 4-19: Minuet
Global Address
Book dialog box.

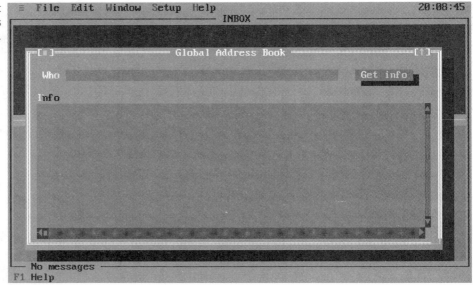

5. Enter the user name of the person you are trying to locate in the username@domain.top-domain format and press **Enter**. The results will be displayed in the lower panel of the dialog box, as shown in Figure 4-20.

Figure 4-20: Minuet
Finger results.

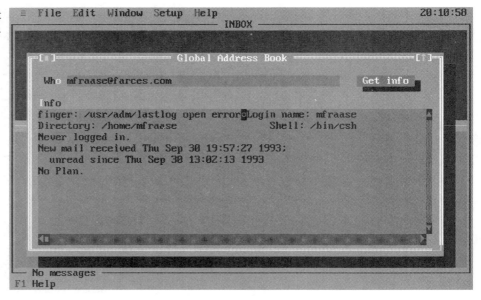

Using MIT's USENET User List

If the person you are trying to locate has ever posted a message to any of the USENET newsgroups, you may be able to locate him or her by using a specialized mail server at the Massachusetts Institute of Technology (MIT). The MIT server constantly monitors incoming USENET postings and extracts each poster's name and e-mail address.

To use MIT's USENET User List service:

1. Establish your connection to the Internet, if necessary. If you're using UMSLIP, type **slip dial** at the command prompt, and the connection will be automatically established.

   ▓ If you are using other SLIP or PPP software, follow the directions provided by your network administrator or service provider to establish the connection.

   ▓ If you enjoy a direct connection to the Internet, there is no need to establish a connection.

2. Launch Minuet (or another e-mail program), by typing **minuet** (or the appropriate command) at the command prompt.

3. Send an e-mail message consisting only of the single line: send usenet-addresses/*name* where *name* is the name of the person you are trying to locate. For example, to search for my e-mail address, the line would be send usenet-addresses/fraase

4. Address the e-mail message to mail-server@pit-manager.mit.edu

5. Send the e-mail message. You'll soon receive a responding message from the MIT mail server that looks something like the one shown in Figure 4-21.

Figure 4-21: MIT
USENET User List
example.

```
≡  File  Edit  Manage  Window  Setup  Help                    23:16:51
══════════════════════════ INBOX Viewer ═══════════ [ ] Index ══[↕]═
                                        Tue, 21 Sep 93 00:12:29 -0400
 To: Michael Fraase <mfraase@farces.com>



 From:   <mail-server@rtfm.MIT.EDU>
 Subject:  mail-server: "send usenet-addresses/fraase"
 ────cut here────
mfraase@farces.com (Michael Fraase) (Aug 3 93)
mfraase@mr.net (Michael Fraase) (Jan 11 93)
Michael Fraase <mfraase@farces.com> (May 21 93)
 ────cut here────




══ Message 18 of 19 ═════════════════════════◄▓▓▓▓▓▓▓▓▓▓═══════►
 F2 Compose  F3 Fetch  F4 Forward  F5 Reply  F6 Delete  F7←Prev Msg  F8→Next Msg
```

Using Whois

Whois is a directory that is maintained by the DDN Network Information Center. Unfortunately, it contains listings only for people who are
responsible for the actual working of the Internet and is useless for
most people in the real world.

The easiest way to access any available Whois server is by using
Gopher. More information on configuring and using Gopher is provided in Chapter 7, "Using Gopher." Search for addresses using Whois
with these steps.

1. Establish your connection to the Internet, if necessary. If you're
   using UMSLIP, type **slip dial** at the command prompt, and the
   connection will be automatically established.

   ▓ If you are using other SLIP or PPP software, follow the directions provided by your network administrator or service provider to establish the connection.

   ▓ If you enjoy a direct connection to the Internet, there is no need
   to establish a connection.

2. Launch Minuet by typing **minuet** at the command prompt.

3. Press **Alt-W** to display the Windows menu.

4. From the Windows menu, select the Gopher command. You'll automatically be logged into the Gopher server you specified during the configuration procedure.

5. Navigate to the Mother Gopher at gopher.tc.umn.edu. The main menu for the University of Minnesota Gopher server appears as shown in Figure 4-22.

Figure 4-22: Main menu for the University of Minnesota Gopher server.

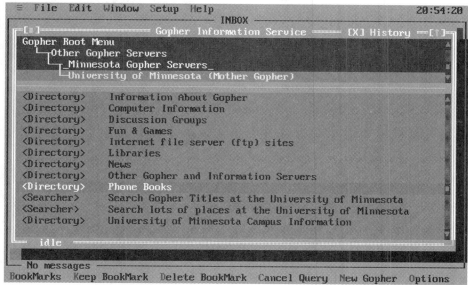

6. Select the Phone Books menu item and press **Enter**. The Phone Books menu is displayed, as shown in Figure 4-23.

Figure 4-23: Gopher Phone Books menu.

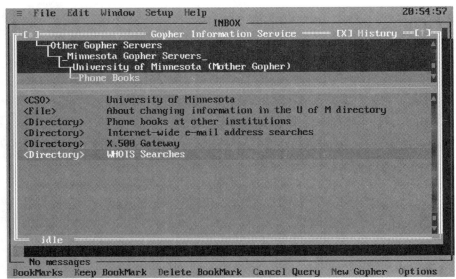

7. Select the Whois Searches menu item and press **Enter**. A list of available Whois servers is displayed in a Gopher window, as shown in Figure 4-24.

Figure 4-24: Gopher Whois servers menu.

8. Select the Whois server you want to access from the list and press **Enter**. A Search Text dialog box appears, as shown in Figure 4-25.

Figure 4-25: Whois server Search Text dialog box within Gopher.

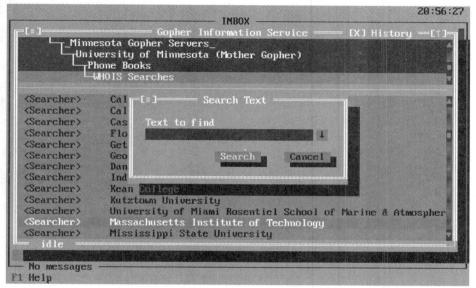

9. Enter the last name of the person you want to search for in the Text to find field and press **Enter**. A menu will appear allowing you to read about the ramifications of the search or to commit to the search.

10. Select the Commit to search item and press **Enter**. The search will be initiated and the results will be displayed in a new window, as shown in Figure 4-26.

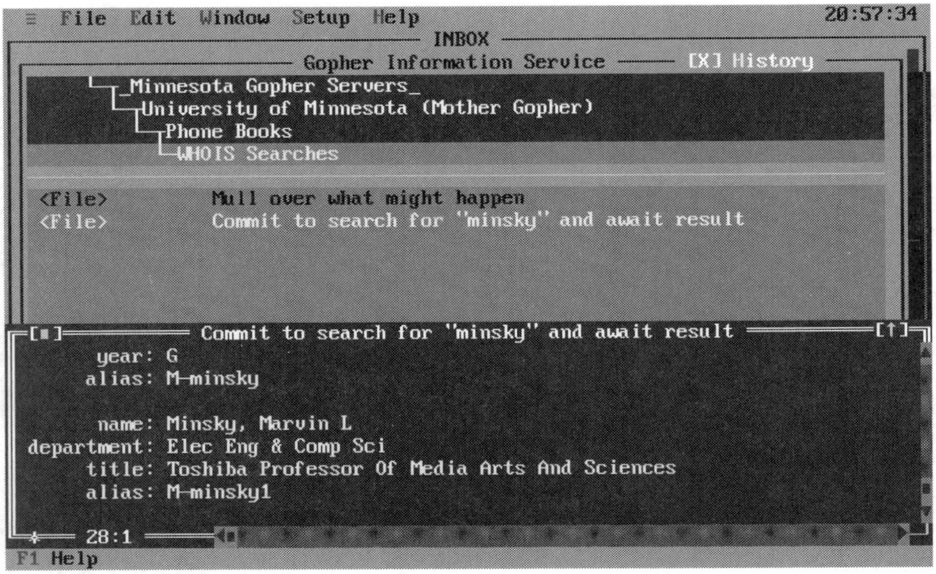

Figure 4-26: Results of a Whois search within Gopher.

```
≡  File  Edit  Window  Setup  Help                    20:57:34
──────────────────── INBOX ────────────────────
──────── Gopher Information Service ──────── [X] History ──────
        └─Minnesota Gopher Servers_
          └─University of Minnesota (Mother Gopher)
            └─Phone Books
              └─WHOIS Searches

<File>         Mull over what might happen
<File>         Commit to search for "minsky" and await result


┌─[■]─────────── Commit to search for "minsky" and await result ═══════[↑]┐
        year: G
       alias: M-minsky

        name: Minsky, Marvin L
  department: Elec Eng & Comp Sci
       title: Toshiba Professor Of Media Arts And Sciences
       alias: M-minsky1

└─ 28:1 ──────◄■                                                         ►┘
F1 Help
```

Using the PSI White Pages

Performance Systems International (PSI)—an Internet service provider—offers a directory service that is accessible to Internet users. Unfortunately, most of the listings are for PSI clients or employees.

The easiest way to access the PSI White Pages is by using Gopher as described in the previous section, "Using Whois." The PSI White Pages appear in the menu of available Whois servers. More information on configuring and using Gopher is provided in Chapter 7.

InterNIC Directory Services

In April 1993, the InterNIC began providing Internet registration and directory services. The InterNIC is a collaboration of General Atomics, AT&T and Network Solutions with a charter of simplifying the use of the Internet. The InterNIC's directory services are provided by AT&T, offering three core resources:

- Directory of Directories
- Directory Services
- Database Services

The InterNIC Directory Services are a sort of electronic White and Yellow Pages for registered Internet users. As of August 1993, the InterNIC had processed more than 100,000 requests for Internet registration information. If you're keeping score, that's more than one request every three minutes, 24-hours-a-day, since the service's inception.

There are various ways to access the InterNIC, but the easiest way to find someone's e-mail address is by using, yup, you guessed it—e-mail. Here's how:

1. Establish your connection to the Internet, if necessary. If you're using UMSLIP, type **slip dial** at the command prompt, and the connection will be automatically established.

   ■ If you are using other SLIP or PPP software, follow the directions provided by your network administrator or service provider to establish the connection.

   ■ If you enjoy a direct connection to the Internet, there is no need to establish a connection.

2. Launch Minuet by typing **minuet** at the command prompt.

3. Send an e-mail message consisting only of the single line: person *firstname lastname, organization, country*

   ■ *firstname* is the first name of the person you are trying to locate.

   ■ *lastname* is the last name of the person you are trying to locate.

   ■ *organization* is the name of the company or institution with which the person you are trying to locate is affiliated.

   ■ *country* is the country in which the person you are trying to find is located.

   ■ For example, to search for my e-mail address, the line would be person michael fraase, arts and farces, us

4. Address the e-mail message to mailserv@ds.internic.net

5. Send the e-mail message. You'll soon receive a responding message from the MIT mail server containing the e-mail address and other contact information for anyone matching the search criteria you entered. The InterNIC also provides a wealth of other services for Internet users, and you can perform directory searches interactively. Look for more information on the InterNIC in Chapter 8, "Other Internet Resources," and in the electronic updates to this book.

E-Mail Address Starter Kit

Lots of PC-related companies and luminaries are accessible by Internet e-mail. A starter kit of some e-mail addresses is provided in Table 4-2.

Table 4-2: PC-related e-mail addresses.

Company/Person	E-Mail Address
PC WEEK	2393520@mcimail.com
Spencer the Katt	spencer@pcweek.ziff.com
John Perry Barlow	barlow@well.sf.ca.us
Jerry Berman	jberman@eff.org
InfoWorld	letters@infoworld.com
Stewart Brand	sbb@well.sf.ca.us
CPSR	cpsr-staff@csli.stanford.edu
Stewart Alsop	stewart_alsop@infoworld.com
Dan Farber	72511.124@compuserve.com
Bob Metcalfe	bob_metcalfe@infoworld.com
Rachel Parker	rachel_parker@infoworld.com
Tom Quinlan	tom_quinlan@infoworld.com
Mitch Kapor	mkapor@eff.org
University of MN SLIP	slip@boombox.micro.umn.edu
Howard Rheingold	hlr@well.sf.ca.us
Whole Earth Review	wer@well.sf.ca.us

And don't worry that you might be annoying these people by sending them mail—they've all published their e-mail addresses.

Electronic Mailing Lists

Electronic mailing lists have very little in common with their paper mail counterparts, even though they work in much the same manner:

- Electronic mailing lists actually serve a useful purpose.
- You have to specifically request to join an electronic mailing list.
- Electronic mailing lists don't overflow landfills.

Electronic mailing lists exist either as a forum for group discussions or as distribution lists. Currently there are close to 3,000 publicly accessible mailing lists on the Internet. They cover a wide variety of subjects, and the number grows daily. You can find a mailing list for just about any subject of interest. If not, you can always start your own.

You can join a mailing list by sending e-mail to the list administrator. Once your name has been added to the list, you'll begin receiving messages from other members of the list, and you can read and respond to any of those messages. Your responses will automatically be forwarded to all the other subscribers on the list.

The quality of mailing lists is generally higher than in USENET newsgroups because the "signal to noise ratio" is higher—there are generally more worthwhile messages in a day's mailing list message traffic than there are in a day's newsgroup message traffic. It's pretty rare to find an Ivy League freshman wanting to sell a microwave oven in a cyberpunk mailing list, but that's a pretty common happening in most any newsgroup (especially in the early autumn).

You can download a list of current mailing lists from ftp.nisc.sri.com in the directory /netinfo/interest-groups/. For more information on using the File Transfer Protocol (FTP) to download files, see "Downloading Files With Minuet" on page 154.

Subscribing to Mailing Lists

Most mailing lists are set up to automatically forward any message sent to the list to all members of the mailing list. You subscribe to an electronic mailing list by sending an e-mail request to the list's administrative address. The list's *administrative address* is almost always different from the list's *submission address*. Many mailing list administrative addresses can be recognized by the word "request" in the list address. Make sure you use the right address for the job.

In general, to subscribe to a mailing list you send a short message requesting a subscription to the mailing list's administrative address. Some mailing lists are automated and have specific subscription requirements.

For example, to subscribe to the automated New Mailing Lists mailing list:

1. Establish your connection to the Internet, if necessary. If you're using UMSLIP, type **slip dial** at the command prompt, and the connection will be automatically established.

   ■ If you are using other SLIP or PPP software, follow the directions provided by your network administrator or service provider to establish the connection.

   ■ If you enjoy a direct connection to the Internet, there is no need to establish a connection.

2. Launch Minuet by typing **minuet** at the command prompt.

3. Send a message consisting only of the single line: subscribe new-list *your name* where *your name* is your first and last name. For example, for my subscription, the line would be subscribe new-list michael fraase

4. Address the e-mail message to listserv@vm1.nodak.edu

5. Send the e-mail message. You'll receive a response introducing you to the mailing list and instructions on how to use it.

The New-List Lists is run by a *Listserv* automated mail server. A Listserv mail server is simply a computer program that accepts and responds to the commands you send it.

Use these steps to subscribe to a manual mailing list, like the Electronic Frontier Foundation's mailing list.

1. Establish your connection to the Internet, if necessary. If you're using UMSLIP, type **slip dial** at the command prompt, and the connection will be automatically established.

   ■ If you are using other SLIP or PPP software, follow the directions provided by your network administrator or service provider to establish the connection.

   ■ If you enjoy a direct connection to the Internet, there is no need to establish a connection.

2. Launch Minuet by typing **minuet** at the command prompt.

3. Send a brief message requesting to be added to the mailing list. Just a simple message like "please add me to the EFF mailing list, thanks" is enough.

4. Address the message to eff-request@eff.org

5. Send the e-mail message. You'll receive a response from the list owner or the person administrating the mailing list.

A general overview for some of the popular mailing lists is provided in Table 4-3.

Table 4-3:
Electronic mailing
list subscription
information.

Mailing List	Administrative Address	Subscription Instructions	Submission Address
EFF	eff-request@eff.org	Send brief request	eff@eff.org
CPSR	listserv@gwuvm.gwu.edu	subscribe CPSR your name in message	cpsr@gwuvm. gwu.edu
New Mailing Lists	listserv@vm1.nodak.edu	subscribe new-list your name in message	new-list@vm1. nodak.edu
Grateful Dead	dead-flames-request@ fuggles.acc.virginia.edu	Send brief request	dead-flames@fuggles. acc.virginia.edu
Computer Risks	risks-request@csl.sri.com	Send brief request	risks@csl.sri.com
NREN	nren-discuss-request@psi.com	Send brief request	nren-discuss@psi.com
Telecom- munications	telecom-request@eecs.	Send brief request nwu.edu	telecom@eecs. nwu.edu
Computer Underground Digest	tk0jut2@mvs.cso.niu.edu cso.niu.edu	Send brief request	tk0jut2@mvs.
Chaos Corner	chaos-request@pelican.	Send brief request cit.cornell.edu	chaos@pelican. cit.cornell.edu

Canceling Subscriptions to Mailing Lists

In general, to cancel your subscription to a mailing list you send a short message requesting to be removed from the list to the mailing list's administrative address. Some mailing lists are automated and have specific subscription cancellation requirements.

For example, use these instructions to cancel your subscription to the automated New Mailing Lists mailing list.

1. Establish your connection to the Internet, if necessary. If you're using UMSLIP, type **slip dial** at the command prompt, and the connection will be automatically established.

- ▨ If you are using other SLIP or PPP software, follow the directions provided by your network administrator or service provider to establish the connection.

- ▨ If you enjoy a direct connection to the Internet, there is no need to establish a connection.

2. Launch Minuet by typing **minuet** at the command prompt.

3. Send a message consisting only of the single line: signoff new-list *your name* where *your name* is your first and last name. For example, for my subscription, the line would be signoff info-mac michael fraase

4. Address the e-mail message to listserv@vm1.nodak.edu

5. Send the e-mail message. You'll receive a response acknowledging your subscription cancellation and removal from the mailing list.

Use these steps to cancel your subscription to a manual mailing list, like the Electronic Frontier Foundation's mailing list.

1. Establish your connection to the Internet, if necessary. If you're using UMSLIP, type **slip dial** at the command prompt, and the connection will be automatically established.

- ▨ If you are using other SLIP or PPP software, follow the directions provided by your network administrator or service provider to establish the connection.

- ▨ If you enjoy a direct connection to the Internet, there is no need to establish a connection.

2. Launch Minuet by typing **minuet** at the command prompt.

3. Send a brief message requesting to be removed from the mailing list. Just a simple message like "please remove me from the EFF mailing list, thanks" is enough.

4. Address the message to eff-request@eff.org

5. Send the e-mail message. You'll receive a response from the list owner or the person administrating the mailing list acknowledging your subscription cancellation and removal from the mailing list.

E-Mail & Attached Files

In addition to sending *messages*, you can also use e-mail to send any sort of *file* through the Internet. Actually, most PC files have to first be converted to a text document before you can send them through the Internet, but the good news is that with the right tool, the process is automatic and transparent. Minuet (which is included on *The PC Internet Tour Guide Companion Disk*) is just such a tool, and it automatically converts any PC file for transmission over the Net.

Sending Files in E-Mail Messages

To attach a file to an e-mail message in Minuet:

1. Create an e-mail message as you ordinarily would (following steps 1–8 in "Creating & Sending an E-Mail Message With Minuet" beginning on page 78).

2. Press **F5**. The Choose file to enclose dialog box appears, as shown in Figure 4-27.

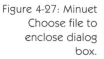
Figure 4-27: Minuet Choose file to enclose dialog box.

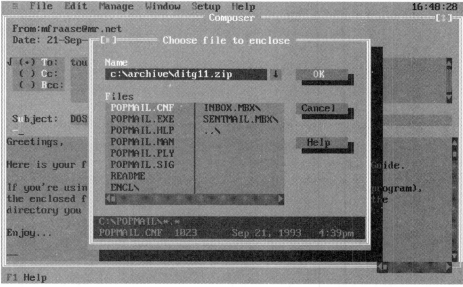

3. Enter the pathname for the file you want to enclose and press **Enter**. The bottom portion of Minuet's Composer screen will be updated to reflect the pathname of the file enclosure, as shown in Figure 4-28.

Figure 4-28: Minuet Composer screen with pathname of file enclosure.

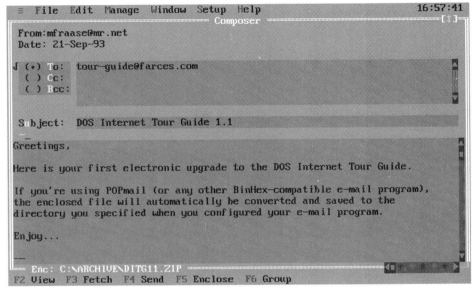

4. Repeat steps 2–3 if you want to enclose additional files.

5. Press **F4** to send your e-mail message and its enclosure(s). Your message will be sent to the mail-server you specified when you configured Minuet. A dialog box is displayed informing you of the status of the message sending process.

Receiving Files in E-Mail Messages

Receiving files enclosed in e-mail messages is automatic in Minuet. The attached files of any e-mail message are automatically converted and saved in the folder you specified for received files when you configured the program. Receiving enclosed files with other e-mail programs may require that the file be processed or decoded after it's received. Refer to the documentation that came with your e-mail program if you have any questions.

Note that many files you receive in e-mail are likely to be compressed. You'll need to use the appropriate file decompression utility to extract the file(s) from the compressed archive. For more information on decompressing files you receive in e-mail see Chapter 6, "Transferring Files."

Files in E-Mail Caveats

From time to time you may receive non-PC files by e-mail. One of the hottest trends in cross-platform software is something called "binary compatibility." That's a software program that runs on different kinds of computer hardware and saves its documents in a format that is common to all the different kinds of computers. FrameMaker documents, for example, are binary compatible regardless of the kind of computer used to create them. I can open NeXT, Macintosh or UNIX FrameMaker files on my PC without converting them.

But since people often compress binary files before sending them, and there are different compression utilities for each kind of computer, you can imagine the problems that can arise. What do you do with UNIX files you receive that have been "tarred and compressed?" Or what about those goofy Mac files that have been "stuffed?" This dilemma is covered in "A Primer on File Types" in Chapter 6, "Transferring Files," on page 148.

Be careful with the size of the files you send by e-mail. Most of the e-mail gateways provided by the commercial information services like CompuServe and America Online have severe file-size limitations, as indicated in Table 4-1.

Moving On

This chapter has given you a thorough overview of electronic mail, from the nuts and bolts of how to send and receive it to the subtleties of e-mail courtesy and etiquette. Look for more in-depth information about using e-mail (plus evaluations of new e-mail products) in this book's electronic updates.

E-mail is most useful for communicating with individuals or small groups of people. But what if you want to exchange information with large groups of people, all over the world? That's what Network News is for, the topic of the next chapter. So let's stop the tour bus at that newsstand just ahead and take a break to learn about reading and posting USENET news articles.

CHAPTER 5

NETWORK NEWS & NEWSGROUPS
Broadsheets of the Broadband

As our tour through the Internet continues, it's easy to become overwhelmed with the size and scope of all that it offers. But one of the most important resources on the Net is easy to overlook: people. Network news and newsgroups are valuable because of the insights and information that people bring to them.

For instance, wouldn't it be great if you could poll all the most knowledgeable folks on the Internet for answers to technical questions or advice on everything from buying the best VCR to cooking the perfect pot roast? While electronic mail is useful for communicating with another individual or small workgroup, you can't send e-mail to thousands of people you don't know, asking questions about topics that don't interest them. (Well, I suppose you *could*, but it probably wouldn't be very productive. And if you think it sounds like it might be a good idea, put this book down and go outside for a walk. A long walk.) But with network news, there's a better way.

What Is Network News & What Are Newsgroups?

Think of network news as a worldwide collection of automatically updated electronic bulletin boards. Except these aren't bulletin boards like the single-line systems set up by thousands of hobbyists in small towns across America. Network news messages are seen by millions of people who generate as much as 40mb of network news information every day.

Electronic bulletin boards are like the cork bulletin boards you see at your local grocery store. You know, where you can find a great deal on a 1955 Buick or a litter of prize poodle puppies. Network news on the Internet is the same concept, only it's all electronic and much more extensive. Imagine the electronic equivalent of 4,000 different grocery store cork bulletin boards, and you've got a pretty good grasp of the thousands of newsgroups that make up network news.

If you've used CompuServe or America Online you're probably familiar with the concept of forums or bulletin boards. Each newsgroup is roughly equivalent to a message area on America Online or CompuServe, except that network news newsgroups are seen by many more people, and on the Internet, highly specialized newsgroups are available for just about any topic.

You'll see everything from announcements for new software products to in-depth technical discussions to candid—and sometimes heated—conversations. These super-heated discussions are called *flame wars*; each individual message in a flame war is called a *flame*. Flames are considered to be in bad taste (except in newsgroups set up just for flames) and starting a flame war will win you lots of enemies with long memories. Each message within an individual newsgroup is called a *post* or an *article*. Articles can be cross-posted to several newsgroups, but this practice is considered to be bad form unless the article is especially relevant to several newsgroups.

Articles within each newsgroup are arranged in *topics*. Topics within a newsgroup about laptop computers, for instance, may include battery conservation tips, problems with a specific model's keyboard or comparisons between different available configurations. Initial queries or informational articles will likely generate several responses. This patchwork of queries and responses form a *message thread* within a specific topic. The software you use to read network news will automatically piece together the various queries and responses in logical order. The original article will appear first, followed by any available *followup* (response) articles in the message thread.

E-mail blind courtesy copies that aren't.

There is a troublesome fluke with most mail servers on the Internet that could prove to be embarrassing for you. If you send an e-mail message to a group of people, with each recipient sent a blind courtesy copy, make sure you also e-mail a copy to at least one address in the To: field. If you send an e-mail message with the To: field empty, most mail servers will insert "Apparently-To:" addresses, neatly listing every recipient of your blind courtesy copy.

Network news is actually not even part of the Internet—although, to the uninitiated, it is probably perceived as being the most easily recognizable part of the Internet. Network news is transmitted on USENET, a network of about 3 million people (mostly UNIX users). USENET is even more disjointed and anarchic than the Internet. Just about the only thing USENET sites have in common is that they communicate using the UNIX-to-UNIX Copy Protocol (UUCP). Some USENET sites have connections to the Internet, which is how network news—and other USENET traffic—gets to the Internet.

Internet sites that provide a network news server use the Network News Transfer Protocol (NNTP) to provide a database for local news clients and to transfer news between servers. In order to read network news on the Internet, you must use NNTP client software (like the kind we'll discuss in this chapter) or use the archaic UNIX commands for navigating and reading newsgroups.

Network news is divided into *newsgroups*. Each newsgroup is devoted to a single topic (at least hypothetically; most newsgroups sort of cross-pollinate one another). Each newsgroup article is received and stored on each participating USENET computer. Unlike e-mail, where the messages are actually sent to your computer and stored on your own hard drive, newsgroup articles are stored on a *news server*, at the site that services your account. The newsgroup articles you read are stored on the news server, not on your own computer.

The network news—or USENET—newsgroups are organized in a hierarchy. Each newsgroup has a name with periods in it similar to the Internet domain name system. The periods (read as "dots") separate the various hierarchical levels. For example, comp.sys.ibm.pc.digest is read as "comp-dot-sys-dot-ibm-dot-pc-dot-digest" or "comp-sys-ibm-pc-digest" and reflects the hierarchy shown in Figure 5-1.

Figure 5-1:
Network news
newsgroups
hierarchy.

comp.sys.ibm.pc.digest

translates in the newsgroup hierarchy to:

Computers

Systems

IBM

PC

Digest

There are several top-level newsgroup categories in the hierarchy, as shown in Table 5-1.

Table 5-1:
Network news
newsgroups top-
level categories.

Category	Topic Explanation
alt	Alternative discussions; not carried by all sites. The newsgroups found here range from the bizarre to the useful. The most useful "alt" newsgroups were created in this top-level hierarchy to avoid going through the bureaucratic hassle of forming a certified newsgroup.
bionet	Biology discussions.
bit	Discussions that originate from Bitnet Listserv mailing lists.
biz	Business discussions. Commercial articles are permitted only in this top-level hierarchy.
comp	Computer discussions.
misc	Miscellaneous discussions—topics that don't fit in any of the other top-level hierarchies.
news	Discussions related to network news and the software used to transmit, read and create articles.

Category	Topic Explanation
rec	Recreation discussions and topics related to the arts.
sci	"Hard" science discussions.
soc	Discussions related to social issues.
talk	Argumentative discussions.

An Overview of Newsgroups

There are more than 4,000 active newsgroups covering virtually every conceivable topic. Some network-savvy observers in mainstream media hypothesize that the Internet will eventually replace most sources of news. It simply won't happen, at least not for another 10 years or so. Computer news and Grateful Dead concert dates travel faster on the Net than they do through other channels, but that's about it.

There was one case of "pseudo-news" on the Internet. In April 1992, an area developed on IRC (Internet Relay Chat—similar to a wide-open international conference call using keyboards instead of phones) that carried news relays of the Los Angeles riots following the first Rodney King verdict. Of course, most of the information came from people who were simply relaying what they had received from local television coverage.

You can always find a regularly updated list of all available newsgroups by reading the news.list newsgroup.

Interesting Newsgroups

Interesting newsgroups exist for just about any topic you can think of. Some of these newsgroups are listed in Table 5-2.

Newsgroup	Description
comp.archives	Listings and descriptions of public-access archives (moderated)[1]
comp.dcom.isdn	Discussions related to the Integrated Services Digital Network (ISDN)
comp.dcom.telcom	Telecommunications digest (moderated)
comp.infosystems.gopher	Discussions related to Gopher
comp.newprod	Computer product announcements (moderated)
comp.org.acm	Discussions related to the Association for Computing Machinery (ACM)
comp.org.eff.news	Electronic Frontier Foundation (EFF) news (moderated)
comp.org.eff.talk	Discussions related to the Electronic Frontier Foundation (EFF)
comp.risks	Discussions related to the risks of computers (moderated)
comp.society.cu-digest	Computer Underground Digest (moderated)
comp.society.privacy	Discussions related to computers and privacy in society (moderated)
comp.text.desktop	Discussions related to desktop publishing
misc.consumers	Discussions related to consumer interest
misc.entrepreneurs	Discussions related to running a business
misc.invest	Discussions related to investing
misc.jobs.contract	Postings of work-for-hire contract availability
misc.jobs.offered	Listings of positions available
misc.jobs.offered.entry	Listings of entry-level positions available
misc.jobs.resumes	Listings of resumes and position queries
news.announce.important	Announcements of general interest (moderated)
news.announce.newgroups	Announcements of new newsgroups (moderated)
news.announce.newusers	Important announcements for new users (moderated)
news.newusers.questions	Questions and answers for new users

Newsgroup	Description
rec.arts.movies	Discussions related to film
rec.arts.movies.reviews	Movie reviews (moderated)
rec.mag	Discussions related to magazines
rec.music.bluenote	Discussions related to jazz and blues
rec.music.dylan	Discussions related to Bob Dylan's music
rec.music.gdead	Dead-head discussions
rec.music.reggae	Discussions related to reggae music
rec.sport.baseball	Discussions related to baseball
soc.culture.japan	Discussions related to Japan and Japanese culture
soc.politics	Political discussions (moderated)
soc.rights.human	Discussions related to human rights and activism

1. Moderated newsgroups are best described as read-only newsgroups. Don't send articles directly to the newsgroup; instead, follow the instructions available in each moderated newsgroup. In general, you send articles to the group's moderator, who posts them as appropriate.

Remember, this is just a tiny sample of the thousands of newsgroups you can access via the Internet.

IBM PC & MS-DOS Newsgroups

Several newsgroups cater specifically to the PC community. A listing of these newsgroups is provided in Table 5-3.

Table 5-3: PC newsgroup descriptions.

Newsgroup	Description
comp.os.msdos.4dos	Discussions related to the 4DOS operating system
comp.os.msdos.apps	Discussions related to MS-DOS software programs
comp.os.msdos.desqview	Discussions related to Desqview
comp.os.msdos.mail-news	Discussions related to MS-DOS e-mail and news programs
comp.os.msdos.misc	Discussions related to miscellaneous MS-DOS issues
comp.os.msdos.pcgeos	Discussions related to the Geos operating system

Newsgroup	Description
comp.os.msdos.programmer	Discussions related to programming for MS-DOS
turbovision	Turbovision
comp.sys.ibm.pc.demos	Discussions related to PC demonstration software
comp.sys.ibm.pc.digest	Discussions related to general PC use; includes listings of additions to major archive sites (moderated)
comp.sys.ibm.pc.games	Discussions related to general PC games
comp.sys.ibm.pc.games.action	Discussions related to arcade and action style PC games
comp.sys.ibm.pc.games.adventure	Discussions related to adventure style PC games
comp.sys.ibm.pc.games.announce	Announcements related to general PC games (moderated)
comp.sys.ibm.pc.games.flight-sim	Discussions related to flight simulator style PC games
comp.sys.ibm.pc.games.misc	Discussions related to miscellaneous PC games
comp.sys.ibm.pc.games.rpg	Discussions related to role playing PC games
comp.sys.ibm.pc.games.strategic	Discussions related to strategy style PC games
comp.sys.ibm.pc.hardware	Discussions related to PC hardware
comp.sys.ibm.pc.misc	Discussions of miscellaneous PC topics
comp.sys.ibm.pc.rt	Discussions related to the RT workstation
comp.sys.ibm.pc.soundcard	Discussions related to various audio and sound hardware for PCs

A Primer on Newsgroup Etiquette

The USENET news system is a remarkable beast. By nature, it is a wide-open terrain with absolutely no restraints on freedom of expression. Each author assumes the responsibility for his or her articles, and the uncensored environment of network news is widely appreciated.

News article posting etiquette is based pretty much on the kind of behavior you'd expect in a college dormitory: don't hit anyone and clean up your own messes. The sole overriding principle is that just about anything is allowed, as long as it does not put the network itself in jeopardy. While you're pondering what that really means, here are a few tips to get you started.

- I remember asking one of my teachers how long an essay I had been assigned should be; her response simultaneously answered my question and taught me about metaphor. She told me the essay should be like a woman's skirt: short enough to be interesting but long enough to cover the subject. Her advice is appropriate for news articles as well.

- Lots of people on the Internet read hundreds of messages each day. You can't reasonably expect someone to remember what has been said in every previous message. Include appropriate background material that will help the reader understand the context of your message.

- By the same token, you don't need to provide 50 lines of background about a message if you're only responding to a small part of it. Don't, for example, quote a 1,000-line article only to add "I agree!"

Evangelizing the Internet.

Paul Jacoby is a consultant with David Mitchell & Associates, on assignment with 3M. He's been working long and hard to introduce 3M employees to the Internet:

"I've been in the process of evangelizing the Internet to the folks I work with here at 3M. The main response I get from people who begin to delve into the depths of the Internet is 'Wow, I had no idea this existed!' Followed closely by 'You mean it's *free*?'

"People are continually amazed at the concepts of software archives ('... filled with *free* software?') and the near instantaneous access to points across the globe. Most are tickled to death to find associates with Internet addresses, exchanging e-mail with turn-around time in the sub-minute range.

"In presenting a summary of the Internet and trying to describe how it works, I boiled all the technical stuff down to one important phrase: It's *automagic*, i.e., don't worry, be happy, use and learn without worrying about the fine points. Most people are quite happy to operate this way :-)"

- Limit your lines to lengths of 80 characters or less.

- Don't use long, rambling signatures or include ASCII graphics—keep it to four lines or less.

- Don't post "me too!" follow-up articles unless you have a worthwhile comment to add.

■ Use the right newsgroup for the job. Some newsgroups are intended for discussions while others are intended for announcements. Don't engage in discussions on newsgroups intended for announcements.

■ Newsgroups are called newsgroups, not bulletin boards, boards or bboards.

■ Don't post private e-mail correspondence in a network news article without the permission of the author. While it may be technically legal to do so, it's rude and could be a copyright violation in some circumstances. (Besides, would you want someone plastering your private e-mail on a network where 10 million people could read it?)

■ Don't ask what ":-)" means (tilt your head ninety degrees to the left and see "Smiley Gallery" on page 123).

■ Don't post flames outside a newsgroup labeled specifically for flames. (See "Flames, Flame-Bait & Flaming" on page 122.)

■ Don't end your post with a snooty comment like "Please send e-mail, because I don't read this newsgroup." If you don't read a newsgroup, why would you be posting messages there?

■ Don't use excessive CAPITALIZATION & punctuation!!!!!!!!!!!!!

■ Don't cross-post to multiple newsgroups unless it's completely relevant and absolutely necessary.

■ If you ask for help with a software program, make sure you state what kind of computer you're using. Not everyone uses a PC. (There are tons of UNIX and Mac users on the Internet too.) Also, include specific details like what brand and model PC you have, how much RAM you have, what version of DOS (or Windows) you're using, what kind of monitor you have, any special cards you've installed or any other particulars about your unique PC configuration.

■ Keep a sense of humor. There's little room for self-righteous stuffed shirts in the world of network news.

■ Don't post articles about what kind of computer is better. Similarly, don't respond to articles arguing the issue.

■ Before posting a question in a newsgroup, read its Frequently Asked Questions (FAQ) file. These files contain answers to—you guessed it—the most frequently asked questions. Most newsgroups post the FAQ file to the newsgroup on a regular basis. The FAQ files for most newsgroups are available by FTP from pit-manager.mit.edu

- Understand that you're going to make mistakes, and as sure as grits is groceries, some jerk's going to let you know about it when you do. Try to keep a thick skin about it. See "My First Network News Mistake" for an example.

My First Network News Mistake.

Just less than a month after I started using the Internet, I asked a stupid question in a newsgroup. I had accumulated quite a few PostScript files—mostly documentation—some of them very large.

I didn't want to waste paper by printing these files out if I could view them on the screen. My assumption was that if there were all these wonderful Internet software tools, there was probably a PostScript viewer somewhere. I had checked every archive I knew about, but I couldn't find one.

Timidity is not usually one of my more defining personality qualities, but I timidly—*yes timidly*—posted a very short query on one of the appropriate newsgroups. Something on the order of "Does anyone know where I can find a PostScript viewer? This is for multi-page, raw PostScript files, not EPS documents."

Within hours I received 10 e-mail responses. The more polite of the bunch were to the effect of "You ignorant *?!)&S. Why don't you read the *S?)#!* FAQ??!!" I didn't have the slightest idea what a FAQ was, and I sure wasn't going to ask.

A day or so later the comp.sys.mac.misc FAQ was posted and, of course, my question was answered.

What continues to confound me is that every one of the pinheads that responded to my original question at length could have saved themselves a lot of trouble with a simple, two-letter, one-word response: NO.

I think it's either a network culture thing ("let's jump the newbie") or these guys have canned messages that they automatically send out as one of their few means of entertainment.

Since then, a PostScript viewer—GhostScript—has been released. It's available in the Oakland University archive if you're interested, but it's useless for multi-page documents.

Flames, Flame-Bait & Flaming

You'll hear a lot about *flames* while reading network news. A flame is an inflammatory message usually posted for no other reason than to start an argument. It's pretty common for someone to login to one of the comp.sys.ibm.pc newsgroups (a stronghold of PC advocates) and post a message with a title like "PCs suck, buy a Mac!" The best response to this sort of wasted bandwidth is to ignore it. Unfortunately, the message always gets answered and a *flame war* erupts with vile epithets hurled in all directions.

Emotion is hard to communicate on the network. Irony and sarcasm are easily misinterpreted without verbal cues or body language. Similarly, terseness can come across as rudeness. And until we can add italics and bold type to our messages, things are even worse—we're limited to ASCII text as the lowest common denominator.

In general, use of capital letters is considered shouting, so be careful how you use them. You can show emphasis by setting off a word or phrase with asterisks: That's *not* what I said. This is considered more polite and respectful than: That's NOT what I said.

Another result of the difficulty of communicating with only ASCII text is the *smiley*. Tilt your head 90 degrees counterclockwise and look at this:

:-)

Remember those yellow "Have a Nice Day" smiley faces? Well, a smiley, like the one shown above, is the electronic equivalent. Smileys are used to convey emotion within an electronic message, and you'll find them widely used throughout the Internet. I hate them, and I almost never use them (in fact, I can't think of a single time I've used one), but they are everywhere, and you'd better learn to decode them. For more information, see the following "Smiley Gallery."

Smiley Gallery.
Here are a few of the more common smileys you're likely to encounter.

Smiley	Meaning
:-)	basic smiley; connotes cheer or a grin, sometimes tongue-in-cheek sarcasm
;-)	wink; connotes light sarcasm
:-I	indifference
:->	devilish grin; connotes heavy sarcasm
:-(	frown; connotes anger or displeasure
@:-)	curly hair
8-)	eye-glasses
:-D	shock or surprise
:-/	perplexed
:-7	tongue sticking out

Now that you know a little about the politics and etiquette of using network news, you can start reading and posting on your own. But first, you'll need a first-class utility for navigating newsgroups and composing and posting articles.

Selecting a News Reader

A news reader is a software program that runs on your PC that simplifies the process of navigating and reading network news articles. You use this program to select which newsgroups you want to monitor on a regular basis and which articles you want to read. You also use the news reader to post new articles or reply to existing ones. It's important that you choose a news reader that you can live with—one that lets you navigate quickly through the thousands of pages of articles available—to target the information you need.

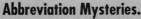

Abbreviation Mysteries.

There is a set of abbreviations that are commonly used as shorthand in network communications. Don't worry too much about decoding abbreviations you see. You'll find that they're pretty self-explanatory in context; sort of like reading real-estate listings or personal ads in the newspaper. Here are some of the abbreviations in widest use.

Abbreviation	Meaning
IMHO	in my humble opinion (it very rarely is)
BTW	by the way
ROTFL	rolling on the floor laughing
TNSTAAFL	there's no such thing as a free lunch
OBO	or best offer
RTFM	read the funny manual
FYI	for your information

There are several good news readers available for the PC, and new ones under development. One of the most popular PC news readers is the one built into the University of Minnesota's Minuet program. Minuet is distributed as *shareware*; if you continue to use the program after the evaluation period, you must pay the $50 shareware registration fee.

Peter Tattam's Trumpet is also a very popular network news reader for PCs. If you don't already have a news reader and you want to get your hands on a great one for free, you can use FTP (the Internet's File Transfer Protocol) to download the most recent version of Trumpet. You'll find it in the Trumpet directory of the University of Tasmania's FTP archive. If you'd like to get a copy of Trumpet but you're unfamiliar with how to download files, "Downloading Files With Minuet" in Chapter 6 gives you complete instructions on how to download files and the Visitors Center will tell you where to find your very own copy of Trumpet.

In this chapter, we'll walk through the steps for configuring and using Minuet for reading network news.

Configuring Minuet

Included on the companion disk to *The PC Internet Tour Guide* is Version 1.0 of Minuet. This version is fully functional and should handle almost all of your network news tasks. You can always find the latest version of Minuet (and the other major freeware and shareware programs covered in this book) in *The PC Internet Tour Guide's* "Visitors Center," at ftp.farces.com. Check the /pub/visitors-center/software/dos/news/ directory for Minuet and other interesting items. You can also always download the latest version of Minuet (and related software and documentation) from the FTP site at boombox.micro.umn.edu in the /pc/minuet/ directory. To configure Minuet for use with your news server:

1. Establish your connection to the Internet, if necessary. If you're using UMSLIP, type **slip dial** at the command prompt, and the connection will be automatically established.

   ▦ If you are using other SLIP or PPP software, follow the directions provided by your network administrator or service provider to establish the connection.

   ▦ If you enjoy a direct connection to the Internet, there is no need to establish a connection.

2. Launch Minuet by typing **minuet** at the command prompt.

   ▦ If you have configured Minuet to automatically check for mail, the program will automatically login to the server and download any e-mail addressed to you. The rest of this section assumes that you will be checking for e-mail manually. In either case, the INBOX Viewer will appear.

3. Press **Alt-W**. The Windows menu is displayed.

4. From the Windows menu, select the News command. The News window appears, with a Help dialog box overlay.

5. Press **Esc** to dismiss the Help dialog box.

6. Press **Alt-N**. The News menu is displayed.

7. From the News menu, select the Show Group Tree command.

   ▦ Minuet will retrieve and build a list of all available newsgroups on your news server. This may take a while. This process occurs only the first time you configure your subscribed newsgroups and whenever you choose the Show Group Tree command. A list of available newsgroups will be retrieved from the news server and displayed in the top panel of the News window, as shown in Figure 5-2.

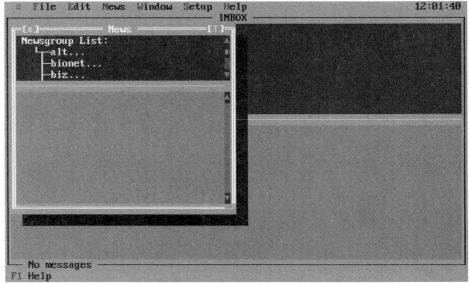

Figure 5-2: Minuet News window with list of available newsgroups.

8. Press **Tab**. The first item in the list of available newsgroups will be highlighted.

9. Use the **Up** and **Down arrow** keys to navigate to the newsgroup hierarchy containing a newsgroup to which you want to subscribe and press **Enter**. The newsgroup hierarchy will be expanded to display subhierarchies and available newsgroups.

10. Use the **Up** and **Down arrow** keys to highlight a newsgroup to which you want to subscribe and press **Enter**. The selected newsgroup will be marked as subscribed.

11. Repeat steps 9–10 for each additional newsgroup to which you want to subscribe.

■ Here's a shortcut for navigating the list of available newsgroups: Enter the first few letters of a newsgroup to scroll immediately to that point in the list. It's much faster than scrolling from top to bottom in long lists.

12. Navigate through the list of available newsgroups, pressing **Enter** when a newsgroup to which you want to subscribe is highlighted. The list of subscribed newsgroups appear in the top panel of the display, as shown in Figure 5-3.

Figure 5-3: Minuet News window with list of subscribed newsgroups and group tree.

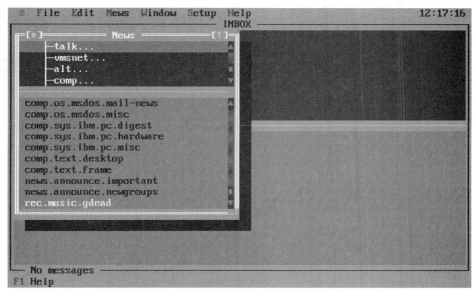

Meckler Publishing.

Meckler Publishing (Westport, CT) is aggressively developing Internet guides for librarians, researchers and information professionals. Contact meckler@jvnc.net for notification of upcoming books on Internet basics, electronic scholarship, Internet directories, WAIS and Gopher servers, citation of electronic sources, Internet/NREN policy, etc. Meckler's quarterly *Electronic Networking* will now be *Internet Research: Electronic Networking, Applications, and Policy.*

Managing network news and newsgroups can quickly become an overwhelming task. A good approach is to begin by selecting only those newsgroups you are especially interested in. Later, if you find you have enough time to read more articles, you can create additional lists or add more newsgroups to existing lists. It's much easier to add newsgroups later than to wade through massive amounts of information you may not be interested in.

Freeware SLIP software.
The programmers at the University of Minnesota have created and released a freeware SLIP driver for MS-DOS computers. SLIP software allows you to login to the Internet (via a SLIP server) using a high-speed modem and ordinary telephone lines. It works quite well and is part of the UMSLIP distribution package. (The companion software included with this *Tour Guide* makes use of this package.) The current version of SLIP is available by anonymous FTP at boombox.micro.umn.edu in the /pub/pc/slip/ directory.

How to Read, Post & Reply to Articles

In a graphical environment like Minuet, each news article is represented individually. You read an article by selecting it. You can reply to an article by selecting the range of text to which you want to respond and using your news reader's Reply command. Sometimes you'll want to create a completely new topic within a newsgroup. To do this, simply create a new message using the appropriate Create New Message command in your news reader. This section shows you how to read, post and reply to network news articles using the news reader module in Minuet.

Using Minuet

Minuet is one of the most popular news readers in the PC community, probably because it's inexpensive, performs well and offers an intuitive interface. Subscribed newsgroups appear in a dialog box, a list of available messages in the current newsgroup appears in the upper panel, and the actual text of selected messages appears in the bottom panel of the display. Reading and posting news articles in Minuet uses the same commands as reading and creating e-mail.

Reading News With Minuet

Use the following steps to read network news articles with Minuet. This section assumes that you have already properly configured Minuet and selected the newsgroups you want to monitor. These examples use the comp.os.msdos and comp.sys.ibm.pc series of newsgroups, but Minuet works the same for all available newsgroups.

1. Establish your connection to the Internet, if necessary. If you're using UMSLIP, type **slip dial** at the command prompt, and the connection will be automatically established.

   - If you are using other SLIP or PPP software, follow the directions provided by your network administrator or service provider to establish the connection.

   - If you enjoy a direct connection to the Internet, there is no need to establish a connection.

2. Launch Minuet by typing **minuet** at the command prompt.

   - If you have configured Minuet to automatically check for mail, the program will automatically login to the server and download any e-mail addressed to you. The rest of this section assumes that you will be checking for e-mail manually. In either case, the INBOX Viewer will appear.

3. Press **Alt-W**. The Windows menu is displayed.

4. From the Windows menu, select the News command. The News window appears and contains a list of newsgroups to which you have subscribed, as shown in Figure 5-4.

Internet Signatures.

Electronic communications—both e-mail and network news postings—are usually much less formal than the typical business letter. Formal salutations are rarely called for and are generally considered something of a waste of bandwidth.

Similarly, formal closings are almost never seen. Instead, most networkers end their messages with a *signature*. A signature is a short—four lines or less—identification tag that includes your full name, organization and contact information.

Signatures range in style from the strictly functional to almost rococo-like. The function of a signature is to provide identification and contact information in case the address header is incorrect or incomplete.

More⟩

The best signatures usually include a quote that tells you something about the person writing the message. Quotes are fine, but should be kept short and pithy.

In creating a signature, remember that ASCII text is still the lowest common denominator for Internet communications. Use a monospaced font and keep the length of each line under 80 characters.

Here's one of the signatures I use:

```
                  —
Michael Fraase,      |"Nothing to tell, let the words be yours
   proprietor        | I am done with mine…" Weir/Barlow
Arts & Farces        |
Saint Paul, MN USA  |————————————————————————————
mfraase@farces.com  | Writing and document design
```

You can gather a lot of interesting information from a person's signature. From mine you could assume that I'm self-employed (the top-level domain is a commercial account and the domain name matches part of my company name); I live in Minnesota; and I like the Grateful Dead more than just a little (and you can draw your own conclusions from that). Sometimes, signatures carry a disclaimer stating that the comments represent the views of the individual posting the message but not necessarily the views of that person's employer, company or organization. Sometimes these disclaimer lines are even written with a sense of humor:

```
Opinions this ludicrous are mine. Reasonable opinions
will cost you.
```

Here are some of the better signature tag lines I've come across lately:

```
I need some indication that all of this is real now.
Slipping into madness is good for the sake of comparison.
"Tens of thousands of messages, hundreds of points of view.
It was not called the Net of a Million Lies for nothing."
-Vernor Vinge
Spread peanut butter, not AIDS.
Fear is a little darkroom where negatives are developed.
Stop yawning. Start yearning.
Bandwidth expands to fit the waste available.
Practice random kindness and senseless acts of beauty.
"I stand behind all of my misstatements." — Dan Quayle
```

Figure 5-4: Minuet
News window
with list of
subscribed
newsgroups.

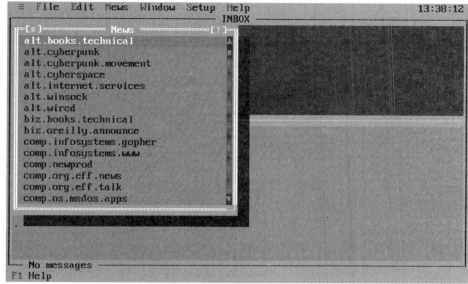

5. Using the **Up** and **Down arrow** keys, navigate to highlight the subscribed newsgroup you want to read and press **Enter**. The available articles will be retrieved from the news server and the Information dialog box appears reporting the number of articles that have been downloaded.

6. Press **Enter** to dismiss the Information dialog box.

  ▓ The list of available articles is displayed in the upper panel of the News Viewer, with the text of the first article displayed in the lower panel, as shown in Figure 5-5.

Figure 5-5: Minuet News Viewer with list of available network news articles and selected news article.

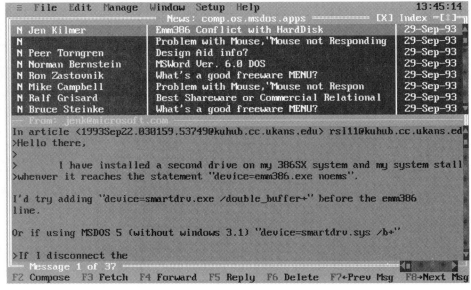

- The author of the article appears in the leftmost column, followed by the subject line of the article, and the date of the article appears in the rightmost column.

- Note that Minuet is different than most network news readers. Most network news readers download only the titles of articles and retrieve an article only when you select it. Minuet automatically downloads to your hard drive all the available news articles in each newsgroup you select. For more information on reading articles offline and managing network news with Minuet, see "Managing Network News With Minuet," beginning on page 137.

7. Navigate to the next message you want to read with any of these techniques:

- Use the **Up** and **Down arrow** keys.

- Press **F7** to view the previous message.

- Press **F8** to view the next message.

8. Repeat step 6 for remaining messages in the current newsgroup.

9. Repeat steps 3–6 for each additional newsgroup you want to read.

   ▤ Note that the article navigation and manipulation commands in Minuet's news reader work exactly the same as the commands available in Minuet's e-mail module. In fact, the articles for each newsgroup you elect to read are stored in Minuet e-mail folders until you delete them.

Posting a News Article With Minuet

Reading news articles is only half the point of participating in newsgroups. To get the most out of your time with network news, you also have to know how to post original articles and responses to existing articles. To post a news article with Minuet:

1. Establish your connection to the Internet, if necessary. If you're using UMSLIP, type **slip dial** at the command prompt, and the connection will be automatically established.

   ▤ If you are using other SLIP or PPP software, follow the directions provided by your network administrator or service provider to establish the connection.

   ▤ If you enjoy a direct connection to the Internet, there is no need to establish a connection.

2. Launch Minuet by typing **minuet** at the command prompt.

   ▤ If you have configured Minuet to automatically check for mail, the program will automatically login to the server and download any e-mail addressed to you. The rest of this section assumes that you will be checking for e-mail manually. In either case, the INBOX Viewer will appear.

3. Press **F2**. The Minuet Composer appears, as shown in Figure 5-6.

Figure 5-6: Minuet
Composer.

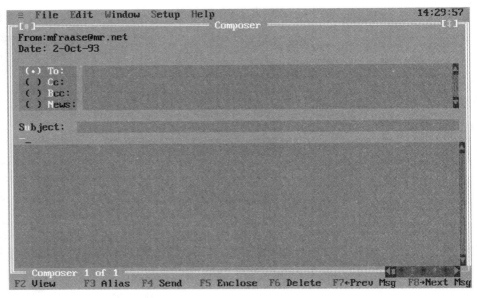

4. Press the **Down arrow** key three times, selecting the News option. A bullet symbol (•) appears next to the News option.

5. Press **Tab**. The cursor will advance to the To: addressee field.

6. Enter the name of the newsgroup (or multiple newsgroups) in which you want to post your article.

   ■ For example, if you want your news article to be posted to the MS-DOS Applications newsgroup, you would enter **comp.os.msdos.apps** in the To field.

7. Press **Tab**. The cursor will advance to the Subject line.

8. Enter a subject or title for your news article and press **Tab**. The cursor will advance to the body section of the Composer.

9. Enter the body text of your news article.

10. Press **F4**. The Information dialog box appears, asking if you want to post the news article to the newsgroup.

11. Press **Enter**. Your news article will be posted to the newsgroup you specified in step 6. Alternatively, if you've made a mistake or have second thoughts about your article, press **Esc** to dismiss the Information dialog box without posting your news article. A dialog box is displayed informing you of the status of the message sending process.

Many times you'll want to respond to something you read in a network news article. Use these steps to reply to a news article with Minuet.

1. Use the steps outlined in the "Reading News With Minuet" section, beginning on page 129, to read the available news articles in the newsgroups to which you have subscribed.

2. Hold the **Shift** key while pressing the **Down arrow** key to select a range of text within the article to which you want to reply as shown in Figure 5-7.

Figure 5-7: Text selected within a news article for reply.

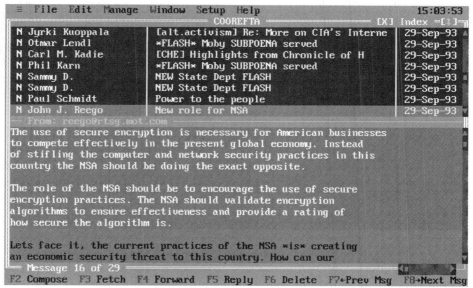

- Alternatively, if you want to reply to the entire message, skip this step.

3. Press **F5**. The original message (or the range of text you selected) will be opened in the Minuet Composer, with a ">" preceding each line, as shown in Figure 5-8.

Figure 5-8:
Replying to a news
article with Minuet.

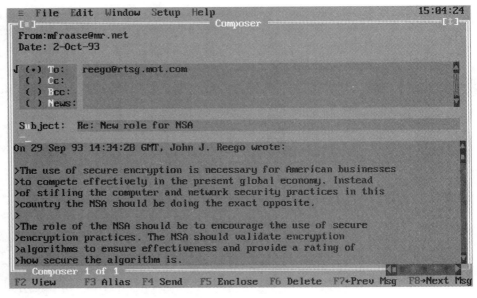

■ For more information on message quoting conventions, see the
Internet quoting conventions sidebar on page 81.

4. Enter the body of your message. You can type or paste text into
this area.

5. Specify the addressing information for the article.

■ The default is to send the reply via e-mail to the news article's
author. If this is what you want to do, skip the rest of this step
and advance to step 6.

■ If you want to post the reply as a follow-up news article, press
Tab to move the cursor into the addressing panel of the Minuet
Composer, press the **Down arrow** key three times to select the
News option, press **Tab** again and enter the name of the
newsgroup in which you want to post the follow-up article.

6. Press **F4**. The Information dialog box appears, asking if you want
to post the news article to the newsgroup.

7. Press **Enter**. Your news article will be posted to the newsgroup
you specified in step 6. Alternatively, if you've made a mistake, or
have second thoughts about your article, press **Esc** to dismiss the
Information dialog box without posting your news article. A
dialog box is displayed informing you of the status of the message
sending process.

How Fast Can UFOs Go?

There are all sorts of strange newsgroups available on the Internet. Here's a sample exchange—the message title is "How fast can UFOs go?"—from the alt.alien.visitors newsgroup.

[Original post] "Putting aside the energy requirements for accelerating to c, how far is 'far into space?' Assuming that their solar system is constructed similarly to ours, and the time spent in 'hyper-space' is effectively none, that would imply a 3.5 hour trip to the jump point on each side of the hyper-flight. I vaguely recall my high school astronomy teacher telling me that Pluto is 5 lighthours from the sun. So in order to reach a point at which the light speed drive can be used, our insystem drive needs to reach 1.4c? I'm available to these guys as an efficiency consultant."

[Follow-up post] "When I think of the problem of needing to get some distance from a gravitational source—Earth, Moon, Sun, whatever—I would not head towards Pluto. I would head straight up the Y-axis. Cartoon analogy: When a truck is headed towards Daffy Duck, he runs away down the road instead of going left or right to get off the road. The solar system is sort of flat, the universe is not."

Managing Network News With Minuet

As mentioned earlier, Minuet is different from most network news readers in that it downloads to your local hard drive all of the available articles in a selected newsgroup, rather than just the title, author and date—or *header* information—for each article. This is useful if you have a SLIP or PPP connection to the Internet, because it allows you to browse and read network news offline, without wasting network resources. The only disadvantage is that you need enough space on your hard drive to store the downloaded news articles, and downloading all the articles in the first place takes a little longer than jumping in, reading a single post and jumping out. Use these steps to manage network news and read news articles offline with Minuet.

1. Use the steps outlined in the "Reading News With Minuet" section, beginning on page 129, to download the available news articles in the newsgroups to which you have subscribed.

   ▪ The downloaded articles for each newsgroup are stored in a Minuet mail folder. Each network newsgroup has its own Minuet mail folder.

2. Press **Alt-M** to display the Manage menu.

3. From the Manage menu, select the Go to folder... command. The Go to folder dialog box appears, as shown in Figure 5-9.

Figure 5-9: Minuet
Go to folder
dialog box.

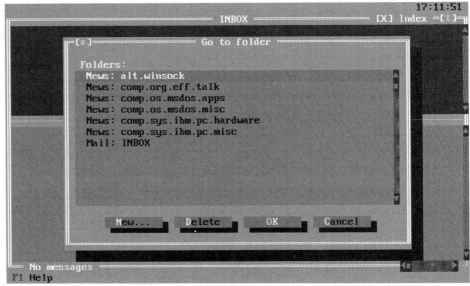

4. Move to any available mail folder by using the **Up** and **Down arrow** keys to select the mail folder and pressing **Enter**.

   ▨ The news articles in the selected newsgroup will be displayed, and you can read, reply and navigate through the available articles as described in the "Reading News With Minuet" section.

You'll probably want to delete news articles that have been downloaded to your local hard drive after you've read them. Use these steps to delete the network newsgroup mail folders *and all the news articles they contain*.

1. From anywhere within Minuet, press **Alt-M** to display the Manage menu.

2. From the Manage menu, select the Go to folder… command. The Go to folder dialog box appears, as shown in Figure 5-9.

3. Navigate to the mail folder you want to delete by using the **Up** and **Down arrow** keys to select the mail folder.

4. With the mail folder you want to delete selected, press **Alt-D**. The Confirm dialog box will appear, asking if you really want to delete the selected mail folder and the messages it contains, as shown in Figure 5-10.

Figure 5-10: Minuet Confirm dialog box for deleting mail folders.

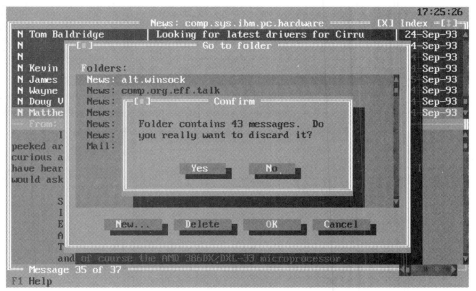

5. Press **Enter**. The selected mail folder *and all of its contents* will be deleted from your hard drive and the mail folder will be removed from the list of available mail folders.

   ▪ Alternatively, press **Esc** if you don't want to delete the mail folder and its contents.

6. Repeat steps 3–5 for each mail folder you want to delete.

MOOGopher.
MOOGopher is an object-oriented, multi-user dimension that uses an integrated Gopher client. Objects in the environment can contain Gopher items, and you navigate the Gopherspace as if you're exploring a game. You can try it by pointing your Gopher program at theory.cs.mankato.msus.edu port 1709. (For more on Gopher and TurboGopher, see Chapter 7, "Using Gopher.")

Moving On

Now you're ready to venture into the thousands of newsgroups on the Internet. But be careful, you can waste a lot of time trolling through network news looking for nuggets of useful information. Unfortunately, there are no proven secrets to tracking down worthwhile articles. I've found that the best information tends to cluster within the smaller newsgroups and those that are moderated. Also, it's usually a better idea to carefully read a few newsgroups than to try to skim scores of them. There are more newsgroups available than anyone can possibly read, so pick your targets wisely.

If hunting for truly informative newsgroups is a challenge, then finding great files is a cakewalk. As our tour bus cruises through the next chapter, you'll learn how to effectively use the Internet's File Transfer Protocol (FTP) and the FTP client built into Minuet to mine these information-rich resources.

CHAPTER 6

TRANSFERRING FILES
The Mother Downlode

Part of the fun of
visiting any distant place is taking snapshots and collecting souvenirs
to take back home. Our tour through the Internet is no exception. There
are plenty of strange and wondrous curios—as well as practical items
you'll use every day—nestled throughout the Net. And you don't have
to hop a steamer or board a plane to collect them all. Thanks to the
Internet's File Transfer Protocol (FTP), it takes only a few commands to
download a shareware program or text file from a computer halfway
around the world. But perhaps the most satisfying thing about using
the Internet's FTP to download files is that you get exactly the information you want without wading through a lot of stuff you don't want.

Depending on how relevant it is to you as an individual, information
has a level of density. E-mail is usually information-dense on one level
because it is of unique concern to you. Network news, on the other
hand, is comparatively information-sparse, because there are a lot of
useless messages you must plow through to get to the information
that's important to you. Files that you download and use on your PC
are information-dense, perhaps more than anything else you will
encounter on the Internet.

In this chapter, we'll cover the basics of the File Transfer Protocol itself, and we'll also go over the details of using a popular software program (the FTP module in the University of Minnesota's Minuet) that lets you transfer files across the Internet. So sit back, get your cameras ready and fish out those traveler's checks—we're going souvenir hunting.

What Is FTP?

FTP is an acronym for File Transfer Protocol, but nobody says File Transfer Protocol; everyone says FTP, as in "you can FTP that file from the Oakland archive" or "that file is available by FTP from the Minnesota archive."

People use FTP as a noun when they refer to the actual File Transfer Protocol, but they also use it as a verb when describing the process of transferring files on the Internet. Technically, FTP is a full-fledged data-transfer protocol like Z-Modem or Kermit. It allows files to be transferred between different kinds of computers, without regard to the operating system used by the computers or even how they are connected.

Why Would You Want to Transfer Files?

You can use MS-DOS applications (like Minuet) that employ FTP to send and receive files between your PC and any other computer on the Internet that supports FTP. There is a wealth of software available through the Internet by *anonymous FTP*. Anonymous FTP is an Internet service that allows anyone to enter publicly accessible file archives, practically anywhere in the world, without having an account on that archive. If an FTP server accepts anonymous logins (and there are thousands that do), you login with the username *anonymous* and any text as a password. It is a generally accepted convention that anonymous FTP users should enter their complete e-mail address—in the username@domain.top-domain format—as their password.

Hot News on the Net.

Savvy folks in public relations and publicity departments know that news travels fast along the Net. That's why you can count on the Internet to be one of the first places to offer news releases from all kinds of sources, ranging from the White House to Microsoft. In short, you can see it on the Net today or read about it in the paper tomorrow.

"INTERNET WORLD '93 and DOCUMENT DELIVERY WORLD '93

"Conference and Exhibition Dealing with the Commercial and Non-Commercial Utilization of these Services and the Impact they Have on Information Providers and Users

"December 6–9, 1993, Jacob Javits Convention Center, New York City

"Sponsored by Internet World Magazine and Document Delivery World Magazine

"Travel into the future of the Internet and electronic Document Delivery and much more. Over 100 speakers and 100 exhibitors present ideas, applications and products that will enable you to take advantage of these important information technology delivery systems.

"Meckler has created workshops and seminars designed for professionals and end-users in several interest categories. You decide which workshops or seminars are right for you. There are 8 pre-conference workshops, 41 seminars and 4 post-conference workshops that address your specific needs. INTERNET WORLD '93 is unequaled in the industry. It is the only program built around the concept of the delivery of information on the Internet.

"Over 100 exhibitors will be showcasing a universe of the latest products, programs and services related to Internet utilization and electronic Document Delivery. You can explore the world of Internet by testing the 'super electronic highway' at numerous hook-ups in our exhibit hall. INTERNET WORLD is the trade show for information and technology related to Internet services. Register now and begin your successful competition in the 'information world' of tomorrow."

Resources available from anonymous FTP archives include fully functional software programs (spreadsheets, text editors, telecommunications programs, databases, graphics programs, utilities and more) as well as graphic images, sounds, animations and texts ranging from President Bill Clinton's speeches to *Macbeth*. Some of the most valuable software resources available on the Internet are updaters and bug fixes for commercially distributed software. Software companies distribute the updaters to the general public via the Internet and various online services. People who own a program that may not be compatible with a new hardware or software release can download the updater and run it on their outdated program to upgrade it to the newest version. It's a classic win-win situation: users get quick updates and the vendor gets inexpensive distribution and loads of goodwill within the community, while at the same time keeping its installed base of users current and up-to-date.

Other valuable resources—information resources—are available by FTP. Developer notes, technical reports, technical support documents, electronic magazines, journals, templates and tutorials are all available. And then there are the thousands of "miscellaneous" resources that seem to find their way to FTP sites: things like musical notation and lyric sheets for just about any piece of music from the last 30 years, and full-text copies of classic literature ranging from *Alice in Wonderland* and *Peter Pan* to the complete works of Shakespeare.

A Primer on Software Resources

For the time being, there are three general types of software resources you can find on the Internet: information resources, software programs and program-specific files for use with those software programs (templates and samples). Information resources—documents that were distributed as ink (or toner) on paper in the past—are widely available from numerous sources on the Internet. Software programs and files for use with those programs are generally less widely available, but plentiful nonetheless.

Dial "S" for Software.

Just about the only kind of software resource you won't find on the Internet is commercially distributed software. And even that may change in the relatively near future. Imagine the benefit MondoCorp can reap if it can distribute within seconds a new version of its MondoWriter software to anyone on the Internet. Users could simply type in a credit card number and instantly download the software and documentation right to their hard drives. Look for this to happen soon and look to see who the initial players are. Chances are the first companies to distribute their software across the Internet will be the most forward-thinking in the industry.

In broadest terms, there are three classifications for the software resources you will find on the Internet: public domain, freeware and shareware. Let's take a look at the differences between these three distribution methods.

Public Domain

Public domain resources are those that carry no copyright. The author or developer has created the resource for the good of the community and has released it for any and every use. There is no limit on redistribution or sale of public domain resources, and it can be modified or transformed by anyone.

Freeware

Freeware resources are those that carry the author's copyright. The author retains copyright, but allows you to use the resource free of charge. There are generally some restrictions on freeware resources, most often regarding distribution and modification. The usual case with freeware is that you can give it away, but you can't sell it, and the author retains copyright.

Shareware

Shareware resources are those that are distributed on a "try-before-you-buy" basis. The author retains copyright and allows you to use the resource on a trial basis for a short evaluation period. At the end of the evaluation period you must either pay the author for the resource or destroy all the copies of the resource in your possession. You are encouraged to make copies for your friends, but you can't charge for them. Shareware resources carry a relatively low price because the author doesn't have to pay distribution or advertising costs. The author cuts out the middlemen like distributors and resellers, dealing with you—the user—directly.

Minuet—one of the programs included on the companion disk—is an example of shareware. If you're a commercial Internet user and decide to continue using Minuet, you must pay a $50 fee to the Regents of the University of Minnesota.

The Beauty of Telix.
Telix is one of the most popular PC shareware programs. It provides terminal emulation, ANSI support and a built-in phonebook. Telix offers various file transfer protocols, including Z-Modem, Kermit, X-Modem and Y-Modem. It's available by FTP from oak.oakland.edu in the /pub/msdos/ telix/ directory.

Making Shareware Work

If shareware is to remain a viable way to distribute and sell software, people who use it must pay the shareware authors. If you regularly use a piece of shareware, it's in your own best interest to pay the shareware fee. Some of the programs included on the companion disk are shareware products and are included for evaluation purposes only. If you continue to use these programs, you must pay the software authors directly. See the documentation for each program for details.

Freeware PPP software.

PPP software allows you to login to the Internet using a high-speed modem and ordinary telephone lines. SLIP is currently more common than PPP, but PPP will probably surpass SLIP in the near future because it offers more features and better throughput during interactive sessions where small bits of information are passed in both directions. EtherPPP, for MS-DOS computers, is available by anonymous FTP at merit.edu in the /pub/ppp/ directory.

A Primer on File Types

Files on the Internet are usually going to have names that are pretty much the same as what you're used to seeing. Most PC files that you find will be listed in this filename format:

filename.ext.

The "ext" part of a file's name represents the compression tool used to create the file. The most common options are: zip, lha and zoo. For more information on what these extensions mean, see Table 6-1. The "exe" or "doc" extension indicates that the file has been placed on the FTP server in its native file format and need not be processed after it's downloaded. An "hqx" extension is rare in the PC world, but indicates that the file has been placed on the FTP server in BinHex format. BinHex is a standard format that allows files to be accessed by virtually any computer, regardless of the hardware or software it uses.

You'll also probably find a lot of files that end with a "txt" or "ps" extension. These are ASCII text and PostScript files, respectively, and are intended for use on all kinds of computers. ASCII text can be read by any word processor, and PostScript files can be printed—fully formatted—by any PostScript-capable output device.

Minuet automatically determines the transfer mode to use based on the type of file you download.

PKWARE's PKUNZIP utility automatically decompresses files created with PKZIP, the most widely used PC compression program. To use PKUNZIP, simply type **pkunzip filename.ext** (where filename.ext is the name and extension of the file you want to decompress) at the command prompt. Of course, the PKZIP family of compression products offers a wealth of other options for compressing and decompressing files, but that's the basic command. For more information, see the PKZIP documentation.

Information about the file extensions and file types used on the Internet is provided in Table 6-1.

Table 6-1:
Archived file type
extensions.

Ext	Compression Program Used
exe, doc	Native file formats created by various software programs (these files aren't processed by PKZIP); note that filenames with an .exe extension may be self-extracting archive files; to decompress them, simply type the filename at the command prompt
hqx	BinHex 4.0
zip	PKZIP
arj	ARJ
lha	LHA
zoo	ZOO
arc	ARC

If you stick to the major PC FTP servers, you'll probably never see any other filename extensions. But then you'd be missing out on most of the software resources available on the Internet. (For a list of the most popular PC FTP sites on the Internet, see "Famous PC FTP Archives" on page 159.)

California Software Design's SHEZ is currently the best program for decompressing files created with different compression utilities. You still have to have the various compression utilities on your hard disk, but SHEZ provides a unified interface for all the most widely used compression tools. For information on downloading SHEZ, see "Downloading Files With Minuet" beginning on page 152.

If you download files almost exclusively from the most popular PC archives, you'll probably be able to decompress them with the free PKUNZIP utility. But if you're planning to wander the Net, sampling files from all over, you'll need several compression utilities; there is no "Swiss army knife" compression utility for PCs. PKZIP is the most widely used, however, and is available as shareware from PKWARE Inc., 9025 North Deerwood Drive, Brown Deer, WI 53223; 414/354-8699; 414/354-8559 (fax). It's also available on all of the popular PC FTP archives, including the Visitors Center.

University of Michigan PC archive.
The PC archive maintained by the University of Michigan is one of the most popular archives on the Internet. Just about any public domain, freeware or shareware software for the PC is available here. It's accessible with Gopher (as well as the traditional methods). Point your Gopher at gopher.archive.merit.net port 7055.

Alternatively, all files are available by anonymous FTP at archive.umich.edu. You can download an index of descriptions of all available files in the /msdos/info/ directory.

A SCAN Utility for Viruses

If you're going to download files from any FTP archive on the Internet, you run the risk of having your system infected with a *virus*. A virus (and similar files like trojan horses or worms) is actually a computer program imbedded within another file you download. It "infects" your computer in one of a number of different ways. Some viruses are merely annoying, but others can cause severe damage by erasing files on your hard disk, scrambling your disk's file catalog or a number of other malicious tricks.

Your computer can't get infected by a text file, only by binary files, but it's generally a good policy to consider any file you download to be a potential source of viruses. While viruses are relatively rare, the Internet is a fertile breeding ground for them. So many files are uploaded and transferred every day, it's impossible to check them all, especially since there's no single system in place for checking for viruses.

The best way to protect yourself is to download the current version of McAfee Associates' SCAN antivirus program. You can always find the latest version of SCAN at oak.oakland.edu in the /pub/msdos/virus/ directory as the filename scanvxxx.zip (where xxx is the current version number).

Etiquette for Uploaders.

Here's a quick checklist of things to keep in mind when you upload files to remote FTP sites:

Make sure you include all relevant documents.

Compress your files using either PKZIP or as a self-extracting archive (these are the two "standard" file compression utilities in the PC community).

Check your files for viruses before uploading them.

Upload your file to the appropriate directory.

Provide a brief, but accurate, description for your uploaded file.

Using SCAN

SCAN is probably the most frequently updated and widely used anti-virus utility for the PC. With it, you can periodically check your hard drive and local area network for viruses and eradicate most any viruses you might find. To scan your hard drive for any known virus and repair the drive if a virus is found:

1. Navigate to the directory that contains the SCAN program.

2. At the prompt, enter **SCAN** and press **Enter**. The SCAN instructions will be displayed, as shown in Figure 6-1.

Figure 6-1: SCAN instructions.

```
SCAN 9.19 V108 Copyright 1989-93 by McAfee Associates. (408) 988-3832
Usage:       SCAN d1: ... d26: /A /ADx /AF filename /AG filename /AV filename
                   /BELL /BMP /CERTIFY /CF filename /CHKHI /CG /CV /D
                   /DATE /E .xxx .yyy /EXT d:filename
                   /HISTORY filename /MAINT /MANY /NLZ /NOBREAK
                   /NOEXPIRE /NOMEM /NOPAUSE /REPORT filename
                   /RF filename /RG /RV /SAVE /SHOWDATE
                   /SUB @filename

Examples:    SCAN C:
             SCAN A: B:
             SCAN C:\TEST\*.* D:\ E:\
             SCAN A:TESTFILE.EXE /BELL /MANY

Options are:
      \                    - Scan root directory and boot area only
      /A                   - Scan all files, including data, for viruses
      /ADx                 - Scan all drives ('L'=local,'N'=network,' '=both)
      /AF filename         - Store recovery data/validation codes to file
      /AG filename         - Add recovery data/validation codes to specified
                             files EXCEPT those listed in filename
      /AV filename         - Add validation codes to specified files EXCEPT
                             those listed in filename
      /BELL                - Ring alarm if virus found
More? ( H = Help )
```

3. At the prompt, enter **SCAN X:** where x is the logical drive location for your hard drive.

▓ For example, if the logical location for your hard drive is C, you would enter **SCAN C:** at the prompt. The contents of your computer's memory and hard drive will be scanned for viruses and the results of the scan appear, as shown in Figure 6-2.

Figure 6-2: SCAN results.

```
C:\DOSAPPS\SCAN>scan C:
SCAN 9.19 V108 Copyright 1989-93 by McAfee Associates. (408) 988-3832
Scanning memory for critical viruses.
Scanning for known viruses.

Scanning Volume: MORIARITY .

Disk C: contains 244 directories and 5168 files.

No viruses found.

SCAN 9.19 V108 Copyright 1989-93 by McAfee Associates. (408) 988-3832

    This McAFEE(TM) software  may  not be used by a business, government
    agency or institution without  payment of  a negotiated license fee.
    To negotiate a license fee contact McAfee Associates (408) 988-3832.
    All use of  this software  is  conditioned upon  compliance with the
    license terms set forth in the LICENSE.DOC file.


    Copyright (c) McAfee Associates 1989-1993. All Rights Reserved.

C:\DOSAPPS\SCAN>
```

The SCAN distribution package contains extensive documentation. Refer to the documentation for further instructions on using SCAN, including the licensing information.

Commercial software updates.
The Oakland University archive offers updater programs for various commercial software programs on its FTP server. Updater programs for AfterDark, Canvas, FileMaker Pro, CrossTalk and ProComm are only a few of those you can download and use completely free. They're available by FTP from oak.oakland.edu in the appropriate directories.

Using FTP to Transfer Files

Minuet contains a complete File Transfer Protocol (FTP) module written by a team of programmers at the University of Minnesota. With Minuet, you can quickly and easily download (get) files from or upload (put) files to a remote host on the Internet. The file transfer speed will vary based on the type of Internet connection you have. I use a Serial Line Internet Protocol (SLIP) connection and a V.32bis modem with error correction and data compression. I almost always get throughput of about 1,300 characters-per-second on compressed data files and significantly faster results on text files. Using a V.32bis modem with error correction and data compression, you can expect to download a 500k file in about five or six minutes. Of course, if you're fortunate enough to enjoy a direct connection to the Internet, you can transfer a 500k file in a few seconds (just a little bit longer than it takes to transfer the same amount of data from your local file server).

Minuet's FTP module is an excellent, full-featured FTP program—in fact, it's the PC FTP tool I use most often. It is simple to use, providing an intuitive directory-tree interface for the FTP process. It automatically translates standard file conventions into the required FTP commands.

Shocking Growth.

Counting the number of nodes on the Internet is sort of like counting the number of stars in the sky. OK, not exactly, but you get the idea.

Vinton Cerf, widely acknowledged to be the "father" of the Internet, made the following observations in September 1993:

June 1991 was the fulcrum point in the commercialization of the Internet. In that month commercial use of the Net exceeded academic use.

As of September 1993, the NSFNet backbone was carrying about 7 terabytes of traffic each month.

As of fall 1993, the Internet is growing at a rate of 12% per month.

By the end of 1993, the Internet will be comprised of more than 2 million hosts on 46,000 registered IP networks within 22,000 registered domains in 91 countries.

A copy of Minuet is included on *The PC Internet Tour Guide Companion Disk*. If you're on the Internet as a commercial user, the program is provided for evaluation purposes only. If you decide to continue to use Minuet, you must pay a $50 fee to the Regents of the University of Minnesota.

Site licenses are also available; please send inquiries via e-mail to minuet@boombox.micro.umn.edu

Locating FTP servers.

Can't get enough of downloading files via FTP? Don't worry, it's not likely you'll run out of files or FTP sites.

A list of publicly accessible FTP sites is available by FTP from pilot.njin.net in the /pub/ftp-list/ directory.

Any FTP site listed allows anonymous logins. It's Internet courtesy to supply your e-mail address—in the username@domain.top-domain format—as your login password.

Downloading Files With Minuet

SHEZ, mentioned earlier in this chapter, is an indispensable compressed file manipulation utility. SHEZ brings a simple but very powerful interface to the Internet, and it's a program every PC Internet user should have. You can use Minuet to download the SHEZ application files.

1. Establish your connection to the Internet, if necessary. If you're using UMSLIP, type **slip dial** at the command prompt, and the connection will be automatically established.

   ▪ If you are using other SLIP or PPP software, follow the directions provided by your network administrator or service provider to establish the connection.

   ▪ If you enjoy a direct connection to the Internet, there is no need to establish a connection.

2. Launch Minuet by typing **minuet** at the command prompt.

    ▓ If you have configured Minuet to automatically check for mail, the program will automatically login to the server and download any e-mail addressed to you. The rest of this section assumes that you will be checking for e-mail manually. In either case, the INBOX Viewer will appear.

3. Press **Alt-W**. The Windows menu is displayed.

4. From the Windows menu, select the FTP command. The FTP dialog box appears, as shown in Figure 6-3.

Figure 6-3: Minuet FTP dialog box.

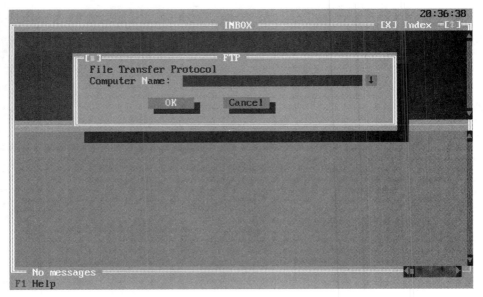

5. In the Computer Name field, type **oak.oakland.edu** and press **Enter**. Minuet will attempt to make contact with the computer you specified in the Computer Name field and, if successful, the FTP login info dialog box appears, as shown in Figure 6-4.

Figure 6-4: Minuet
FTP login info
dialog box.

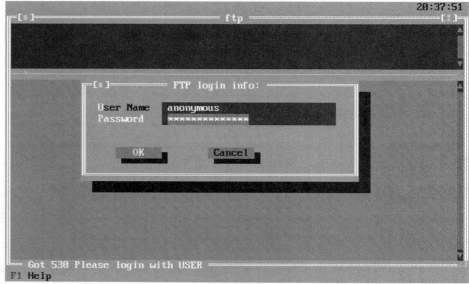

■ Here's a great shortcut. You only have to remember the domain address of the computers you access regularly one time. When you successfully login to a remote computer with FTP, Minuet remembers both the domain name of the site and the User Name and Password you used to login. Sites that are known to Minuet can be accessed with the **Up** and **Down arrow** keys while the FTP dialog box is active.

■ If the attempt to make contact with the computer you specified is unsuccessful, a dialog box noting the failure will be displayed.

■ Minuet automatically inserts a User Name of anonymous and your e-mail address as a password. Change these values if you have a predefined account on the computer you are accessing.

6. Press **Enter**. You will be logged into the computer. A welcome message (if any) will be displayed in the bottom portion of the ftp window and the hierarchical directory tree appears in the upper portion of the ftp window, as shown in Figure 6-5.

Figure 6-5: Minuet
ftp window.

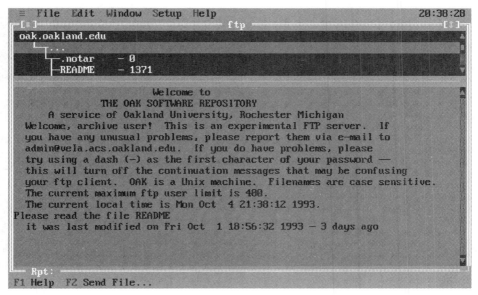

7. Use the **Up** and **Down arrow** keys to navigate the directory tree to locate the /pub/ subdirectory.

8. Press **Enter**. The contents of the /pub/ subdirectory are added to the directory tree in the upper panel of the ftp window.

9. Use the **Up** and **Down arrow** keys to navigate the directory tree to locate the /pub/msdos/ subdirectory.

10. Press **Enter**. The contents of the /pub/msdos/ subdirectory are added to the directory tree in the upper panel of the ftp window.

11. Use the **Up** and **Down arrow** keys to navigate the directory tree to locate the /pub/msdos/arcutils/ subdirectory.

12. Press **Enter**. The contents of the /pub/msdos/arcutils/ subdirectory are added to the directory tree in the upper panel of the ftp window.

13. Use the **Up** and **Down arrow** keys to navigate the directory tree to locate the /pub/msdos/arcutils/shez93.zip file, as shown in Figure 6-6.

Figure 6-6: Minuet
ftp window with
file selected.

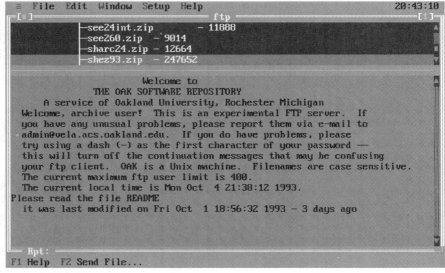

14. Press **Enter**. The download will begin and the file transfer's progress will be updated in the lower-left portion of the ftp window. When the transfer is complete, a tone will sound.

15. When the transfer is complete, press **Alt-W** to display the Window menu.

16. From the Window menu, select the Close command. The connection to the remote computer will be broken and Minuet's INBOX Viewer will reappear.

File Extensions.

Every file you download from the Internet will probably have at least one—and perhaps several—*filename extensions*. This is a method used to identify the types of files (and the software program used to create the files). Filename extensions have become a veritable alphabet soup, and often end up confusing people more than they inform.

The filename extension will give you a clue about which transfer mode (ASCII or Binary) to use in your FTP program. The good news is, if you're using Minuet, all this is automatically handled for you.

If you're using another FTP program, files that end with hqx, txt or ps extensions are the *only* files that can be downloaded in ASCII mode. All other types of files *must* be downloaded in Binary (also called Image) mode. Chances are that if you get errors during file decompression indicating that your file is corrupt, it's because you used ASCII mode when you should have used Binary mode.

For more information, see "A Primer on File Types" earlier in this chapter on page 144.

Uploading Files With Minuet

Downloading files is just one side of the file transfer coin. You can also *upload*, or send, files to a remote FTP server using Minuet. If you have a file that you want to share with the rest of the world, consider uploading it (as long as there are no restrictions on its distribution) to your favorite FTP site. To upload files to a remote FTP server with Minuet:

1. Establish your connection to the Internet, if necessary. If you're using UMSLIP, type **slip dial** at the command prompt, and the connection will be automatically established.

   ▧ If you are using other SLIP or PPP software, follow the directions provided by your network administrator or service provider to establish the connection.

   ▧ If you enjoy a direct connection to the Internet, there is no need to establish a connection.

2. Launch Minuet by typing **minuet** at the command prompt.

   ▧ If you have configured Minuet to automatically check for mail, the program will automatically login to the server and download any e-mail addressed to you. The rest of this section assumes that you will be checking for e-mail manually. In either case, the INBOX Viewer will appear.

3. Press **Alt-W**. The Windows menu is displayed.

4. From the Windows menu, select the FTP command. The FTP dialog box appears, as shown in Figure 6-3.

5. In the Computer Name field, type the domain address of the computer you want to access—in the format domain.top-domain—and press **Enter**.

   ▧ Alternatively, select the domain address of the computer you want to access from the list of known sites (with the FTP dialog box active, use the **Up** and **Down arrow** keys to select the site and press **Enter**).

   ▧ Minuet will attempt to make contact with the computer you specified in the Computer Name field and, if successful, the FTP login dialog box appears, as shown in Figure 6-4.

   ▧ If the attempt to make contact with the computer you specified is unsuccessful, a dialog box noting the failure will be displayed.

- Minuet automatically inserts a User Name of anonymous and your e-mail address as a password. Change these values if you have a predefined account on the computer you are accessing.

6. Press **Enter**. You will be logged into the computer. A welcome message (if any) will be displayed in the bottom portion of the ftp window, and the hierarchical directory tree appears in the upper portion of the ftp window, as shown in Figure 6-5.

7. Use the **Up** and **Down arrow** keys to navigate the directory tree to the directory in which you want to upload your file.

- Note that most FTP archives have a special directory set aside for uploads. These directories are usually labelled something like /pub/incoming/ or /pub/uploads/

8. Press **F2**. The File to Send dialog box is displayed, as shown in Figure 6-7.

Figure 6-7: Minuet File to Send dialog box.

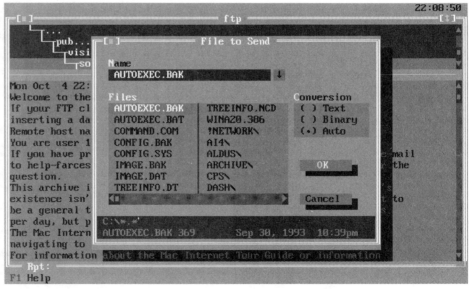

Chapter 6: Transferring Files

Famous PC FTP Archives.

Here are the most popular PC-specific FTP sites. All accept anonymous logins, but be sure to use your full e-mail address—in the username@domain.top-domain format—as a password.

domain name	directory
oak.oakland.edu	/pub/msdos/
archive.umich.edu	/msdos/
ftp.microsoft.com	/pub/
microlib.cc.utexas.edu	/microlib/pc/
ftp.funet.fi	/pub/pc/
ftp.lu.se	/pub/pc/

Here are the most popular PC mirror FTP sites. A *mirror site* is an exact copy of another site. They are designed to relieve the heavy traffic in the major FTP sites. If you find that you can't login to one of the sites in the above listing, try one of these mirror sites.

domain name	directory
archie.au	/micros/msdos/
ftp.lth.se	/msdos/
minnehaha.rhrk.uni-kl.de	/pub/pc/
utsun.s.u-tokyo.ac.jp	/msdos/
wuarchive.wustl.edu	/mirrors/msdos/
shark.mel.dit.csiro.au	/pc/

More information on these and other FTP sites is provided in Chapter 8, "Other Internet Resources," and in the electronic updates for this book.

9. Press **Tab**. The cursor will advance to the Files list.

10. Using the **Up** and **Down arrow** keys, navigate to the file you want to upload.

   ▓ Press **Enter** to open directories in the Files list.

11. With the file you want to upload selected, press **Enter**. The upload will begin, and the file transfer's progress will be updated in the lower-left portion of the ftp window. When the transfer is complete, a tone will sound.

   ▓ If you attempt to upload a file to a read-only directory, a dialog box appears informing you that you do not have the proper access privileges to upload files to that directory. Check to make sure that you are uploading to the appropriate directory.

12. When the transfer is complete, Press **Alt-W** to display the Window menu.

13. From the Window menu, select the Close command. The connection to the remote computer will be broken, and Minuet's INBOX Viewer will re-appear.

Nice Pictures.
Hiview is a freeware multi-format graphics image viewer. It's a simple, no-nonsense viewer that offers a very clean interface and outstanding performance. It requires at least an 80386 processor and is available by FTP from oak.oakland.edu in the /pub/msdos/graphics/ directory. The filename is hv12.zip.

Moving On

There are huge repositories of very interesting files scattered throughout the thousands of FTP servers available on the Internet. With a little perseverance—and more importantly, knowing where to look—you can use FTP to find files on just about any topic. There is an important Internet resource that can help you navigate many of the available FTP servers—its name is Archie, and you'll learn about it in Chapter 8,

"Other Internet Resources." Of course, the electronic updates to this book are another important resource available to you.

One of the best ways to navigate quickly and effectively through the Internet is the University of Minnesota's Gopher, covered in the next chapter. When it comes to touring the Net, Gopher is a knowing native, helpful concierge and savvy travel agent, all rolled into one.

CHAPTER 7

USING GOPHER
Burrowing for Information

So far, our tour
has covered the many strange languages and customs of the Internet,
but we've barely scratched the surface of the vast resources the Net has
to offer. And when navigating unexplored territories, even pioneers
need all the help they can get. It's always a relief to find an amicable
cab driver or savvy concierge who can clue you in to those great out-of-
the-way spots where most tourists never venture. In this chapter we'll
explore how to use Gopher—the Internet's most sociable, well-con-
nected pathfinder—to browse aimlessly or search specifically for
everything from Russian poetry to local weather reports.

What Is Gopher?

Network news, e-mail and FTP are great tools for specific tasks. As
you've seen, it's simple enough to use Minuet's e-mail module to dash
off an e-mail message to someone, and it's a snap to use the news
reader to look for PC-specific information in some place like the
comp.os.msdos newsgroups. Even finding and downloading a specific
file from an FTP archive is a cinch if you're using Minuet's FTP capabilities. These programs and Internet resources are all specific tools for
specific jobs.

But what if you don't know exactly what you're looking for, or only
have a broad idea about a topic of interest? What if you just want to
surf through the oceans of information available on the Internet? That's
where Gopher comes in.

Gopher is one of the most powerful resources available to Internet users, and Minuet's Gopher module is one of the easiest to use and fastest implementations of the Gopher protocol. Written by a team of programmers at the University of Minnesota, Gopher puts a menu-based interface on many of the Internet's resources, making moving from spot to spot on the Net as easy as picking options from a numbered list—and often easier.

Whole Earth 'Lectronic Link (WELL) Gopher.
The Whole Earth folks have put some of the best articles from the *Whole Earth Review* in a Gopher server. You'll find articles by Bruce Sterling, Stewart Brand and many others. This is one of the best information resources on the Internet. You can access it by pointing your Gopher program at nkosi.well.sf.ca.us port 70.

If Gopher had been developed in California, instead of on the far edge of Minnesota, it might have been called Surfer. Its name comes from the University of Minnesota's mascot, the Golden Gopher. Information servers on the Internet that support access with the Gopher software are always called *Gopher sites*, *Gopher servers* or *Gopher holes*. The software's actual communication and database protocol is also referred to as *Gopher*. The software you run on your PC to browse through Gopher holes is also called *Gopher*.

What Can I Use Gopher For?

Gopher (the protocol) lets you burrow through information resources using a series of easy-to-navigate menus that appear as numbered lists. Gopher (the program) lets you navigate through Gopher information resources using standard menus and submenus. You can use Gopher on the PC to navigate huge "dataspaces" by simply navigating menu structures.

Gopher is best used as a browsing tool. It doesn't matter where an information resource you find with Gopher is physically located. As long as it is compatible with Gopher, it simply appears as another menu item in the hierarchy. You don't have to worry about IP addresses or even domain names with Gopher—when you find a resource you want to browse, just select it from the menu.

Extensions to the Gopher protocol allow you to browse through different kinds of information resources—pictures, sounds, video, computer files, as well as text. Instead of groping around blindly through a series of interconnected servers, connecting and disconnecting with each one in turn, you can use Gopher to wander aimlessly without worrying about the process of connecting and disconnecting. This chapter also explains how you can wander around through *Gopherspaces* (those areas that support the Gopher protocol) purposefully, as if you had a well-trained research librarian helping out.

Why Should I Use Gopher Instead of FTP?

Gopher is a *stateless* software program, making the most efficient possible use of network resources. Instead of keeping a connection to a remote site continuously open, Gopher opens a connection to initiate your request, closes the connection, and then reopens a connection to receive the host's response. By comparison, FTP maintains a continuous connection while you are browsing directories and transferring files. Many of the best archive sites restrict FTP access, while allowing unrestricted Gopher access. You can be a good Internet citizen by using Gopher whenever you can. Most of the major FTP archives also support Gopher access, and more Gopher servers are continually being added. Some sites support only FTP access, though, so it's important that you use the right tool for the job.

Using Gopher

The elegant simplicity of Gopher is that its developers didn't reinvent the wheel. They configured Gopher, and the Gopher software you use from your PC, to take advantage of existing network conventions. When you use the Gopher application to login to a Gopher server and select a network resource, Gopher automatically determines the right tool for the job. If you're accessing a computer file, it will be sent to you using FTP. If you select a login resource, Gopher automatically opens a TELNET session. It's all handled transparently and automatically.

Browsing Information With Gopher

The latest versions of various Gopher software programs are available from a number of FTP sites throughout the Internet. The current version of Minuet and the University of Minnesota's Gopher client for the

PC are available by anonymous FTP from boombox.micro.umn.edu. Complete instructions for downloading files on the Internet are provided in "Using FTP to Transfer Files" beginning on page 151.

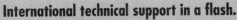

International technical support in a flash.

North Americans take technical support for granted because the vast majority of software developers are located in the United States and Canada. International users are faced with a host of problems when they have technical questions. Many use the Internet as their sole avenue of support. Zviki Cohen of Israel is a good example:

"I'm from Israel, and I work and study at the Technion—Israel Institute of Technology. I use the Internet as an important tool to get support. Last month I was interested in buying some products. In America or Europe you can pick up a phone, dial a toll-free number and hear all about it, but here, when you are interested in a product the local salesman hasn't heard of (and there are plenty...) you can forget about it.

"Well, not with the Internet. A few e-mails to the companies sorted out the problem and I got a few suggestions for the products I needed. When I found a serious bug in a software program I bought, I didn't wait until the tech support people here get me the answer from across the sea. I got it myself the next day from the companies headquarters in the USA."

If you know how to use the **Up** and **Down arrow** keys to navigate a hierarchical menu tree, you already know how to use Gopher. Navigate Gopherspace—that is, browse through those resources accessible via the Gopher protocol—by selecting any menu item that looks interesting and press **Enter**. It's as simple as that. Really!

- Selecting any menu item generally opens that item and displays its contents or provides a dialog box for additional information.

- Selecting a <Directory> item opens that directory and displays its contents.

- Selecting a <File> item displays the text of that document on your screen. If the file is larger than about 32k you'll be prompted to save the file to disk.

- Selecting a <Bin File> item downloads that software resource to your PC; you'll be prompted to save the file to disk.

- Selecting a <Telnet> item opens a TELNET remote login session on the specified computer.

- Selecting a <Searcher> item displays a Search for text dialog box.

Use these steps to browse vast stretches of Gopherspace.

1. Establish your connection to the Internet, if necessary. If you're using UMSLIP, type **slip dial** at the command prompt, and the connection will be automatically established.

   ▪ If you are using other SLIP or PPP software, follow the directions provided by your network administrator or service provider to establish the connection.

   ▪ If you enjoy a direct connection to the Internet, there is no need to establish a connection.

2. Launch Minuet by typing **minuet** at the command prompt.

   ▪ If you have configured Minuet to automatically check for mail, the program will automatically login to the server and download any e-mail addressed to you. The rest of this section assumes that you will be checking for e-mail manually. In either case, the INBOX Viewer will appear.

3. Press **Alt-W**. The Windows menu is displayed.

4. From the Windows menu, select the Gopher command. You'll be logged into the root level of the Gopher server you specified when you configured Minuet. For example, my home Gopher server's root level is shown in Figure 7-1.

Figure 7-1: Minuet home Gopher server root level.

```
≡  File  Edit  Window  Setup  Help                          16:49:36
┌──────────────────────── INBOX ─────────────────────────────────┐
┌─[■]────────────── Gopher Information Service ══════ [X] History ═[↑]─┐
│ Gopher Root Menu                                                 ▲
│                                                                  
│                                                                  
│                                                                  ▼
│ <File>          About this Gopher and MRNet                      ▲
│ <Directory>     MRNet Anonymous FTP Archives                     
│ <Directory>     NREN                                             
│ <Directory>     NSFNET Info                                      
│ <Directory>     Other Gopher Servers                            
│ <Directory>     Popular FTP Sites via Gopher                    
│ <Directory>     Search FTP Sites using Archie                   
│ <Directory>     Search titles in Gopherspace using veronica     
│ <Directory>     Weather Forecasts                               
│ <Directory>     dialIP clients & other Mac network software     ▼
│                                                                  
└─ idle ──────────────────────────────────────────────────────────┘
── No messages ──
BookMarks  Keep BookMark  Delete BookMark  Cancel Query  New Gopher  Options
```

5. Using the **Up** and **Down arrow** keys, navigate the menu to select an item that interests you.

6. Press **Enter** to open the selected item.

   ▪ Note that most Gopher servers provide an item named "Other Gopher Servers" or something similar. From within this item you can usually find an item named "All the Gopher Servers in the World," which contains alphabetical and geographic listings of every available Gopher Server, as shown in Figure 7-2.

Figure 7-2: All the Gopher Servers in the World Gopher menu item.

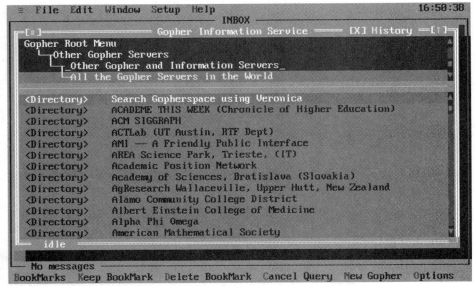

7. Using the **Up** and **Down arrow** keys, continue to navigate your way through the available Gopher servers, selecting any item that interests you.

Eventually you'll find that you've followed the Gopher too deep into one of the many Gopher holes on the Internet. Here's how to backtrack your way out of a Gopher hole.

1. With your Internet connection established and the Gopher window active within Minuet, press **Tab** twice. The cursor will move to the upper panel of the window, containing the hierarchical menu of items leading to your current position in Gopher hole.

2. Use the **Up** and **Down arrow** keys to select the level to which you want to return.

3. With the level to which you want to return selected, press **Enter**. The menu hierarchies will collapse and you'll be returned to the selected level.

The Politics of Gopher

As the Internet changes from a network of networks dominated by research and education institutions to one populated by a mixture of commercial and academic users, the Internet community itself is experiencing great stress.

Nowhere has this stress been more apparent recently than with Gopher and the University of Minnesota's Gopher development team.

Gopher, like most other Net resources, had always been made available for use by anyone, free of charge. In March 1993, however, the Gopher team decided it was time to recover some of their expenses and issued a policy statement that requires commercial sites to pay an annual license fee for any Gopher servers they operate.

Under the initial policy, the Gopher team was charging a first-year license fee of $5,000 per server ($2,500 license fee for succeeding years) to any commercial site accessible from the Internet that offers only free information. For commercial sites that sell their information or charge a fee for access, an additional license fee of 7.5 percent of receipts was required.

Needless to say, a firestorm erupted in the comp.infosystems.gopher newsgroup—the spot on the Net where users discuss Gopher-related issues. Charges of "greed killing Gopher" were fired off by angry Gopher users. People who had contributed to the development of Gopher publicly wondered how they would be compensated for their work. Others wondered how a tax-payer-supported University could attempt to turn a profit on something they had already been compensated for. A few days later, the University of Minnesota's Gopher development team posted an article stating that the Gopher server license fees would be "negotiable."

Within a month, a freeware Gopher-compliant server (software that would allow administrators to set up their own Gopher servers without using the University of Minnesota's software) was available on the Internet, with no license fee for commercial use. It was reportedly somewhat buggy, but it was available. The new software was provided by a consortium of programmers, in the spirit of the free-flow of information that characterizes the Internet.

Should the University of Minnesota be able to charge license fees for what they used to give away free of charge? Sure. Gopher is theirs to do with as they please. That doesn't prohibit someone else from developing a competing product and giving it away. And in fact that's what happened.

More▸

A few months later, the University of Minnesota announced a modified fee structure for the use of Gopher servers. Organizations that do not charge for access to their Gopher server and do not offer products or services for sale are required to pay $100 per year per server.

Organizations with less than $3.5 million gross income (from the Gopher server alone) per year who use a Gopher server to offer products or services for sale (but do not charge for access to the server) are required to pay the University of Minnesota $500 per year per server.

For organizations with less than $3.5 million gross income per year (from the Gopher server alone) who use a Gopher server to offer products or services for sale and charge access fees on the server, the license fee is the greater of $500 per server or 2.5% of the amount charged for access to the server each year.

Organizations with more than $3.5 million gross income per year (from the Gopher server alone) who use a Gopher server to offer products or services for sale and charge access fees on the server are required to pay the greater of $2,500 per server or 2.5% of the amount charged for access to the server each year.

This problem of fee structures isn't going to go away and the commercialization of the Internet is something the researchers and academics are going to want to accept.

Now that you know the basics of how to navigate through Gopherspace using four keys (Up arrow, Down arrow, Tab and Enter), let's take a look at using Gopher to actually retrieve useful information.

1. Establish your connection to the Internet, if necessary. If you're using UMSLIP, type **slip dial** at the command prompt, and the connection will be automatically established.

   ▦ If you are using other SLIP or PPP software, follow the directions provided by your network administrator or service provider to establish the connection.

   ▦ If you enjoy a direct connection to the Internet, there is no need to establish a connection.

2. Launch Minuet by typing **minuet** at the command prompt.

   ▦ If you have configured Minuet to automatically check for mail, the program will automatically login to the server and download any e-mail addressed to you. The rest of this section assumes that you will be checking for e-mail manually. In either case, the INBOX Viewer will appear.

3. Press **Alt-W**. The Windows menu is displayed.

4. From the Windows menu, select the Gopher command. You'll be logged into the root level of the Gopher server you specified when you configured Minuet.

5. Navigate to the University of North Carolina's SUNsite Gopher server.

   ■ The actual procedure for navigating to a particular server will vary, based on your home Gopher server. From within the "Other Gopher Servers" (or similar) menu item, select the "North America," "United States," "North Carolina," "University of North Carolina at Chapel Hill (Ogphre/SUNsite)" menu items in succession. When you get there, your Gopher window should look similar to the one shown in Figure 7-3.

Figure 7-3:
Gopher window
for the University
of North Carolina's
SUNsite Gopher
server.

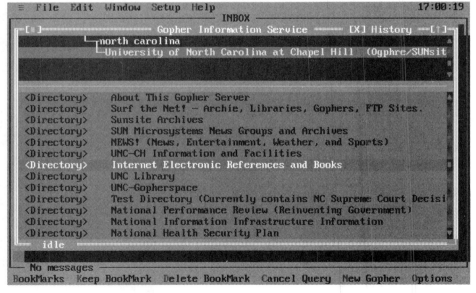

6. Select the Internet Electronic References and Books <Directory> menu item and press **Enter** to open that directory, as shown in Figure 7-4.

Figure 7-4: Gopher
Internet Electronic
References and
Books menu.

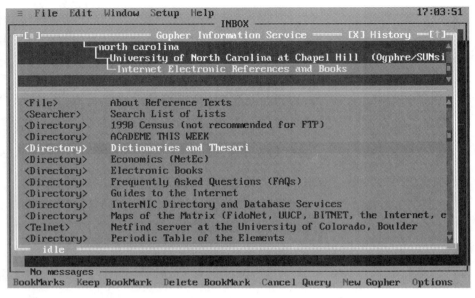

7. Select the Dictionaries and Thesauri <Directory> menu item and press **Enter** to open that directory, as shown in Figure 7-5.

Figure 7-5: Gopher
Dictionaries and
Thesauri menu.

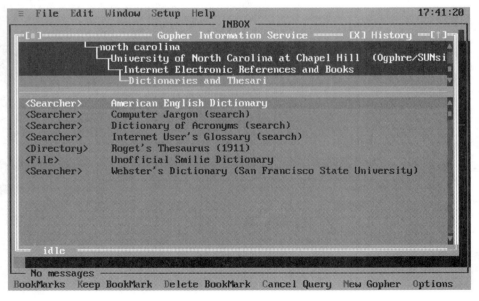

8. Select the American English Dictionary <Searcher> menu item and press **Enter**. A Search Text dialog box appears, as shown in Figure 7-6.

Figure 7-6: Gopher
Search Text
dialog box.

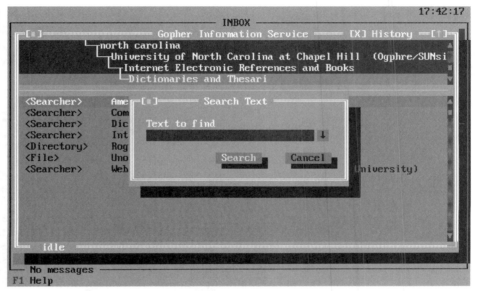

9. Enter the word you want to search for in the Text to find field and
   press **Enter**. This example uses the word "intrepid" as the search
   item. A menu of matched items appears, as shown in Figure 7-7.

Figure 7-7:
Gopher list of
matched items
menu.

```
≡  File  Edit  Window  Setup  Help                    17:43:37
┌─────────────────────── INBOX ───────────────────────┐
│┌[■]──────────── Gopher Information Service ═══ [X] History ═[↑]┐
││         └north carolina                                      ▲│
││           └University of North Carolina at Chapel Hill  (Ogphre/SUNsi│
││             └Internet Electronic References and Books       ▒│
││               └Dictionaries and Thesari                     ▼│
││                                                              ▲│
││ <File>         intrepid [exact match]                        │
││ <File>         immaterial [soundex match]                   ▒│
││ <File>         immature [soundex match]                      │
││ <File>         immaturity [soundex match]                    │
││ <File>         immoderacy [soundex match]                    │
││ <File>         immoderate [soundex match]                    │
││ <File>         immoderately [soundex match]                  │
││ <File>         indirect [soundex match]                      │
││ <File>         indirection [soundex match]                   │
││ <File>         indirectly [soundex match]                    │
││ <File>         indoor [soundex match]                        │
││ <File>         indoors [soundex match]                       │
││ <File>         indorse, [soundex match]                     ▼│
││═ idle ═══════════════════════════════════════════════════════│
│└──────────────────────────────────────────────────────────────┘
└─ No messages ─────────────────────────────────────────────────┘
BookMarks  Keep BookMark  Delete BookMark  Cancel Query  New Gopher  Options
```

10. Select the appropriate matched item and press **Enter**. The results of the search appear in the bottom panel of the Gopher window, as shown in Figure 7-8.

Figure 7-8:
Gopher window
with results of a
search.

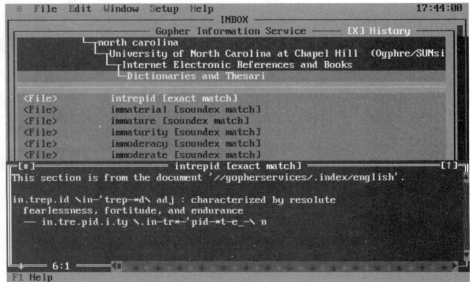

11. Press **Alt-W** to display the Window menu.

12. From the Window menu, select the Close command. The topmost window—in this case, the results of the text search—will be dismissed.

13. Repeat steps 11–12 as necessary to close all open Gopher windows, returning to the Minuet INBOX Viewer.

Barney the Dinosaur.

I don't know about you, but I just don't understand this Barney the Dinosaur phenomenon. At the April Fools Day 1993 Grateful Dead concert, Barney appeared on stage. Everyone there except the kids thought it was bassist Phil Lesh in a purple suit. The kids knew it was Barney.

But lately, there's been a kind of strange, grassroots Barney backlash. Kids across America are singing macabre songs defaming Barney's name and mocking his message of caring and sharing. Two Texas youths even attacked an unsuspecting Barney—pummeling him and trying to rip his head off—during his visit to a shopping mall. (Whether it was the real Barney or one of Barney's many look-alike "helpers" we still don't know.)

And on the Internet there are dozens of savvy adults, wise to Barney's global conspiracy to brainwash kids into spewing a mindless doctrine of vapid grins and hyperkinetic world-glee. In fact, one guy even started a newsgroup, alt.barney.dinosaur.die.die.die, to help rally opposition against the "Great Evil Purple One."

Downloading Files With Gopher

Some of the most popular FTP sites (especially archives rich with PC software) on the Internet offer access to their files via Gopher. This means you can use Gopher instead of another program to download files from those sites, conserving network resources.

To download files with Gopher:

1. Establish your connection to the Internet, if necessary. If you're using UMSLIP, type **slip dial** at the command prompt, and the connection will be automatically established.

   ▧ If you are using other SLIP or PPP software, follow the directions provided by your network administrator or service provider to establish the connection.

   ▧ If you enjoy a direct connection to the Internet, there is no need to establish a connection.

2. Launch Minuet by typing **minuet** at the command prompt.

   ▧ If you have configured Minuet to automatically check for mail, the program will automatically login to the server and download any e-mail addressed to you. The rest of this section assumes that you will be checking for e-mail manually. In either case, the INBOX Viewer will appear.

3. Press **Alt-W**. The Windows menu is displayed.

4. From the Windows menu, select the Gopher command. You'll be logged into the root level of the Gopher server you specified when you configured Minuet.

   ▤ Telix is one of the most popular MS-DOS telecommunications programs. An example of excellent shareware, the program is as good as many commercial products. Telix is available at many FTP archives on the Internet, and this section will show you how to use Gopher to download the program from the Merit Software Archives.

5. Navigate to the Merit Software Archives at the University of Michigan.

   ▤ The actual procedure for navigating to a particular server will vary, based on your home Gopher server. From within the "Other Gopher Servers" (or similar) menu item, select the "North America," "United States," "Michigan," "Merit Software Archives" menu items in succession. When you get there, your Gopher window should look similar to the one shown in Figure 7-9.

Figure 7-9: Gopher window for the Merit Software Archives.

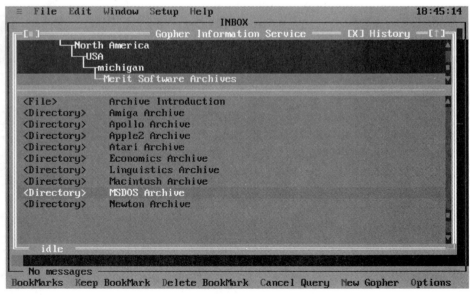

6. Select the MSDOS Archive <Directory> menu item and press **Enter** to open that directory, as shown in Figure 7-10.

Figure 7-10:
Gopher MSDOS
Archive menu.

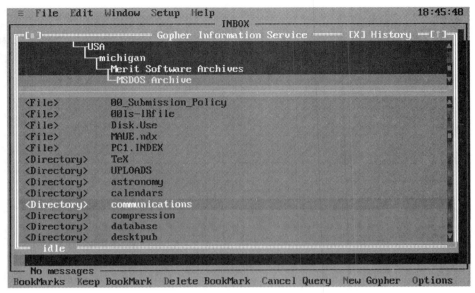

7. Select the communications <Directory> menu item and press **Enter** to open that directory, as shown in Figure 7-11.

Figure 7-11:
Gopher
communications
directory menu.

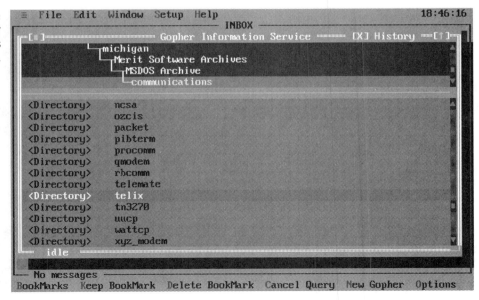

8. Select the telix <Directory> menu item and press **Enter** to open that directory, as shown in Figure 7-12.

Figure 7-12:
Gopher telix
directory menu.

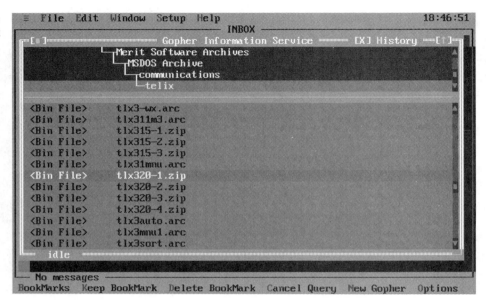

9. Select the tlx320-1.zip <Bin File> item and press **Enter**. The Save
Binary file as dialog box appears, as shown in Figure 7-13.

Figure 7-13:
Gopher Save
Binary file as
dialog box.

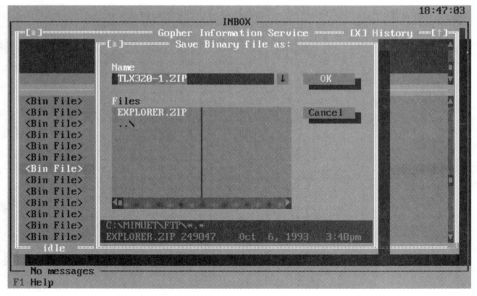

■ Files you download with Gopher are stored in the /MINUET/
FTP/ directory on your local hard drive.

10. Press **Enter**. The file transfer will begin, with its status reported in the Gopher window, as shown in Figure 7-14.

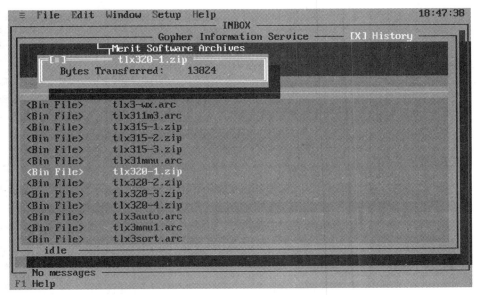

Figure 7-14: Gopher file transfer progress display.

▦ When the file transfer is complete, a tone will sound and the status display reporting "done."

11. Repeat steps 9–10 for the remaining core telix files: tlx320-2.zip, tlx320-3.zip and tlx320-4.zip.

12. Press **Alt-W** to display the Window menu.

13. From the Window menu, select the Close command. The topmost window will be dismissed.

14. Repeat steps 12–13 as necessary to close all open Gopher windows, returning to the Minuet INBOX Viewer.

Sometimes you just want to browse through a Gopher server looking for interesting files and documents. This is a great way to keep up with what's happening on the Net. One of the most interesting Gopher holes on the Internet is the Whole Earth 'Lectronic Link (WELL) Gopher server.

To browse through the WELL Gopher server:

1. Establish your connection to the Internet, if necessary. If you're using UMSLIP, type **slip dial** at the command prompt, and the connection will be automatically established.

- ▓ If you are using other SLIP or PPP software, follow the directions provided by your network administrator or service provider to establish the connection.

- ▓ If you enjoy a direct connection to the Internet, there is no need to establish a connection.

2. Launch Minuet by typing **minuet** at the command prompt.

   - ▓ If you have configured Minuet to automatically check for mail, the program will automatically login to the server and download any e-mail addressed to you. The rest of this section assumes that you will be checking for e-mail manually. In either case, the INBOX Viewer will appear.

3. Press **Alt-W**. The Windows menu is displayed.

4. From the Windows menu, select the Gopher command. You'll be logged into the root level of the Gopher server you specified when you configured Minuet.

5. Navigate to the Whole Earth 'Lectronic Magazine—The WELL's Gopherspace.

   - ▓ The actual procedure for navigating to a particular server will vary, based on your home Gopher server. From within the "Other Gopher Servers" (or similar) menu item, select the "North America," "United States," "General," "Whole Earth 'Lectronic Magazine—The WELL's Gopherspace" menu items in succession. When you get there, your Gopher window should look similar to the one shown in Figure 7-15.

Figure 7-15:
Gopher window
for the WELL's
Gopher server.

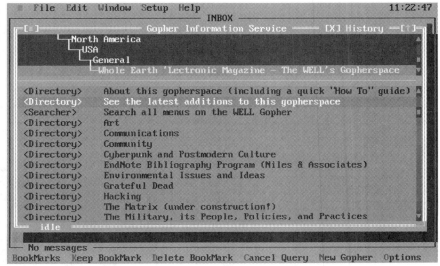

■ The WELL's Gopher server is a very fertile information resource. You can browse around on your own, or you can come
along on the guided tour. We'll begin the tour by taking a look
at "What's New in the WELL."

6. Select the See the latest additions to this gopherspace <Directory>
menu item and press **Enter** to open that directory, as shown in
Figure 7-16.

Figure 7-16:
Gopher's "What's
New in the WELL"
directory.

7. Select the About "What's New in the WELL" <File> menu item and press **Enter**. A text file explaining how to retrieve new information appears.

8. Press **Alt-W** to display the Window menu.

9. Select the Zoom command. The topmost window (the WELL instruction file in this case) will be enlarged to fill the screen, as shown in Figure 7-17.

Figure 7-17: Gopher "What's New in the WELL" instruction file.

```
≡  File  Edit  Window  Setup  Help                              11:36:48
┌[■]───────────────── About 'What's New in the WELL' ═════════════════[↕]┐
│About 'What's New in the-well":                                          │
│                                                                         │
│To search for items that have been created or changed                   │
│since some date, give that date as the search string.                   │
│                                                                         │
│Dates can be specified in two formats. For example:                     │
│    1 day 35 min ago                                                     │
│and                                                                      │
│    19921104040013 gophergmt                                            │
│                                                                         │
│In general the formats are:                                             │
│    {W w{weeks}} {D d{ays}} {H h{hours}} {M m{inutes}} {S s{econds}} ago│
│and                                                                      │
│    YYYYMMDDHHMMSS gophergmt                                            │
│                                                                         │
│The last three items listed will be:                                    │
│        **About 'What's New in the-well"                                │
│        **The top of the "the-well"'                                    │
│        **Bookmark for future new "the-well" items (...)                │
│                                                                         │
│If you save the bookmark now and "enter" it in the the future, it will │
└── 28:1 ──────────◄■                                                   ►│
 F1 Help
```

10. Press **Esc** to dismiss the WELL instruction file.

11. Select the What's New in the WELL? <Searcher> menu item and press **Enter**. The Search Text dialog box appears, as shown in Figure 7-18.

Figure 7-18:
Gopher Search
Text dialog box.

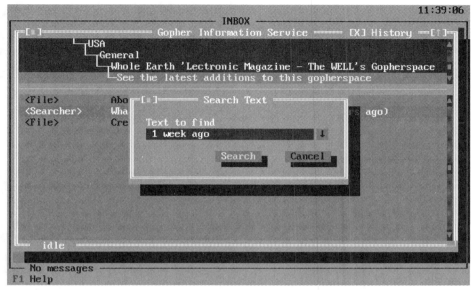

12. Enter **1 week ago** in the Text to find box and press **Enter**. A menu of items added in the last week appears, as shown in Figure 7-19.

Figure 7-19:
Gopher menu of
new items added
in the last week.

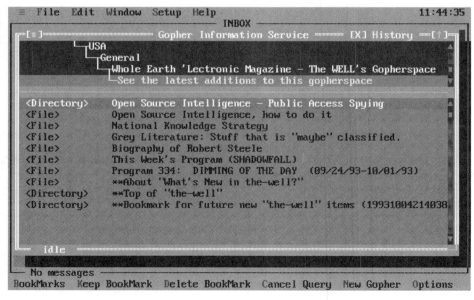

13. Select an item that interests you and press **Enter**. Alternatively, select the Top of "the well"<Directory> item and press **Enter** to return to the WELL's top directory.

14. When you're finished browsing, press **Alt-W** to display the Window menu.

15. From the Window menu, select the Close command. The topmost window—in this case, the results of the text search—will be dismissed.

16. Repeat steps 14–15 as necessary to close all open Gopher windows, returning to the Minuet INBOX Viewer.

Using Gopher Bookmarks

Gopher is great for browsing through lots of different kinds of information resources on the Internet. As you gain more experience prowling these resources, you'll probably start wishing for a way to leave a crumb trail to your favorite Gopher servers, so you can easily find your way to them again. Gopher's Bookmark feature lets you define a trail to your favorite Gopher servers. This allows you to quickly and easily login to your favorite Gopher servers by selecting a single menu item.

To set Bookmarks within Gopher:

1. Establish your connection to the Internet, if necessary. If you're using UMSLIP, type **slip dial** at the command prompt, and the connection will be automatically established.

   ▓ If you are using other SLIP or PPP software, follow the directions provided by your network administrator or service provider to establish the connection.

   ▓ If you enjoy a direct connection to the Internet, there is no need to establish a connection.

2. Launch Minuet by typing **minuet** at the command prompt.

   ▓ If you have configured Minuet to automatically check for mail, the program will automatically login to the server and download any e-mail addressed to you. The rest of this section assumes that you will be checking for e-mail manually. In either case, the INBOX Viewer will appear.

3. Press **Alt-W**. The Windows menu is displayed.

4. From the Windows menu, select the Gopher command. You'll be logged into the root level of the Gopher server you specified when you configured Minuet.

5. Navigate through Gopherspace by selecting menu items until you reach the resource for which you want to create a Bookmark.

6. With the resource selected, press **Alt-K**. The Keep Bookmark dialog box appears, as shown in Figure 7-20.

Figure 7-20:
Gopher Keep
Bookmark
dialog box.

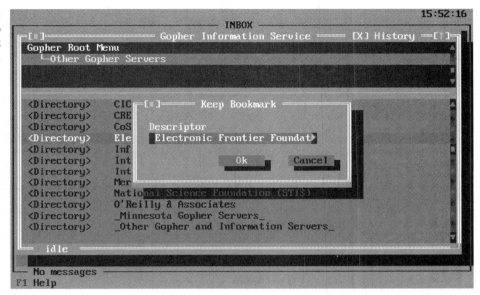

7. Enter a name for the Bookmark in the Descriptor box and press **Enter**.

8. Repeat steps 5–7 for each additional Bookmark you want to add.

Use these steps to use the Bookmarks you have created.

1. Establish your connection to the Internet, if necessary. If you're using UMSLIP, type **slip dial** at the command prompt, and the connection will be automatically established.

   ▪ If you are using other SLIP or PPP software, follow the directions provided by your network administrator or service provider to establish the connection.

   ▪ If you enjoy a direct connection to the Internet, there is no need to establish a connection.

2. Launch Minuet by typing **minuet** at the command prompt.

   ▪ If you have configured Minuet to automatically check for mail, the program will automatically login to the server and download any e-mail addressed to you. The rest of this section assumes that you will be checking for e-mail manually. In either case, the INBOX Viewer will appear.

3. Press **Alt-W**. The Windows menu is displayed.

4. From the Windows menu, select the Gopher command. You'll be logged into the root level of the Gopher server you specified when you configured Minuet.

5. Press **Alt-B**. A list of available Bookmarks will be displayed, like the example shown in Figure 7-21.

Figure 7-21:
Gopher
Bookmarks.

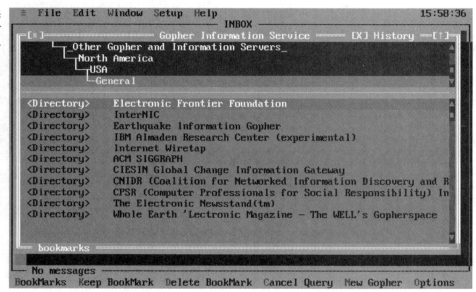

6. Using the **Up** and **Down arrow** keys, select the Bookmark you want to use and press **Enter**. The Gopher resource represented by the Bookmark will be activated.

   ▪ If the Bookmark you selected is a <Directory> menu item, you will be logged into that Gopher server.

   ▪ If the Bookmark you selected is a <File> menu item, the file will be displayed (if it's a text file) or downloaded to your hard drive (if it's a binary file).

   ▪ If the Bookmark you selected is a <Telnet> menu item, the login process will be initiated on the remote computer.

You can delete any Bookmark by selecting it and pressing **Alt-D**.

You can set Bookmarks for any resource within Gopherspace. For instance, if you're constantly downloading telecommunications software from the /msdos/communications/ directory of the Merit Software Archives, you can set a Bookmark specifically for the communications directory. Selecting the communications Bookmark will cause Gopher to immediately login to the Merit archive's /msdos/communications/ directory, rather than forcing you to navigate through the directory hierarchy. You don't even have to be logged into the Merit Gopher server for this to work. Selecting the communications Bookmark and pressing **Enter** will automatically login to the Merit server and navigate instantly to the /msdos/communications/ directory.

Locating e-mail addresses.
You can locate the e-mail address of anyone who has posted a network news article by sending this message to mail-server@pit-manager.mit.edu
   send usenet-addresses/*name*
where *name* is the name of the person for whom you want an e-mail address.

Remote Login With Gopher
Gopher can be used to login remotely to distant computers on the Internet using the TELNET protocol. Of course, you can use a terminal emulation program to login to remote computers, but Gopher provides you with a way of browsing terminal-based information in the same manner as any other information resource that is accessible with Gopher. Terminal emulation programs provide the advantage of complex emulations for various hardware terminals. Gopher's implementation is very simple and will not work with some Internet resources accessible by remote login, but Gopher offers the advantage of ease-of-use—you don't have to know or remember machine addresses; just select the resource you want to use from the Gopher menu.

Use these steps to login to remote computers with Gopher.

1. Establish your connection to the Internet, if necessary. If you're using UMSLIP, type **slip dial** at the command prompt, and the connection will be automatically established.

   ▓ If you are using other SLIP or PPP software, follow the directions provided by your network administrator or service provider to establish the connection.

   ▓ If you enjoy a direct connection to the Internet, there is no need to establish a connection.

2. Launch Minuet by typing **minuet** at the command prompt.

   ▓ If you have configured Minuet to automatically check for mail, the program will automatically login to the server and download any e-mail addressed to you. The rest of this section assumes that you will be checking for e-mail manually. In either case, the INBOX Viewer will appear.

3. Press **Alt-W**. The Windows menu is displayed.

4. From the Windows menu, select the Gopher command. You'll be logged into the root level of the Gopher server you specified when you configured Minuet.

5. Navigate to the remote login resource you want to access.

   ▓ Remote login resources appear as <Telnet> menu items in Gopher directories.

   ▓ This section uses MIT's TechInfo as an example. The actual procedure for navigating to this resource will vary, based on your home Gopher server. From within the "Other Gopher Servers" (or similar) menu item, select the "North America," "United States," "Massachusetts," "Massachusetts Institute of Technology," "Network Navigation Tools," "Terminal-based TechInfo services" menu items in succession. When you get there, your Gopher window should look similar to the one shown in Figure 7-22.

Figure 7-22:
Gopher window
for the MIT
TechInfo remote
login resource.

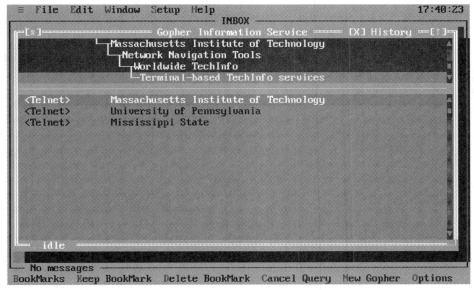

6. Press **Enter.** You will be logged into the MIT TechInfo system as a
   remote user and a Minuet TELNET window will be opened, as
   shown in Figure 7-23.

Figure 7-23: Minuet
TELNET window
opened within a
Gopher session.

7. Enter the **number** of a menu item that interests you and press
   Enter. The screen will be updated to reflect your selection.

8. Continue to navigate through the various menu items using these methods:

- Enter the **number** of a menu item and press **Enter**.
- Enter an available **command** (commands are usually displayed along the bottom of the window) and press **Enter**.

9. Disconnect from the remote computer by pressing **Alt-F2** when you are finished browsing the available resources. The connection to the remote computer will be broken and the last Gopher menu you used will be displayed.

- Note that only the network connection to the remote computer is broken; your connection to the Internet is still live.

Gopher Servers

There are a number of unique and information-rich sites throughout the Internet that support the Gopher protocol. A listing of just a few of the more interesting Gopher servers available on the Internet is provided in Table 7-1.

Table 7-1:
Gopher servers.

Domain Address	Comments
boombox.micro.umn.edu	Gopher distribution archive
gopher.uis.itd.umich.edu	University of Michigan archive
ashpool.micro.umn.edu	Washington University (St. Louis) archive
wx.atmos.uiuc.edu	Weather maps
gopher.eff.org	Electronic Frontier Foundation archive
ashpool.micro.umn.edu	Supreme Court rulings
gopher.well.sf.ca.us	Whole Earth 'Lectronic Link (WELL) archive
gopher.bu.edu	Boston metropolitan guide
gopher.concert.net	University of North Carolina archives
gopher.unc.edu	SUNsite archives at UNC
wiretap.spies.com	White House press release service

Domain Address	Comments
siggraph.org	Conference proceedings and materials from the graphics special interest group (SIGGRAPH) of the Association for Computing Machinery
ashpool.micro.umn.edu	Internet Resource Guide
hunter.cs.unr.edu	Search Gopherspace using Veronica
wcni.cis.umn.edu	Academic Position Network
gopher.cpsr.org	Computer Professionals for Social Responsibility archive
gopher.msen.com	Search for individuals on the Internet
akasha.tic.com	Sample issues of John Quarterman's *Matrix News* Internet newsletter
internic.net	Internet directory services

The Gopher of the Future.

Although the original Gopher protocol is frozen, a forward-compatible protocol (called Gopher +) is currently in development by the Gopher Team at the University of Minnesota.

Gopher is currently the tenth-most-used protocol in terms of number of connections, and the ninth-most-often-used protocol in terms of the number of bytes transferred.

Gopher + will support multiple views of a document, allowing information providers to include Microsoft Word, PostScript, RTF and ASCII text versions of a single document, for example.

Support for forms is also planned for inclusion in Gopher +. This will allow an interface to database back-ends as well as user information ranking, user-created items and directories, and conferencing systems.

Authentication support will be included in Gopher +. This will allow a finer control of information access on Gopher servers. Although it's not designed to replace public-key encryption or Kerberos, Gopher + authentication will allow access to particular information to be granted on an individual basis. Interestingly, the password is never sent across the network, so security will also be enhanced.

Moving On

Gopher is the best way to navigate parts of the Internet you aren't familiar with, because it sports a familiar interface of directories and subdirectories. And because Gopher is a *stateless* software program, it makes the most efficient possible use of network resources.

While previous chapters of this book have focused on the most widely used programs and most frequently visited spots on the Internet, the next chapter will take a look at the dozens of other small but important Internet resources. You'll learn about TELNET, another software program widely used to access Internet resources, and we'll visit a few of the more secluded cul-de-sacs on the Net.

Our tour bus is making only one more excursion before our trip is over. If there's a program, resource, organization or site on the Internet that you're still wondering about, odds are we'll be visiting it in the next chapter. So now would be a good time to stock up on provisions and get a little rest, because the final leg of our tour promises to be the most exciting one yet.

CHAPTER 8

OTHER INTERNET RESOURCES
Geez, what is all this stuff?

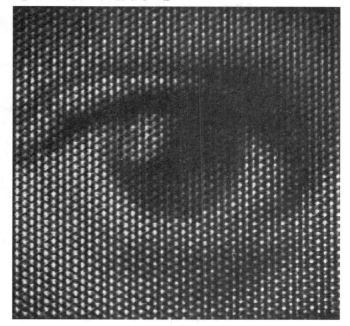

By this point in our tour, you're an old pro at cruising the Internet. You've learned the terrain of the network, the language and customs of its inhabitants, and the quickest routes to the information you need. Yet there are still dozens of helpful but lesser-known resources that can make your time online more productive and enjoyable. For this last leg of our tour, we're loading up the bus for a final loop around the outer fringe of the Net. We'll be moving pretty fast, so climb aboard and hang on.

For those who use PCs on the Internet, electronic mail, network news, FTP and Gopher are four of the most widely used resources. TELNET is also a commonly used Internet resource. Specialized, task-specific software programs keep appearing that make TELNET less necessary on the Internet. But some applications will probably always require the use of TELNET. This chapter offers a look at TELNET, as well as some of the many organizations and resources available via the Internet. We'll also cover some of the less commonly used software tools available for use on the Internet.

What Is TELNET?

Using TELNET, you can login to other computers on the Internet in an interactive, command-line mode. You use TELNET to access experimental services, library card catalogs, weather reports and various other specialized databases. If you have a UNIX account on another computer on the Internet, you use TELNET to login remotely to your account on that computer.

In the early days of the Internet, TELNET was one of the few tools available to the infonaut. Today, many of the services available by TELNET also provide an alternative method of access, like WAIS or WWW or Gopher (covered in detail in Chapter 7, "Using Gopher"). Although more and more TELNET services are becoming accessible via other methods, some Internet services still require a TELNET connection.

The TELNET module in Minuet is very basic in nature. Some users will prefer a more powerful implementation. NCSA TELNET is a freeware application program for the PC that lets you take full advantage of the TELNET protocol. It is available by anonymous FTP from ftp.ncsa.uiuc.edu in the /pc/ directory. Extensive documentation is also available in the same directory.

Using TELNET

You use TELNET to login remotely across the Internet to virtually any computer that offers public access or on which you have an account. While there are more powerful implementations of TELNET available, Minuet will meet the needs of most users, and this section focuses on the fundamental aspects of using TELNET effectively.

To open a TELNET session with Minuet:

1. Establish your connection to the Internet, if necessary. If you're using UMSLIP, type **slip dial** at the command prompt, and the connection will be automatically established.

   ■ If you are using other SLIP or PPP software, follow the directions provided by your network administrator or service provider to establish the connection.

   ■ If you enjoy a direct connection to the Internet, there is no need to establish a connection.

2. Launch Minuet by typing **minuet** at the command prompt.

■ If you have configured Minuet to automatically check for mail, the program will automatically login to the server and download any e-mail addressed to you. The rest of this section assumes that you will be checking for e-mail manually. In either case, the INBOX Viewer will appear.

3. Press **Alt-W**. The Windows menu is displayed.

4. From the Windows menu, select the Telnet command. The Telnet dialog box appears, as shown in Figure 8-1.

Figure 8-1: Minuet Telnet dialog box.

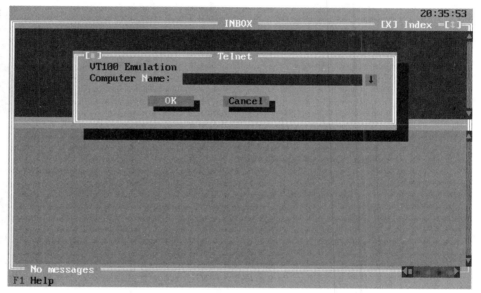

5. In the Telnet dialog box's Computer Name box, enter the domain name—in the domain.top-domain format—for the host to which you want to login.

■ This exercise will use the weather information available from the University of Michigan's Weather Underground as an example, so if you're up for it, enter **downwind.sprl.umich.edu 3000** in the Computer Name box. Alternatively, several other TELNET resources—including online library card catalogs, Supreme Court rulings and major league baseball schedules—are mentioned later in this chapter.

6. Press **Enter**. Minuet will establish a connection to the host you specified, and a Telnet window will be opened, as shown in Figure 8-2.

Figure 8-2: Minuet
Telnet window.

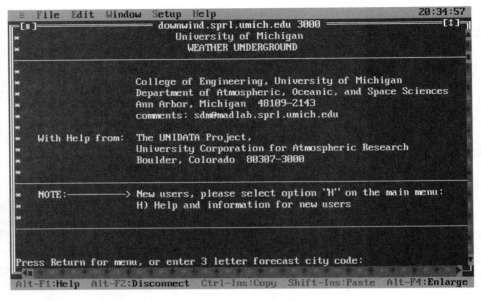

■ Note that some hosts may prompt you for a terminal type. (The University of Michigan's Weather Underground service doesn't.) Sometimes there is a menu selection available, but many times there is simply a TERMINAL: prompt. Minuet emulates a VT102 terminal, so you can enter VT100 (or VT102) at the prompt. Almost every host supports a VT102 terminal.

■ Note that if you are logging into a remote host on which you have an account, you may have to set the terminal type yourself. For a UNIX host, using the C shell, enter **set term=vt100;tset** at the command prompt. For a VAX/VMS host, enter **set term /inq** at the command prompt.

7. You can navigate through the choices and information on the host by entering commands and menu selections at the command prompt.

■ Menu selections are usually self-explanatory. The commands available to you vary from host to host; refer to each specific host's documentation for an explanation of the commands that may be available.

8. Enter **exit** or **logout** at the command prompt to logout, ending the remote session. Alternatively, press **Alt-F2** or the Close command from the Window menu. The Telnet window will disappear when the connection is closed.

Knowbots

Knowbots are knowledge robots—or at least that's the theory behind them. Think of them as electronic librarians that can help you find what you're looking for when you don't know where to look. Currently, Knowbots are used mostly for looking up Internet addresses, but the potential for using Knowbots for other uses is very exciting. (Vice President Al Gore is fond of touting the possibilities of knowbots in his frequent writings and speeches about the electronic superhighway.) Theoretically, you should be able to send a Knowbot into the Internet with a set of search criteria. When it finds sources for the information you're looking for, the Knowbot would return with the information it finds.

Unfortunately, I've never been able to login to a site where the Knowbots live, and the general consensus of those on the Net is that Knowbots aren't quite ready for prime time. Look for more information about Knowbots in one of the electronic updates to this book.

MS-Kermit.
MS-Kermit is a complete implementation of the Kermit file transfer protocol for IBM PCs and compatibles. Both host and client modes are supported, as are script files for automated use. Various versions of the program and companion utilities are available by FTP from oak.oakland.edu in the /msdos/kermit/ directory.

Netfind

Netfind is a program that searches certain databases to help you find an e-mail address. It's not very easy to use and requires that you login remotely using TELNET, but Netfind can be useful when other options prove fruitless.

To use Netfind to locate someone's e-mail address:

1. Use Minuet's TELNET implementation to login to bruno.cs.colorado.edu.

2. At the login: prompt enter **netfind** and press **Enter**.

3. Select the Search item from the menu.

4. At the prompt, enter the name and general location (called "keys") for the person you're looking for.

   ■ For example, let's say you're trying to find the e-mail address of your pal, Wanda Caldwell, at the University of Georgia. You think she might have "wanda" as part of her address, but it's a pretty good bet that she'll have "caldwell" in her address, so you would enter caldwell uga edu at the prompt. A list of people named Caldwell at the University of Georgia will be displayed, and you can select the entry that matches the person you're looking for.

5. Select the Exit item from the menu.

The key to working with Netfind is to learn how to conduct searches that are neither too vague nor too specific. If you enter a search that is too vague—like Caldwell Georgia—the search will return too many possible choices. Conversely, if you enter a search that is too specific—like Caldwell peachnet uga edu—the search will yield no results.

Finger

As discussed in Chapter 3, "Network Infrastructure," Finger is a useful program for searching the user log on a computer connected to the Internet. This allows you to find someone's e-mail address provided you know the name of the computer he or she uses.

The word "Finger"—like many of the other Internet terms including "FTP" and "TELNET"—is used as both a noun and a verb. You use the word "Finger" to refer to the program you use to "finger" (the process of obtaining information with the Finger program) a person or resource on the Net.

Although Finger is most commonly used to find someone's e-mail address or to get a list of everyone currently logged into a computer, it can also be used for some other, sometimes unusual, things. You can use Finger as a sort of general information server. Finger has the ability to display a text file (named .plan if you're curious) to any Finger query. You can find all sorts of interesting information on the Internet by using Finger. If you're interested in baseball, for example, Finger jtchern@ocf.berkeley.edu for a list of today's scores.

Making the world a smaller place.

Sheldon Smith forwarded news of a project undertaken by his wife's 5–6 grade class in San Luis Obispo, Calif.

"This is an example of how the Internet brings the world into the classroom. We, as educators, cannot take the kids out into the world, but Internet can bring the world to the kids.

"About the time when Ross Perot re-announced his candidacy, an American ship accidentally shot a Turkish ship during a NATO exercise, killing the captain and three crew members. Because of the Presidential election, there was not much about it in the news.

"My wife's students heard about the accident and felt the U.S. should apologize. The kids wrote notes of apology which was compiled into a class letter.

"I sent their letter to the Turkish newsgroup, and I also forwarded it to my sister, who moderates a Middle Eastern conference on PeaceNet. She works for AWAIR, which is a non-profit group that produces curriculum materials on the Middle East. In any case, after posting their letter my wife and I received about 30 replies over a two week period."

Here are excerpts from two students' letters:

"Hi my name is Jesse Cutburth. I do not understand why we shot your ship I think we should apologize and this is what I am doing. I don't understand how we shot your ship on accident I think we should replace your ship with one of ours but we can't replace four people."

"Hi, my name is Brianne Reimer. As an American, I am very sorry about what we did. I don't know what we were doing there. But I am only a child. Someday, I hope I will go to Turkey. And if I do go I will surely apologize to you face to face. Sorry."

If you Finger buckmr@rpi.edu, a list of this week's top U.S. popular music recordings will be displayed.

Perhaps the strangest Finger resources are the cold-drink vending machines that some universities have connected to the Internet. When Fingered, these machines report which bins in the vending machine are empty and which bins hold the coldest drinks, as shown in Figure 8-3.

The PC Internet Tour Guide

Figure 8-3: Finger
cold-drink
vending
machine.

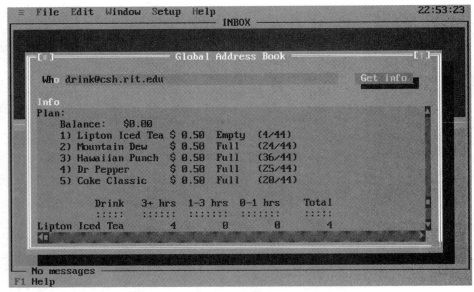

Since I'm sure you're going to ask for it later if I don't include it now, here's a list of vending machines attached to the Internet.

coke@cs.wisc.edu
@coke.elab.cs.cmu.edu
mnm@coke.elab.cs.cmu.edu
bargraph@coke.elab.cs.cmu.edu
drink@csh.rit.edu

LHA.

LHA is a popular (though not as popular as PKZIP) file compression utility for IBM PCs and compatibles. With LHA, you can create self-extracting archive files, and in some cases the program's archiving capabilities are quicker than those of PKZIP. LHA is available by FTP from oak.oakland.edu in the /msdos/archivers/ directory. Don't let the .exe file extension scare you; it's distributed as a self-extracting archive.

Archie

Archie is an Internet service, originally developed at McGill University, that allows you to search indexes of available files on publicly accessible FTP servers. In other words, you can ask Archie if a certain file exists on the Internet, and if so, where is it? Archie can be helpful in a number of circumstances. You can use it to search for files when you know their names. You can enter just part of a file's name, like "Minuet," to search for the popular program.

You search Archie's indexes by specifying a string of characters. Archie returns a list of filenames that match your search criteria and the name of the FTP servers where they're located.

As a PC user, you have three options for using Archie:

- You can TELNET to an Archie server and muddle through a command-line interface.

- You can use the MS-DOS-specific Archie client, available by FTP from oak.oakland.edu in the /pub/msdos/lan/ directory.

- You can use Gopher to search the Archie database.

A list of Archie servers is available in Table 8-1.

Table 8-1: Archie servers.

Archie Server	Geographic Area
archie.ans.net	ANS Network sites
archie.au	Australia and Pacific Basin
archie.doc.ic.ac.uk	United Kingdom and Ireland
archie.funet.fi	Europe
archie.mcgill.ca	Canada
archie.rutgers.edu	Northeastern United States
archie.sura.net	Southeastern United States
archie.unl.edu	Western United States

Try to use the Archie server that is geographically closest to you. This will help balance network traffic.

Using the Gopher Archie Client

The Gopher Archie client is extremely easy to use.

1. Establish your connection to the Internet, if necessary. If you're using UMSLIP, type **slip dial** at the command prompt, and the connection will be automatically established.

   - If you are using other SLIP or PPP software, follow the directions provided by your network administrator or service provider to establish the connection.

■ If you enjoy a direct connection to the Internet, there is no need to establish a connection.

2. Launch Minuet by typing **minuet** at the command prompt.

■ If you have configured Minuet to automatically check for mail, the program will automatically login to the server and download any e-mail addressed to you. The rest of this section assumes that you will be checking for e-mail manually. In either case, the INBOX Viewer will appear.

3. Press **Alt-W**. The Windows menu is displayed.

4. From the Windows menu, select the Gopher command. You'll be logged into the root level of the Gopher server you specified when you configured Minuet.

5. Navigate to the Search FTP Sites with Archie menu item.

■ If you're using the University of Minnesota's "mother" Gopher as your Home Gopher server, it's located inside the Internet file server (ftp) sites directory, as shown in Figure 8-4.

Figure 8-4: Gopher Archie Internet file server (ftp) sites directory.

```
≡  File  Edit  Window  Setup  Help                                   14:49:39
───────────────────────────────── INBOX ─────────────────────────────
─[■]═══════════════════ Gopher Information Service ══════ [X] History ══[↑]═
         ┌Other Gopher Servers
         └─Minnesota Gopher Servers_
            └─University of Minnesota (Mother Gopher)
               └─Internet file server (ftp) sites

    <File>          About FTP Searches
    <Directory>     InterNIC: Internet Network Information Center
    <Directory>     Popular FTP Sites via Gopher
    <Searcher>      Query a specific ftp host
    <Directory>     Search FTP sites (Archie)
    <Mac File>      UnStuffIt.hqx




══ idle ══════════════════════════════════════════════════════════════
── No messages ──────────────────────────────────────────────────────
BookMarks  Keep BookMark  Delete BookMark  Cancel Query  New Gopher  Options
```

6. With the Search FTP sites (Archie) menu item selected, press **Enter**. The directory will be opened displaying two <Searcher> items, as shown in Figure 8-5.

Figure 8-5: Gopher
Archie search
directory.

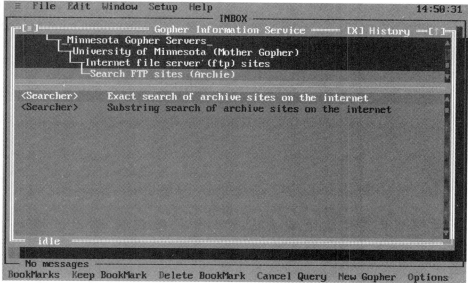

7. Select the Exact search of archive sites on the internet <Searcher>
   item and press **Enter**. The Search Text dialog box will appear, as
   shown in Figure 8-6.

Figure 8-6: Gopher
Search Text
dialog box.

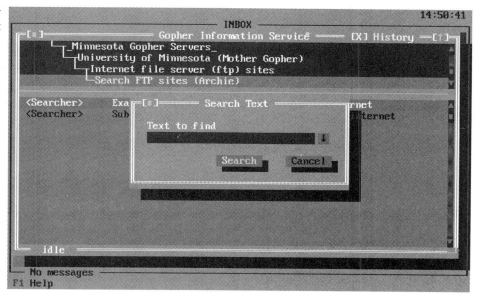

8. Enter a word or series of words contained in the document or
   filename you wish to download and press **Enter**.

■ Gopher will search within the Archie database for documents and filenames matching the search words you specified. A new Gopher directory will appear, showing a list of the documents and files matching your search words, like the example of a search for "minuet" shown in Figure 8-7.

Figure 8-7: Gopher Archie search results.

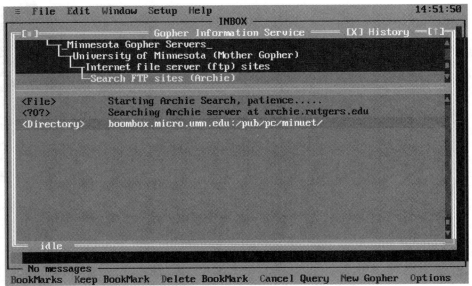

An advantage of using Gopher for Archie searches is that the search results window contains "live" Internet resources. You can simply select any item in the search results window and press **Enter** to automatically login to an anonymous FTP archive or download a file.

RFCs

An RFC (Request for Comments) is a document that defines a specific part of the Internet itself. Because of the anarchic nature of the Internet, anyone can write an RFC. Most are highly technical and relate to topics that are of little interest to the average user. Some RFCs, however, are veritable goldmines of useful information for real people. RFCs are always referred to by their number and may be available in either text or PostScript formats (text versions have a .txt suffix; PostScript versions have a .ps suffix).

RFCs are available from many FTP archives, including the "official" depositories shown in Table 8-2.

Table 8-2: Official RFC depositories.

FTP Site	Directory
nic.ddn.mil	/rfc/
nis.jvnc.net	/rfc/
nisc.sri.com	/rfc/
wuarchive.wustl.edu	/doc/rfc/
nnsc.nsf.net	/rfc/
src.doc.ic.ac.uk	/rfc/

Because all RFCs are available only by RFC number, it's a good idea to first download the index of RFC files (rfc-index.txt). This file contains a complete index of all currently available RFCs.

You can also obtain RFCs by e-mail with these steps:

1. Launch your e-mail program.

2. Create a new message to the address mail-server@nisc.sri.com

3. Enter a one-line message consisting of send rfcxxx.txt (where xxx is the number of the RFC you want to receive.

   ▨ To receive the index, enter a one-line message consisting of send rfc-index.txt

4. Send your e-mail message.

A list of some of the RFCs that are useful for average users is provided in Table 8-3.

Table 8-3:
Useful RFCs.

RFC	Title
1432	Recent Internet books
1402	There's Gold in them thar Networks! or Searching for Treasure in all the Wrong Places
1392	Internet Users' Glossary
1359	Connecting to the Internet: What connecting institutions should anticipate
1325	FYI on questions and answers: Answers to commonly asked "new Internet user" questions
1296	Internet Growth (1981-1991)
1259	Building the open road: The NREN as test-bed for the national public network
1244	Site Security Handbook
1208	Glossary of networking terms
1207	FYI on Questions and Answers: Answers to commonly asked "experienced Internet user" questions
1192	Commercialization of the Internet summary report
1180	TCP/IP tutorial
1178	Choosing a name for your computer
1175	FYI on where to start: A bibliography of internetworking information
1167	Thoughts on the National Research and Education Network
1118	Hitchhiker's guide to the Internet

FAQs

A FAQ (Frequently Asked Question) is a collection of questions (and their answers) most often asked by new Internet users. FAQs exist for all network news newsgroups and most mailing lists. Until you get your Internet legs, read the FAQ for the newsgroups you frequent. You can save yourself a lot of embarrassment by skimming FAQ files.

Most FAQs are posted to their related newsgroups on a monthly basis. In addition, FAQs for all the newsgroups are consolidated and posted to the news.answers newsgroup. You can also obtain FAQs by FTP from pit-manager.mit.edu in the /pub/usenet/ directory.

Internet Organizations

As the Internet has evolved from a project researching ways to ensure communications in the event of a nuclear attack into a research and business tool used by millions of individuals, a number of diverse and vital organizations have sprung up. The actions of two of these organizations—the Internet Society and the Electronic Frontier Foundation—have repercussions for every Internet user.

FTPNuz.

FTPNuz is a fully implemented network news reader for IBM PCs and compatibles. Distributed as shareware, FTPNuz requires access to an NNTP server. The program is available by FTP from oak.oakland.edu in the /pub/msdos/lan/ directory.

Electronic Frontier Foundation

On July 10, 1990, two unlikely cohorts announced they were forming a foundation to "address social and legal issues arising from the impact on society of the increasing pervasive use of computers as a means of communication and information distribution." Mitch Kapor is best known as the founder of Lotus Development Corporation, the publisher of the Lotus 1-2-3 spreadsheet program. John Perry Barlow is a sometimes lyricist for the Grateful Dead, one-time Congressional candidate and Wyoming rancher.

A number of factions are battling for control and influence over cyberspace, and the Electronic Frontier Foundation (EFF) is entrenched in the front lines of the battlefield. On one side of the battle lines are a number of government agencies, corporations and other entities that want to limit access to information and dictate what people can do in cyberspace. On the other side, there are those—like the members of the EFF—who want to widen (and deepen) everyone's access to information and extend the rights most Americans enjoy in physical reality to cyberspace.

Kapor and Barlow came together when both were questioned by the FBI following an incident at Apple Computer where a group calling itself the NuPrometheus League had distributed the Color QuickDraw source code to members of the computer press and luminaries in the computer industry.

John Perry Barlow was amazed at the level of computer ignorance exhibited by the FBI agent who visited him in May 1990. Barlow had been a longtime member of the Internet-connected Whole Earth 'Lectronic Link (WELL) and describes himself as a "techno-crank." From the agent, Barlow learned that computer hackers—*all* computer hackers—were under suspicion as Evil Criminals. He also learned that the FBI was tracing anyone who had visited the Hackers Conference, an invitation-only affair begun in 1984 that drew attendees from the top levels of the computer industry, including executives, consultants, pundits and journalists.

It's important to draw the distinction between hackers (those who like to explore systems for the sake of learning something about those systems) and crackers (those who are out to wreak havoc by breaking into systems, deleting files and reaping financial gain illegally).

Barlow, alarmed at the implications of computer ignorance within the FBI (and the possibility of a high-tech witch hunt), sounded the alarm on the WELL. One of the many WELL inhabitants who took note of Barlow's outcry was Mitch Kapor, who had already endured being fingerprinted by the FBI.

Kapor flew to Barlow's Wyoming ranch in June 1990 to lay the groundwork for the EFF, and Barlow wrote "Crime and Puzzlement," an article announcing the pair's intention of forming a political organization intent on extending Constitutional rights to cyberspace.

The response from the computing community was astounding. Original funding for EFF was provided by Kapor and Apple co-founder Steve Wozniak. John Gilmore (one of the founders of Sun Microsystems) contributed, and others quickly followed.

The Electronic Frontier Foundation continues to fight for a careful balance of freedom, access and privacy throughout the networks, and they've even won a few battles.

You can download a wealth of information from the EFF's FTP or Gopher server at ftp.eff.org and gopher.eff.org respectively. Here's a sampling:

- Back issues of *EFFector Online*, the electronic newsletter of the EFF.

- Testimony of EFF staff and board members.

- Papers and articles by EFF staff and board members.

- EFF Newsnotes and informational postings.

- Papers and articles about cyberspace from luminaries including Bruce Sterling, John Perry Barlow and Dorothy Denning.

- Information about various legal issues affecting the Internet.

- Text of various laws and proposed laws relevant to the electronic frontier.

> Electronic Frontier Foundation
> 666 Pennsylvania Avenue, SE
> Suite 303
> Washington, DC 20003
> 202/544-9237
> 202/547-5481 (Fax)
> 617/576-4510 (Legal hotline)
> eff@eff.org

Internet Society

The Internet Society exists to encourage cooperation among the various networks that comprise the Internet, fostering a global communications infrastructure. The organization focuses on the future of the Internet and the emerging and established technologies that impact the Net. The Internet Society appoints a small group of members to the Internet Architecture Board—the closest thing the Internet has to a board of governors, although its more accurate to think of the body as a group of tribal elders.

The Internet Architecture Board (IAB) is responsible for the technical management of the Internet. It adopts proposed standards and allocates addresses. The Internet Architecture Board also oversees two groups:

- The Internet Engineering Task Force (IETF), which is responsible for the technical operation of the Internet.

- The Internet Research Task Force (IRTF), which is responsible for research and development issues surrounding the Internet.

The Internet Society sponsors an annual conference, publishes a quarterly newsletter and supports an electronic mail distribution list.

>Internet Society
>1895 Preston White Drive
>Suite 100
>Reston, VA 22091
>703/620-8990
>isoc@nri.reston.va.us

Neat Stuff

New information resources are added to the Internet every minute. It's impossible to keep up with everything on the Net—about the best you can do is seek out those things that specifically interest you. Keep in close touch with your friends and associates, tipping them off to new files, sites and resources that they might be interested in—and ask them to do the same for you. When you find something worth sharing, e-mail pointers (a "trail" through the Net) to each other. Exchange Gopher bookmarks.

The electronic updates that come with this book are another great way to keep up with what's new and worthwhile on the Internet. For more details, see "Electronic Updates & Visitors Center" beginning on page 249.

As your tour guide, it's impossible for me to show you *all* of the Internet. (That's like trying to ride every ride at Disneyworld in just one day!) Because the Net is constantly changing, any collection of Internet resources is only a snapshot of what's interesting *right now* (Fall 1993). Of course, what's interesting to me may not be interesting to you at all, so I'm providing pointers of general interest.

Besides, who would want to ride *every* ride at Disneyworld? There are always lemons—disappointing resources (or amusement park rides)—that don't deliver what they promise. So rather than bury you under mountains of untested, untried programs, sites or resources, you'll only find the most stable, useful and widely acclaimed resources listed in this chapter. For information on a wide variety of interesting Net items, be sure to check *The PC Internet Tour Guide* electronic updates.

Naturally, many of you will wonder why your favorite site or resource isn't listed with those that follow. The most likely answer is space limitations, but you should still e-mail your favorite Internet finds to me for inclusion in future editions and electronic updates. Send your useful, bizarre and otherwise enticing resources to me at: mfraase@farces.com.

Here's how the resource entries that follow are organized:

■ The **Type**: field tells you what software tool or protocol you need to use to access the resource.

■ The **Address**: field tells you the domain name address for the resource.

■ The **Pathname**: field tells you the pathname for the directory or file of the resource.

■ The **Summary**: field provides a brief description of the resource and any necessary login information.

Acronyms by E-Mail

Type: E-mail
Address: freetext@iruccvax.ucc.ie
Summary: The Irish have always had a way with the language, and the University of Cork offers an e-mail based Acronym Server.

Send an e-mail message with the word "help" (without the quotes) in the body of the message to get instructions on using the server.

Alex

Type: FTP
Address: alex.sp.cs.cmu.edu
Pathname: /doc/README/
Summary: Alex provides a way to transparently read remote files at anonymous FTP sites.

Almanac

Type: Finger
Address: copi@oddjob.uchicago.edu
Summary: Provides a list of notable birthdays, events in history, and planetary occurrences for each day.

AskERIC

Type: Gopher (also available via TELNET)
Address: ericir.syr.edu
Login: gopher (TELNET only)
Summary: Electronic library access (also available via Gopher) for querying education-related questions.

Aspen Gopher

Type: Gopher
Address: aspen.com
Summary: A Gopher hole devoted to topics of relevance to Aspen, Colorado.
Contact: aspen@aspen.com

Bookstore (University of California, San Diego)

Type: TELNET
Address: ucsdbkst.ucsd.edu (132.239.83.66)
Summary: Provides information about titles in stock as well as titles on-order and the *New York Times* best seller lists.

California Common Cause
Political Contributors Report

Type: FTP
Address: synnyside.com
Pathname: /ccause/
Summary: An electronic version of California Common Cause's report on the top ten political contributors in 1991–1992.

Carnegie Mellon University English Server

Type: Gopher
Address: english-server.hss.cmu.edu
Summary: A Gopher server developed by the graduate students in the English department of Carnegie Mellon University designed to freely distribute documents and information on a wide range of subject matter. This is truly one of the most comprehensive information resources on the Net.

Chess Server
Type: TELNET
Address: 128.2.209.147 5000 or 130.225.16.162 5000 (in Europe)
Summary: Observe or play chess matches against human opponents in real-time.

Clearinghouse for Networked Information Discovery and Retrieval (CNIDR)
Type: FTP
Address: cnidr.org
Summary: The Clearinghouse for Networked Information Discovery and Retrieval is an organization dedicated to aiding Internet citizens in their searches for information throughout the network. CNIDR works with a number of other organizations to make information more accessible and standardized across the Internet.

Colorado Alliance of Research Libraries (CARL)
Type: TELNET
Address: pac.carl.org
Summary: The Colorado Alliance of Research Libraries provides access to a number of different academic and public library online catalogs, current article indexes, the Internet Resource Guide, and the Academic American Encyclopedia. CARL also offers a service through which you can request (for a small fee charged to your credit card) a fax copy of any journal article in its catalog, as well as access to other services, such as Journal Graphics, which offers transcripts of popular news and public affairs television programs. A gateway to other library systems is also offered.

Commerce Business Daily
Type: Gopher
Address: cscns.com
Summary: CNS, one of the regional service providers in the United States, is offering free Gopher access to the Commerce Business Daily. The service is updated each evening with information for the next day.
Contact: info@cscns.com or 800/748-1200.

Community Computer Networks:
Building Electronic Greenbelts

Type: FTP
Address: ftp.apple.com
Pathname: /alug/communet/
Summary: Steve Cisler's excellent overview of community networks examining what kinds of information and services can be found on these systems, what groups are running community networks, and cost aspects. The essay discusses current models for community networks and the impact these networks have on their local (physical) environment.
Contact: Steve Cisler
Apple Library
4 Infinite Loop
MS 304-2A
Cupertino, CA 95014
408/974-3258
sac@apple.com

Computer-Mediated Communication

Type: FTP
Address: ftp.rpi.edu
Pathname: /pub/communications/internet-cmc
Summary: John December's compiled list of resources describing the Internet, computer networks and computer-mediated communication.

Computer Professionals For
Social Responsibility (CPSR) Mailing List

Type: Mailing List
Address: listserv@gwuvm.gwu.edu
Summary: Send a one-line message in e-mail:
        subscribe CPSR *your name*
where *your name* is your full name (not your e-mail address).
        Computer Professionals for Social Responsibility is a professional organization that concerns itself with the social and political aspects of computing. Mailing list

subscribers will receive updates on CPSR's current Freedom of Information Act (FOIA) requests, position statements and news releases on topics including privacy and cryptography.

Consumers Access Service

Type: TELNET

Address: columbia.ilc.com (38.145.77.221)

Login: cas

Summary: Browse listings and place online orders for audio CDs, videotapes and computer software.

Cookie Server

Type: TELNET

Address: astro.temple.edu 12345 (129.32.1.100)

Summary: Displays a quote whenever you TELNET in to this address.

Current Cites

Type: TELNET

Address: melvyl.ucop.edu

Summary: Provides a bibliography of current journal articles related to computers and information technology.

Enter **SHOW CURRENT CITES** at command prompt.

More information is available from drobinson@library.berkeley.edu

Dictionary Server

Type: TELNET

Address: cs.indiana.edu 2627

Summary: Provides access to an online Webster's Ninth Collegiate Dictionary.

Login as webster

Enter **HELP** for online help system.

E-Mail Address Locator

Type: E-mail
Address: mail-server@pit-manager.mit.edu
Summary: In body of letter enter:
    send usenet-addresses/*name*
where *name* is the name of the person you want to locate.
    The service will return the e-mail address of the person in the username@domain.top-domain format. This service works only if the person you are looking for has posted an article to one of the USENET newsgroups.

Earthquake Information

Type: Finger
Address: quake@geophys.washington.edu
Summary: Reports recent earthquake information including location, magnitude and time of occurrence.

Electronic Frontier Foundation (EFF) Mailing List

Type: Mailing List
Address: eff-request@eff.org
Summary: Send a brief e-mail message requesting to be added to the mailing list. The Electronic Frontier Foundation is a professional organization concerned with the legal, social and political aspects of civilizing cyberspace. If you subscribe to the EFF mailing list, you'll receive copies of the *EFFector Online* electronic newsletter and news releases.

Electronic Journal on Virtual Culture

Type: FTP
Address: byrd.mu.wvnet.edu
Pathname: /pub/ejvc/
Summary: Very interesting and well-written journal of virtual community and the Internet. Each issue contains three or four feature articles, non-refereed opinion columns and essays, and the Cyberspace Monitor (a listing of important happenings, publications, products, and services related to cyberspace and the Net).

Electronic Newsstand

Type: Gopher

Address: gopher.netsys.com port 2100 (also available via TELNET: gopher.netsys.com login: enews)

Summary: The New Republic Inc. of Washington, D.C. and Hudson, Mass.-based The Internet Company created the Electronic Newsstand Inc. on July 25, 1993 to provide a marketing vehicle for magazine publishers on the Internet.

According to Jeffrey Dearth, president of *The New Republic* magazine and founder and CEO of Electronic Newsstand, "The estimated 10 to 15 million Internet users can browse the table of contents and selected articles from publications on our newsstand 24 hours a day, seven days a week, and send orders to us electronically."

Publications available on the Electronic Newsstand are *The New Yorker, The Economist, The New Republic, Foreign Affairs, National Review, Technology Review, Eating Well, Outside, The Journal of NIH Research, The Source* and *New Age Journal.*

The marketing concept behind the Electronic Newsstand, according to Robert Raisch, president of The Internet Company, and COO of Electronic Newsstand, is that "the more people are exposed to a magazine's editorial content, the more likely they are to be interested in subscribing to a hard copy, or in purchasing a single issue."

Contact: Paul Vizza
202/331-7494
info@enews.com
staff@enews.com
Rob Raisch
raisch@netsys.com

Electronic Publications

Type: Gopher
Address: gopher.cic.net
Summary: CICNet is probably the biggest archive available for electronic publications. Publications are organized by both alphabetical order and subject matter.

Electronic Serials List

Type: E-Mail
Address: listserv@uottawa.bitnet
Summary: An automated distribution server of a comprehensive list of electronic serials on various topics including computers, science, politics, literature, etc.
Send the following lines in an e-mail message:
GET EJOURNL1 DIRECTORY
GET EJOURNL2 DIRECTORY

EPA Gopher Server

Type: Gopher
Address: gopher.epa.gov
Summary: The Environmental Protection Agency has established a Gopher server to provide information about the agency's work on futures research. Pointers to all other Gopher servers operated by the federal government are also available.
Contact: Dave Rejeski
Head, Future Studies Unit
EPA
202/260-6523
rejeski.dave@epamail.epa.gov

Fax (Remote Printing) Experiment

Type: E-mail
Address: tpc-faq@town.hall.org
Summary: Based on the notion that sending packets of data across the Internet is significantly less expensive than placing long-distance telephone calls, a group of researchers began an experiment in providing fax services on the Internet during July 1993. To use the fax system, based on remote printing services available on the Internet,

you send an e-mail message with the destination fax telephone number in the address field. MIME is supported, allowing you to include styled text and graphic images in your message. The e-mail message is automatically routed to an Internet site that has agreed to serve a local geographic "cell" for delivery of the fax message.

Participating regions, as of July 1993, include all of Japan, Australia, the Netherlands and Ireland. In addition, metropolitan Washington D.C., Silicon Valley and parts of the San Francisco Bay area are also participating in the experiment.

For more information on the service, send an e-mail message (the subject and message content are ignored) to tpc-faq@town.hall.org

FTP Sites List
Type: FTP
Address: pilot.njin.net
Pathname: /pub/ftp-list/ directory (download the file ftp.list).
Summary: Provides a list of publicly accessible FTP sites.

Geographic Server
Type: TELNET
Address: martini.eecs.umich.edu 3000
Summary: Provides geographic information including population, elevation, latitude, longitude and more by city or area code. You navigate the information with onscreen menus.

Government Policy Statements re: Internet

Acceptable Use Policies
Type: FTP
Address: nic.merit.edu
Pathname: /acceptable.use.policies/*.txt
Summary: Acceptable Use Policies for several networks that are part of the Internet. Policies are available for CICnet, CREN, JVNCnet, MICHnet, NorthWestNet, NSFnet, OARnet, and SURAnet.

Cable-Telco Local Exchange Competition Bill

Type: FTP
Address: ftp.eff.org
Pathname: /pub/EFF/legislation/infra-act-s1086*
Summary: The full text of the Senate bill, introduced during Summer 1993, lifting the ban on cable television and telephone companies from entering the local exchange market. At the bill's first hearing, almost no support was heard, but the Committee Chair, Inouye, and ranking minority member, Danforth, seemed determined to enter the bill for consideration.

Economic Case for Public Subsidy of the Internet

Type: FTP
Address: ssugopher.sonoma.edu
Pathname: /pub/schickele.txt (or schickele.ps for PostScript version)
Summary: Sandra Schickele's economic analysis of a publicly funded Internet.

FEDLINE

Type: FTP
Address: ftp.nwnet.net
Pathname: /user-docs/government/fedline.*
Summary: Not just politicians are interested in the electronic distribution of government information. "FEDLINE: A Feasibility Study of Establishment and Operation of FedWorld, A Government-Wide Information Locator System at NTIS," is a document that outlines a governmental study on electronic distribution of information our tax dollars have already paid for. ASCII-text, WordPerfect 5.1, and PostScript versions of the study are available on the NorthWestNet FTP server.

High Performance Computing Act (HPCA)

Type: FTP
Address: nic.merit.edu
Pathname: /nren/hpca.1991/nrenbill.txt

Summary: The House-Senate final version of S. 272 (passed House on Nov. 20, 1991; passed Senate on Nov. 22, 1991; signed by President Bush on Dec. 9, 1991), forming the National Research and Education Network (NREN). The bill was originally authored by then-Senator Al Gore.

Information Infrastructure and Technology Act (IITA)

Type: FTP

Address: nic.merit.edu

Pathname: /nren/iita.1992/gorebill.1992.txt

Summary: The press release, summary, and draft text of then-Senator Al Gore's Information Infrastructure and Technology Act of 1992.

National Research and Education Network (NREN)

Type: FTP

Address: nic.merit.edu

Pathname: /nren/nrencongr.txt (or nrencongr.ps for PostScript version)

Summary: The Director of the Office of Science and Technology's report to Congress on the National Research and Education Network (NREN).

OMB Circular A-130

Type: FTP

Address: nic.merit.edu

Pathname: /omb/omb.a130.rev2

Summary: The Office of Management and Budget's report on Management of Federal Information Resources. This report specifies how federal information is to be made publicly accessible in electronic form.

Health Security Act

Type: WWW, FTP, Gopher, WAIS

Address: sunsite.unc.edu

URL: http://sunsite.unc.edu/nhs/NHS-T-O-C

Summary: The Clinton administration's Health Security Act is available on the University of North Carolina's sunsite. The full text of the report and the full text of the legislation are available by FTP, Gopher, WAIS and WWW. A full hypertext version of the legislation for access via WWW clients was under development as of early November 1993.

FTP: sunsite.unc.edu in the /pub/academic/political-science/Health-Security-Act/ directory

Gopher: sunsite.unc.edu (select item 13 from the menu)

WAIS: sunsite.unc.edu port 210 in the Health-Security-Act database

Hot off the Tree (HOTT)

Type: TELNET

Address: melvyl.ucop.edu

Summary: Provides excerpts and abstracts of information technology articles from trade journals and online news services. HOTT is updated every week by the Technology Watch Information Group at the University of California at San Diego. Only two issues at a time are available online, so check this resource regularly if it's of interest to you.

Enter command **SHOW HOTT** at the command prompt. A menu of items will appear; enter your selection at the prompt. An example is shown in Figure 8-8.

Figure 8-8: HOTT example session.

```
≡  File  Edit  Window  Setup  Help                              15:28:39
┌[■]══════════════════ melvyl.ucop.edu ═════════════════════[↕]┐
Information Group (TWIG) from the Library, UCSD.  HOTT contains excerpts and
abstracts of articles from trade journals, online news services and electronic
bulletin boards.  Only 2 issues at a time are available online.  Comments
about HOTT can be sent via an e-mail message to Susan Jurist, sjurist@ucsd.edu
or sjurist@ucsd.bitnet.


   64.  HOT OFF THE TREE, No. 93.09.28
        64.1  If all you Want for Christmas / It Ain't Pretty,
              But It's got a Great Personality?
        64.2  OK, I'm Ready, What are They Waiting for?
        64.3  Chicago Without O'Hare
        64.4  It is 6:05 P.M. — Do you Know Where Your PC Is?
        64.5  For a Good Time, Try Newton


Type the NUMBER for the article you want to read or type just the ISSUE number
to begin with the first article and continue on through the issue.

CAT->
Alt-F1:Help  Alt-F2:Disconnect  Ctrl-Ins:Copy  Shift-Ins:Paste  Alt-F4:Enlarge
```

HPCwire

Type: TELNET

Address: hpcwire.ans.net

Summary: Provides menu-driven information searches related to high-performance computing and information services. Information about everything from workstations to supercomputers is available. Login as hpcwire. An example is shown in Figure 8-9.

Figure 8-9: HPCwire example session.

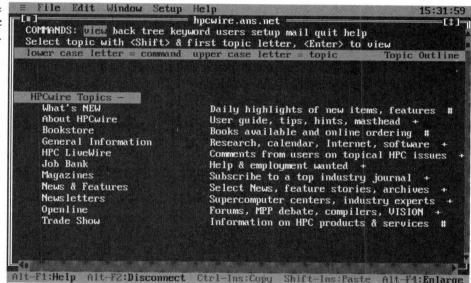

Hytelnet Documentation

Type: FTP

Address: access.usask.ca

Pathname: /pub/hytelnet/README/

Summary: Access TELNET resources using a hypertext browser. Hytelnet is Peter Scott's implementation of a hypertext database of publicly accessible Internet sites. More than 1,300 sites are currently listed, including libraries, campus-wide information systems, Gopher, WAIS and WWW servers.

You can use the UNIX version of Hytelnet with a terminal emulator:

Type: TELNET
Address: access.usask.ca
Login: hytelnet
    A Hytelnet mailing list is also available:
Type: E-mail
Address: listserv@kentvm.kent.edu
Summary: Send a one-line mail message:
      subscribe hytel-l *your name*
  where your name is your first and last name (not your e-mail address).

Hytelnet Server

Type: TELNET
Address: access.usask.ca
Summary: Provides access to several university and library card catalogs. This is a useful way to search for books and journal articles on a specific topic, but you will not be able to access the full text of these resources via a remote Internet login.
    Login as hytelnet

IEEE Document Vending Machine

Type: E-mail
Address: info.new.technology@ieee.org
Summary: If you have problems navigating the Internet, information vending machines offer an answer. Right now most of these vending machines are free, but expect to pay for the information they dispense in the future. These vending machines work by responding to e-mail messages.
    Send a message—the contents of the message or the subject line doesn't matter. You'll receive an e-mail message containing an index of available files. Here are some of the more interesting files available as of Summer, 1993:

- info.new.tech.bt@ieee.org (Broadcast Technology Society)
- info.new.tech.ce@ieee.org (Consumer Electronics Society)

- info.new.tech.e@ieee.org (Education Society)
- info.new.tech.it@ieee.org (Information Theory Society)
- info.new.tech.pc@ieee.org (Professional Communication Society)
- info.new.tech.sit@ieee.org (Society on Social Implications of Technology)

Incomplete Guide to the Internet

Type: FTP
Address: ftp.ncsa.uiuc.edu
Pathname: /misc/ directory
Summary: An excellent guide to the Internet written by the NCSA Education Group. Contains coverage of SLIP connections and the use of various freeware and shareware Net utilities.

Internet Company E-Mail Forwarding Service

Type: E-mail
Address: messenger@internet.com
Summary: In mid-August 1993, the Internet Company announced a service that allows Internet users to receive e-mail sent to addresses within their domains, even if they have only a single account on a commercial service. Called Messenger, the new service is designed to provide domain name type services for individuals and small businesses that do not enjoy full Internet connectivity. For example, a user with an MCI Mail account can use the Messenger service to establish a sort of pseudo domain name. Instead of an address like joeuser@mcimail.com, for instance, a series of addresses—joeuser@company.com, support@company.com, info@company.com, etc.—can all be created with all e-mail routed to the original e-mail address (joeuser@mcimail.com).

Three levels of Messenger service are available:
- **Personal Messenger** routes all mail sent to any username within a registered domain to one or more e-mail accounts, anywhere on the Internet.

■ **Corporate Messenger** allows specific addresses within the domain to forward mail to several e-mail accounts. This permits "virtual organizations" to be designed, where e-mail addressed to joeuser@company.com is routed differently than that addressed to jilluser@company.com.

■ **Organization Messenger** allows large organizations to offer distinct e-mail addresses within their domain.

Internet Information Mailing List

Type: E-mail

Address: tristan@gibbs.oit.unc.edu

Summary: A general information distribution list related to services, programs, guides and frequently asked questions (FAQs) about the Internet and various services offered on it.

To subscribe:

send a brief message requesting to be added to the distribution list to tristan@gibbs.oit.unc.edu

Internet Maps

Type: FTP

Address: ftp.merit.edu

Pathname: /maps/ directory

Summary: A collection of PostScript-format maps of the Internet. You must have a PostScript-capable printer to be able to print and view these maps.

Internet Monthly Report

Type: FTP

Address: nis.nsf.net

Pathname: /internet/newsletters/internet.monthly.report/ directory

Summary: Monthly Internet usage reports. The reports contain information from the Internet Research Group concerning the accomplishments and problems of the participating organizations. Each report usually contains an article from the Internet Architecture Board and a few

Internet Engineering reports. Brief articles are also submitted by the various regional networks, and a calendar of upcoming events is included.

Internet Society Archive

Type: FTP
Address: nnsc.nsf.net
Pathname: /internet-society/ directory
Summary: Contains a collection of Internet Society materials, including status reports, position statements, etc.

Internet Talk Radio Archives

Type: FTP
Address: ftp.uu.net
Pathname: /usenet/news.answers/internet-talk-radio/anonymous-ftp-list.z
Summary: A listing of FTP archive sites that make the Internet Talk Radio sound files available via anonymous FTP. Current FTP archive sites in the United States include (*make sure to use the site that's geographically closest to your physical location*):

Address	Pathname
ftp.nau.edu (134.114.64.70)	/talk-radio/
csn.org (128.138.213.21)	/pub/internet-talk-radio/
ftp.cic.net (192.131.22.2)	/pub/talk-radio/
sunsite.unc.edu (152.2.22.81)	/pub/talk-radio/
ftp.sterling.com (192.124.9.1)	/talk-radio/
ftp.acsu.buffalo.edu (128.205.7.9)	/pub/talk-radio/
ftp.uoregon.edu (128.223.32.35)	/pub/internet-talk-radio/
ftp.utexas.edu (128.83.185.16)	/pub/itr/
ecosys.drdr.virginia.edu (128.143.86.233)	/pub/talk-radio/
radio.ans-core.com (192.77.167.77)	/pub/radio/

Internet World

As of September 1993, *Internet World* is no longer a newsletter and is now an advertiser-supported magazine. *Internet World* is published by Meckler Corp. and appears bi-monthly. Subscriptions are available for $30 per year. The first magazine issue includes articles by Mike Godwin (EFF), Peter Deutsch (Archie), Jane Smith (CNIDR), Mike Barrow (Boston Computer Society), Mary Reindeau (The World) and others. The first magazine issue was available at the Interop/Fall show (August 23–27, 1993) in San Francisco.

Contact: Meckler Corporation
11 Ferry Lane West
Westport, CT 06880
800/632-5537
203/454-7269 (Fax)
meckler@jvnc.net

Daniel Dern, Editor
Internet World
P.O. Box 309
Newton Center, MA 02159
617/969-7947
617/969-7949 (Fax)
ddern@world.std.com

InterNIC

Type: Organization
Address: info@ls.internic.net
Summary: A set of three organizations funded in part by the National Science Foundation dedicated to serving the needs of the Internet community. The InterNIC specializes in helping new users and in compiling registration, directory and database information. You can call their hotline at 800/444-4345 for more details.

Interpersonal Computing and Technology Electronic Journal

Type: E-mail

Address: listserv@guvm.georgetown.edu

Summary: *Interpersonal Computing and Technology* (IPCT: An Electronic Journal for the 21st Century) is a peer-reviewed electronic journal focusing on topics including the use of electronic networks in the classroom, electronic publishing, library applications, professional relationships, and the general use of electronic communication. The IPCT-J distribution list will carry only abstracts and a table of contents for each issue.

To subscribe:

send a one line e-mail message:

subscribe ipct-j *your name*

where *your name* is your first and last names (not your login name).

A general discussion list (IPCT-L) for the same range of topics is also available.

To subscribe:

send a one line e-mail message:

subscribe ipct-l *your name*

where *your name* is your first and last names (not your login name).

Articles can be submitted to Gerald Phillips, editor-in-chief: gmp3@psuvm.psu.edu

Introduction to TCP/IP

Type: FTP

Address: topaz.rutgers.edu

Pathname: /tcp-ip-docs/ directory

Summary: An excellent guide to TCP/IP. This is the best and most clearly written reference available for installing, configuring and administering a TCP/IP connection.

IP Address Resolver

Type: Directory Service

Address: resolve@cs.widener.edu

Summary: In body of e-mail message, enter:

site *address*

where *address* is the name of the site in the domain.top-domain format.

The service will return the IP address of the site.

Law Library

Type: TELNET

Address: liberty.uc.wlu.edu

Summary: Provides law libraries and legal research. Information on law library archives, White House electronic access, the United Nations, gay rights, adoption laws, privacy rights, copyright and much more is available.

Login as lawlib. An example session is shown in Figure 8-10.

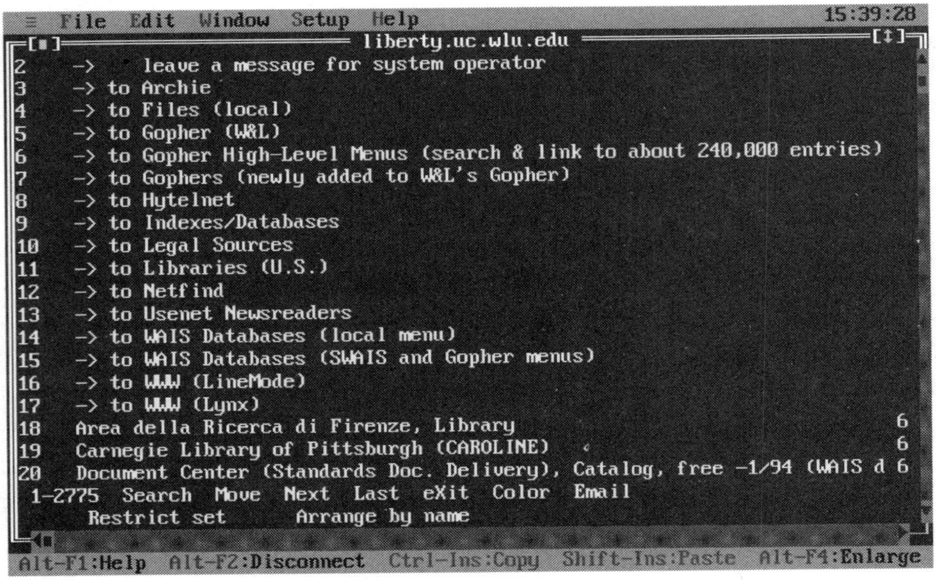

Figure 8-10: Law Library example session.

```
≡  File  Edit  Window  Setup  Help                            15:39:28
┌[■]─────────────── liberty.uc.wlu.edu ───────────────────[‡]┐
│2     ->    leave a message for system operator
│3     -> to Archie
│4     -> to Files (local)
│5     -> to Gopher (W&L)
│6     -> to Gopher High-Level Menus (search & link to about 240,000 entries)
│7     -> to Gophers (newly added to W&L's Gopher)
│8     -> to Hytelnet
│9     -> to Indexes/Databases
│10    -> to Legal Sources
│11    -> to Libraries (U.S.)
│12    -> to Netfind
│13    -> to Usenet Newsreaders
│14    -> to WAIS Databases (local menu)
│15    -> to WAIS Databases (SWAIS and Gopher menus)
│16    -> to WWW (LineMode)
│17    -> to WWW (Lynx)
│18    Area della Ricerca di Firenze, Library                    6
│19    Carnegie Library of Pittsburgh (CAROLINE)                 6
│20    Document Center (Standards Doc. Delivery), Catalog, free -1/94 (WAIS d 6
│ 1-2775  Search  Move  Next  Last  eXit  Color  Email
│         Restrict set        Arrange by name
Alt-F1:Help  Alt-F2:Disconnect  Ctrl-Ins:Copy  Shift-Ins:Paste  Alt-F4:Enlarge
```

LawNet

Type: TELNET

Address: dessert.law.columbia.edu or lawnet.law.columbia.edu

Summary: Offers legal information and card catalog access. Columbia University's Law School library card catalog, information server, academic services and career services are all accessible.

Login as lawnet. An example session screen is shown in Figure 8-11.

Figure 8-11: LawNet example session.

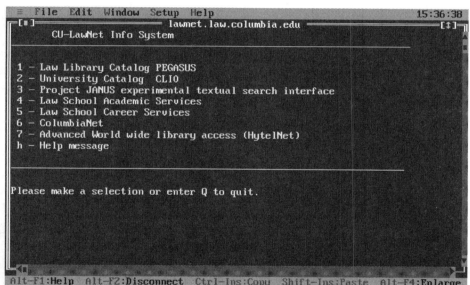

Library of Congress

Type: TELNET

Address: dra.com

Summary: Provides access to the catalog of the Library of Congress. Again, you won't be able to access the full text of the library's holdings, but this is a very useful resource when simply compiling a list of possible sources for a topic of research.

Library of Congress Information System (LOCIS) Quick Search Guide

Type: FTP
Address: seq1.loc.gov
Pathname: /pub/LC-On.line/
Summary: A guide to using the Library of Congress Information System (LOCIS). Available in both ASCII and Microsoft Word formats. Note that the ASCII format version is not properly formatted for an 80-character per line display.

LIBS

Type: TELNET
Address: nessie.cc.wwu.edu
Summary: Provides gateway access to many TELNET services. Library card catalogs in various countries are accessible, as are several campus-wide information systems. This service is referred to as a gateway because you can access other services through this portal.

Login as LIBS. An example session is shown in Figure 8-12.

Figure 8-12: LIBS example session.

```
≡  File  Edit  Window  Setup  Help                          15:37:58
[■]━━━━━━━━━━━━━━━━ nessie.cc.wwu.edu ━━━━━━━━━━━━━━━[↕]


              LIBS - Internet Access Software v2.0
          Mark Resmer, Sonoma State University, Dec 1992
                     WWU rev. 5/17/93

          On-line services available through the Internet:

          1 United States Library Catalogs
          2 Library Catalogs in other countries
          3 Campus-wide Information Systems
          4 Databases and Information Services
          5 Wide-area Information Services
          6 Information for first time users
          7 Special Internet Connection List

          Press RETURN alone to exit now or
          press Control-C Q <return> to exit at any time

          Enter the number of your choice:

Alt-F1:Help  Alt-F2:Disconnect  Ctrl-Ins:Copy  Shift-Ins:Paste  Alt-F4:Enlarge
```

Mailing Lists List

Type: E-Mail

Address: listserv@vm1.nodak.edu

Summary: An automated distribution server of a comprehensive list of e-mail mailing lists. For more information on mailing lists, see "Electronic Mailing Lists" in Chapter 4, beginning on page 102.

Send the following lines in an e-mail message:
LIST GLOBAL

Mbone FAQ

Type: FTP

Address: venera.isi.edu

Pathname: /mbone/faq.txt

Summary: The Mbone provides live audio and video multicasting across a virtual network that lives on top of the Internet.

MELVYL

Type: TELNET

Address: melvyl.ucop.edu

Summary: The MELVYL database contains the entire catalog of the University of California's monographs and periodicals. Several California state universities' holdings are accessible via MELVYL. The system also provides access to MEDLINE and Current Contents. Other systems are accessible by a gateway. Access to some resources is restricted by password.

MicroMuse

Type: TELNET

Address: michael.ai.mit.edu

Summary: MicroMuse is a text-only virtual environment under development at MIT. It's like the old-style text adventure games, with a politically correct spin. Education, cooperation and concern for the environment are stressed in this game-like environment. MicroMuse is something easier experienced than explained; give it a try.

Login as guest. An example session screen is shown in Figure 8-13.

Figure 8-13:
MicroMuse
example session.

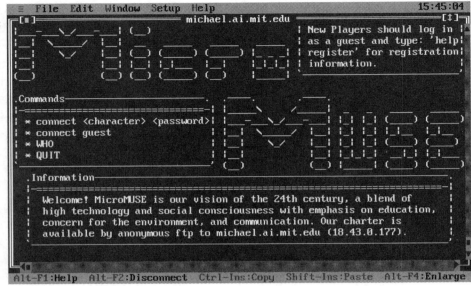

Mining the Internet

Type: FTP

Address: ucdavis.edu

Pathname: /ucd.netdocs/mining/ directory

Summary: This text file offers a good overview of the information resources offered on the Internet, using a mining meta-phor.

MIT Media Lab ACCESS Service

Type: FTP

Address: media-lab.media.mit.edu

Pathname: /access/

Summary: MIT's Media Lab has established an anonymous FTP server to provide information about current projects, publications, and sponsors.

MIT Media Lab Online World

Type: E-mail

Address: online-world-request@media-lab.mit.edu

Summary: Online World is a low-volume electronic mailing list originating at MIT's Media Lab focused on discussions related to electronic publishing, the future of news media, and the social impact of networks.

Contact: Gilberte Houbard
MIT Media Lab
Room E15-430
20 Ames Street
Cambridge, MA 02139
617/253-9787
617/258-6264 (Fax)
gilberte@media-lab.mit.edu

Movie Database

Type: E-mail

Address: movie@ibmpcug.co.uk

Summary: Provides a database of movies, actors and directors via e-mail. Send an e-mail message with the single line "help" (without quotes) to receive complete instructions on using the database.

Command	Returns
TITLE	information about the movie specified
DIRCT	information about the director specified
ACTOR	information abut the actor specified
COMPO	information about the composer specified
WRITE	information about the writer specified
CINEM	information about the cinematographer specified
MOVIE	full list for movie plus lists of all other movies by cast and crew

For example:

    MOVIE O Lucky Man
    DIRECTOR Kubrick, Stanley
    ACTOR McDowell, Malcolm

Would return full information on the movie *O Lucky Man*, the director Stanley Kubrick and the actor Malcolm McDowell.

MTV Hits the Net

Type: FTP, Finger, and Gopher
Address: mtv.com
Pathname: /various/
Summary: MTV vee-jay Adam Curry has registered the mtv.com domain name and has begun to provide popular-music-related information accessible via Gopher and FTP. Curry is also publishing a shareware electronic newsletter focusing on the popular music scene. Eventually graphic images, lyrics and audio files will be available.

MUD FAQ

Type: FTP
Address: ftp.math.okstate.edu
Pathname: /pub/muds/misc/mud-faq/part*
Summary: MUD is an acronym for Multi-User Dimensions (or Dungeons). A MUD is a real-time interaction that is usually based upon some sort of social role-playing.

Music Server

Type: FTP
Address: ftp.uwp.edu
Pathname: /pub/lyrics/ directory
Summary: This site is popular with college students. It provides lyrics, pictures, guitar chords and tablature for a wide array of popular music.

Nasdaq Financial Executive Journal

Type: WWW
Address: http://fatty.law.cornell.edu:80/usr2/wwwtext/nasdaq/nasdtoc.html
Summary: The Nasdaq Stock Market and the Legal Information Institute at Cornell Law School have made available a hypermedia version of the *Nasdaq Financial Executive Journal* (NFEJ). The NFEJ is accessible via the World Wide Web in HTML format:

Network News Mailing List

Type: Mailing List

Address: listserv@vm1.nodak.edu

Summary: A collection of Internet resources and facts. Since this resource exists as a mailing list, you can expect fairly regular updates—and they will be mailed to you automatically until you revoke your subscription to the list. This is a handy tool for staying current with the Net's resources.

Send a one-line message in e-mail:
subscribe nnews *your name*
where *your name* is your full name (not your e-mail address).

New Users' Guide

Type: FTP

Address: nysernet.org

Pathname: /pub/resources/guides/ directory

Summary: New Users' Guide to Unique and Interesting Resources on the Internet is authored by the New York State Education and Research Network (NYSERNet). It covers about 50 Internet resources in more than 145 pages.

NorthWestNet User Services Guide

Type: FTP

Address: ftphost.nwnet.net

Pathname: /nic/nwnet/user-guide/ directory

Summary: NorthWestNet User Services Internet Resource Guide (about 300 pages) covers electronic mail, FTP, remote login, supercomputer access and online library catalogs.

NREN Information

Type: FTP

Address: nis.nsf.net

Pathname: /nren/ directory

Summary: Collection of information on the National Research and Education Network (NREN).

The Online World

Type: FTP

Address: oak.oakland.edu

Pathname: /pub/msdos/info/online10.zip

Summary: Norwegian author Odd de Presno has released his book, *The Online World*, as shareware. *The Online World* was previously published in Norwegian as a 275-page hardcover (ISBN: 82-90628-67-6) and is still available in bookstores. The work covers the practical side of using the global networks and provides examples ranging from databases to entertainment. The FTP-accessible file is in ASCII text format and can be read with any text editor or word processing program.

Contact: opresno@extern.uio.no

PGP v2.2 Encryption Utility

Type: FTP

Address: soda.berkeley.edu

Summary: PGP 2.2 is a data encryption utility that uses the IDEA cipher patented in Switzerland. This utility is of special interest because it has not been sanctioned for general use by the National Security Agency (NSA), which governs issues of coding and encryption in the United States. (This means that data encoded with PGP is probably safer from prying eyes than it would be if you used a "government-approved" encryption method.)

Anonymous public key server sites:

pgp-public-keys@junkbox.cc.iastate.edu
tbird.cc.iastate.edu [/usr/explorer/public-keys.pgp]
pgp-public-keys@toxicwaste.mit.edu
toxicwaste.mit.edu [/pub/keys/public-keys.pgp]
pgp-public-keys@phil.utmb.edu
phil.utmb.edu [/pub/pgp/public-keys.pgp]

Project Gutenberg

Type: FTP
Address: mrcnext.cso.uiuc.edu
Pathname: /etext/ directory
Summary: Project Gutenberg was formed to encourage the creation and distribution of electronic text, hoping to have one trillion volumes available by the end of 2001. Texts currently available include *Alice in Wonderland*, *Peter Pan*, Shakespeare's complete works and Milton's *Paradise Lost*.

Prospero Documentation

Type: FTP
Address: prospero.isi.edu
Pathname: /pub/prospero/doc/README-prospero-documents
Summary: Prospero provides a user-centered view of remote files on FTP servers.

Public Network News Servers

Type: Network News
Address: various, see Summary
Summary: These publicly accessible network news servers are sites where you can login to read (and in some places, respond to) network news articles.

cc.usu.edu (read only)
etl.go.jp (read/post)
europa.eng.gtefsd.com (read only)
fconvx.ncifcrf.gov (read only)
gaia.ucs.orst.edu (read only)
hermes.chpc.utexas.edu (read only)
mailer.cc.fsu.edu (read only)
munnari.oz.au (read/post)
netnews.cc.lehigh.edu (read only)
news.funet.fi (read only)
news.unomaha.edu (read only)
news.yale.edu (read only)
news.ysu.edu (read only)
newshub.nosc.mil (read only)

newsserver.jvnc.net (read only)
newsserver.jvnc.net (read only)
quip.eecs.umich.edu (read/post)
sbcs.sunysb.edu (read/post)
sol.ctr.columbia.edu (read/post)
suntan.ec.usf.edu (read/post)
uicvm.uic.edu (read only)
umd5.umd.edu (read only)
usenet.coe.montana.edu (read only)
uunet.ca (read/post)
uwec.edu (read/post)
vax1.mankato.msus.edu (read only)
vaxc.cc.monash.edu.au (read/post)
willis1.cis.uab.edu (read only)

SIGGRAPH Publications

Type: FTP
Address: siggraph.org
Pathname: /ftp/publications/May_93_online
Summary: The Association of Computing Machinery's (ACM) special interest group for graphics (SIGGRAPH) publications for May 1993.

Special Internet Connections

Type: FTP
Address: csd4.csd.uwm.edu
Pathname: /pub/inet.services.txt
Summary: Scott Yanoff's excellent guide to Internet services. Also available by mailing list by sending a subscription request to yanoff@csd4.csd.uwm.edu. The list is also posted regularly to several USENET newsgroups including biz.comp.services and alt.internet.services.

Sports Schedules

Type: TELNET

Address: culine.colorado.edu

Summary: Provides daily schedules for a wide array of professional sporting events, including hockey, basketball and football.

TELNET to the specified port for the sport schedule you want:

NBA: culine.colorado.edu 859
NHL: culine.colorado.edu 860
MLB: culine.colorado.edu 862
NFL: culine.colorado.edu 863

Enter **HELP** for online help.

After login, press **Enter** for today's schedules.

Terminal Compromise

Type: FTP

Address: ftp.netsys.com or soda.berkeley.edu

Pathname: /pub/novel/

Summary: The first novel distributed on the Internet, Winn Schwartau's *Terminal Compromise* is a high-tech thriller about the invasion of the United States by computer terrorists. The novel was first published in print (ISBN: 0-962-87000-5) by INTER.PACT Press. *Terminal Compromise* is being distributed electronically, on the Internet, as shareware.

Travel Agency on the Net

Type: E-mail

Address: fly@hpcwire.ans.net

Summary: This is a travel agency connected to the Internet. For a price quote on air fare, send a request for a quote, including the departure city, departure date, destination, and return date. They'll either call you voice or send you e-mail with the best fare they can find.

Travel Information

Type: FTP
Address: ccu.umanitoba.ca
Pathname: /pub/rec-travel/ directory
Summary: Provides worldwide travel information including travel guides and FAQs. Here's a brief excerpt from Gary Fischman's entry for St. Maarten:

"There isn't much in the way of tourist sights in St. Maarten/St. Martin. There is the old ruins of the fort in Marigot. It's up on a small hill next to the Marigot waterfront. The fort itself isn't much to see, but there is a great view of the northwest corner of the island."

University of North Carolina LaUNChpad

Type: TELNET
Address: launchpad.unc.edu
Summary: Provides access to a wide variety of Campus Wide Information Servers (CWIS). From LaUNChpad, you can also use a menu-driven interface to access a number of other Internet resources, including WAIS searches, Gopher servers, Supreme Court ruling databases, CARL and many of the other resources listed here. The advantage is that, as when working with Gopher, LaUNChpad automatically logs you in and out of each site—you don't have to memorize domain addresses and login passwords.

Login as launch

At the main menu, select item 3, "On-line Information Systems (LIBTEL)."

U.S. State Department Travel Advisories

Type: FTP
Address: world.std.com
Pathname: /obi/US.StateDept/Travel/ directory
Summary: Foreign travel advisories provided by the U.S. State Department. The advisories are stored by country name, and each new advisory is appended to the end of the file.

VAX Manual

Type: FTP

Address: decoy.uoregon.edu

Pathname: /pub/vaxbook/vms.ps (make sure you also get the errata files that are updated on a regular basis).

Summary: Joe St. Sauver's excellent guide to the University of Oregon's VAX8000 system. At more than 300 pages, the guide provides information that is useful for general network users, not just VAX users.

Veronica FAQ

Type: FTP

Address: veronica.scs.unr.edu

Pathname: /veronica/veronica-faq

Summary: Veronica is used to search for title keywords of Gopher items.

Voices From the Net

Type: E-mail

Address: swilbur@andy.bgsu.edu or mgardbe@andy.bgsu.edu

Summary: *Voices from the Net* is an electronic publication that focuses on providing an "outlet for the expression of views on and about the 'Net.'" These views will include interviews, essays, and other expository forms. The first issue is scheduled for release in early August 1993 and will include an interview with Tom Maddox, an essay by Andy Hawks, and comments from others. The second issue (scheduled for release about a month following the first issue) will include interviews with Adam Curry and Billy Idol.

    To subscribe:

    send a one line e-mail message with the word:
      Subscribe
    with the Subject line:
      Voices From the Net

Washington University Gateway
Type: TELNET
Address: wugate.wustl.edu
Summary: Provides gateway access to many TELNET services. Login as services

Weather Maps
Type: FTP
Address: vmd.cso.uiuc.edu
Pathname: /pub/wx/ directory
Summary: Provides current infrared weather maps and surface analysis.

Weather Service
Type: TELNET
Address: downwind.sprl.umich.edu 3000
Summary: Provides complete weather forecasts as well as other related information, such as earthquake reports, ski conditions and more.

White House Almanac Information Server
Type: E-mail
Address: almanac@esusda.gov
Summary: E-mail accessible documents from the White House concerning press briefings, Executive Orders, photo opportunities and other information. Gopher, WAIS and Xmosaic access is also available.

To request a specific document, send an e-mail message to:
almanac@esusda.gov
and in the body of the message:
send white-house *nn*
where nn is the number of the document you wish to receive.

To receive a guide to other documents available from the USDA Extension Service Almanac, in the body of the message:
send catalog

To receive instructions for using Almanac, in the body of the message:
send guide
Contact: wh-admin@esusda.gov

White House E-Mail
Type: E-mail
Address: president@whitehouse.gov and vice.president@whitehouse.gov
Summary: Send e-mail to the president and vice president of the United States.

White House Press Releases
Type: E-mail
Address: clinton-info@campaign92.org
Summary: This e-mail server is not designed to answer e-mail letters, comments or requests for specific information. It is designed solely to distribute press releases.

The e-mail server works by reading the subject line of your message and taking an appropriate action based on that subject line.

Subject: RECEIVE HELP
Help file for the e-mail server.
Subject: RECEIVE ECONOMIC POLICY
Press releases related to the economy including budget news, technology policy reviews, etc.
Subject: RECEIVE FOREIGN POLICY
Press releases related to foreign policy.
Subject: RECEIVE SOCIAL POLICY
Press releases related to social issues.
Subject: RECEIVE SPEECHES
All speeches made by the President and the most important speeches made by other administration officials.
Subject: RECEIVE NEWS
Transcripts of White House Communications office press conferences.
Subject: RECEIVE ALL
All releases from all subject areas.

(More) White House Press Releases
Type: FTP
Address: sunsite.unc.edu
Pathname: /home3/wais/white-house-papers/ directory
Summary: News and press releases related to economic policy, foreign policy, social policy, press conferences and speeches.

Conclusion

So now you're a pro at practically all things Internet. What's that? You feel like we've just gone around the world in 80 days (or perhaps only eight)? You're still overwhelmed with all the things you can do, people you can meet and places you can visit? The secret to finding your way around the Internet is to forget about where you're going and just go. Explore. Take a sidetrip. Have fun.

The good news is, you're not on your own. There are plenty of friendly people all over the Net who can offer you help whenever you need it. And just by buying this book, you'll get two electronic updates free. (For more details on taking advantage of the electronic updates, see "Electronic Updates & Visitors Center" beginning on page 249.)

But for now, you might want to get back out into the Net to check out a few of the resources listed in this chapter. And don't forget to drop me a line if you spot something extraordinary.

Electronic Updates
& Visitors Center

Appendix A
Electronic Updates & Visitors Center

New services are added to the Internet on a daily—sometimes hourly—basis. It's impossible for one person to keep up with everything that's happening on the Net.

I grew up in the 1960s, and I was constantly told by my elders that there was no such thing as a free lunch. I think the saying originated with signs that used to hang in taverns offering free lunches.

I've got good news for you: there is a free lunch. (OK, you had to buy this book to get the free updates, but you had to buy a drink or two to get a free lunch in the taverns of my youth.)

Because the Internet is in a constant state of flux, Ventana Press and Arts & Farces are offering you two free electronic updates to this book. The updates will include: reviews of the latest Internet client software releases, summaries of new information resources, tips and tricks for finding your way around the Net, news about trends and industry developments, and much more.

Updates Are Just a Postcard Away

It's easy to make sure you receive your exclusive electronic updates, which are available only to owners of the *Tour Guide*. Updates will be distributed via e-mail. This way, they'll be sent directly to your electronic mailbox. To receive your free updates:

- Fill out the response card bound into the back of the book. Make sure you've completed every portion of the card. (Incomplete cards will not be acknowledged and will not qualify for the two free updates.)

- Make certain you've included your Internet-accessible e-mail address in the standard format: username@domain.top-domain. (Addresses in any other format will not be acknowledged and will not qualify for the two free electronic updates.)

- If you'd like to receive occasional informational mailings about other books and materials about the Internet and the PC, simply check the appropriate box on the card.

- Note that the updates may be larger than can fit through the e-mail gateways of some of the commercial information services like CompuServe and America Online. If so, the updates will be sent to you in multiple segments.

The Electronic Visitors Center

It's always nice to have a "home base" when traveling in strange and foreign territory. The Visitors Center is a place where *Tour Guide* owners can stop and rest on their ramblings through the Net. And better still, it's also where you'll find the latest versions of all the great freeware and shareware software discussed in the *Tour Guide*, as well as the latest updates, news, tips, tricks and other hot information.

Access *The PC Internet Tour Guide* Visitors Center by FTP at ftp.farces.com.

Current versions of interesting PC programs for use on the Internet are available via anonymous FTP. Special ReadMe files and other goodies are available there. The Visitors Center is open to anyone, not just *Tour Guide* readers, so spread the word.

Also in the Visitors Center you'll find the latest versions of the programs discussed and demonstrated throughout the *Tour Guide*.

PKZIP204.exe is a file compression and decompression program that you'll need to process many of the files and other software resources you download from various sites on the Internet. The current version of PKZIP is always available in the Visitors Center. (This program is included on the companion disk.)

UMSLIP is a program that allows you to establish a SLIP connection and automated login to a SLIP server provided by your organization or Internet service provider. The current version of UMSLIP is always available in the Visitors Center. (This program is included on the companion disk.)

Minuet is software developed by the University of Minnesota that provides you with a complete solution to navigating the major Internet services: e-mail, network news, FTP, Gopher, TELNET and directory services. The current version of Minuet is always available in the Visitors Center. (This program is included on the companion disk.)

How to Subscribe to a Full Year of Updates

The PC Internet Tour Guide electronic updates will be published and distributed on a quarterly basis. As a purchaser of this book, you'll receive the first two updates free of charge. If you want to subscribe to additional quarterly updates, the current subscription rate is $25 per year (4 issues).

To receive a full year of updates, simply send a check for $25 (U.S. funds only) payable to Arts & Farces to:

> Arts & Farces
> 2285 Stewart Avenue
> Suite 1315
> Saint Paul, MN 55116

For more information on subscribing to future updates, send e-mail to: tour-guide-request@farces.com

A Note About Privacy

The Internet is a place where privacy has to be balanced against the free flow of information. The real world is no different. You'll notice there's a good deal of information you're providing on *The PC Internet Tour Guide* electronic update request postcards. But how that information is used is up to you. If, like many Internet and PC enthusiasts, you like to stay informed about the latest publications and related materials that are relevant to your interests, simply check the appropriate box on the card. Otherwise, the information you provide is for use by Arts & Farces only. I don't sell, lend or rent our mailing list. The transactional information you provide is between the two of us, and is no one's business but our own.

Quick-Reference Page

Use this page and its reverse side to keep track of important information about your Internet account. The information will always be close at hand, even when you aren't logged on to the Internet. You can also copy this page and fax or mail it to vendors and software developers to aid them in their technical support efforts.

Frequently Used Addresses & Other Information

User Name	_____
Computer Name	_____
Domain Name	_____
E-mail Address	_____
IP Address of Your Computer	_____
IP Subnet Mask of Your Computer	_____
IP Address of Domain Name Server	_____
IP Address of Domain Name Server	_____
IP Address of Local Gateway	_____
SLIP/PPP or Dial-Up Access Number	_____
Address of News Server	_____
Address of Mail Server	_____
Network Administrator E-mail	_____
Frequently Used E-mail Addresses	_____
Frequently Used E-mail Addresses	_____
Frequently Used E-mail Addresses	_____
Frequently Accessed Resources	_____
Frequently Accessed Resources	_____
Frequently Accessed Resources	_____

Popular PC FTP Sites

Site	FTP Address	Notes
Oakland University	oak.oakland.edu	_____
University of Michigan	archive.umich.edu	_____
University of Minnesota	boombox.micro.umn.edu	_____
Washington University (mirrors)	wuarchive.wustle.edu	_____
Microsoft (general archive)	ftp.microsoft.com	_____
Arts & Farces (Visitors Center)	ftp.farces.com	_____

Technical Support Information

Software/Service	E-mail	Phone
Network Administrator		
Connection Problems		
Network Service Problems		
Gopher	gopher@boombox.micro.umn.edu	612/626-4276
UMSLIP	slip@boombox.micro.umn.edu	612/626-4276
Minuet	minuet@boombox.micro.umn.edu	612/626-4276
Telnet	telnet@ncsa.uiuc.edu	N/A

PC Internet Tour Guide Visitors Center

Access *The PC Internet Tour Guide* Visitors Center by FTP at:
ftp.farces.com

Current versions of interesting PC programs for use on the Internet are available via anonymous FTP. The latest versions of all the key shareware and freeware programs discussed in this book will be available for downloading.

Author

Michael Fraase
Arts & Farces
2285 Stewart Ave., Suite 1315
Saint Paul, MN 55116
mfraase@farces.com

Publisher

Ventana Press
PO Box 2468
Chapel Hill, NC 27515
919/942-0220 (voice)
919/942-1140 (fax)

Notes

DISK PREVIEW
The PC Internet Tour Guide
Companion Disk

The software on the companion disk accompanying *The PC Internet Tour Guide* is distributed with the permission of its authors and is provided here for evaluation purposes. You may try it without obligation, but if you decide to keep a program permanently, please check the related ReadMe documents and make the appropriate shareware payment whenever applicable. Ventana Press and the author provide this software for your use as is and make no guarantee or warranty regarding its performance or compatibility.

Before you begin, we suggest making a careful backup of the contents of your hard drive and a backup of the companion disk. To install the software from the companion disk, you will need about 2mb of free space on your hard drive.

UMSLIP

The UMSLIP software allows you to route Internet information over a standard telephone line with a modem. Installing the University of Minnesota's UMSLIP software package is straightforward and very simple; step-by-step instructions are provided in Chapter 2, "Getting Connected."

Minuet

Minuet—Minnesota Internet User's Essential Tools—provides all the basic client services you need to access the Internet in a single program. E-mail, network news, File Transfer Protocol (FTP), Gopher and directory services are all available with Minuet's consistent user interface. Instructions for installing the University of Minnesota's Minuet software package are provided in Chapter 2.

Important Note

UMSLIP and Minuet are provided for evaluation purposes only. If you decide to continue using this software after a period of 30 days, you must pay $50 to the Regents of the University of Minnesota, 133 Shepherd Laboratory, 100 Union Street SE, Minneapolis, MN 55455.

Glossary

access method: The rules that manage how all the computers and other devices on a network can send information through the same physical medium in an orderly fashion.

access privileges: The privileges to open and make changes to directories and their contents; they are given to or withheld from users. By setting access privileges, you can control access to confidential information stored in directories on a server.

acronym: A word formed from the initial letter or letters of the main parts of a compound term, such as ROM (read-only memory).

activate: To make a nonactive window active by clicking anywhere inside it.

active window: The frontmost window on the desktop; the window where the next action will take place. An active window's title bar is highlighted.

addressing: A scheme, determined by network protocols, for identifying the sending device and destination device for any given item of information traveling on a network.

administrator: The person who sets up a network resource, registers users and their passwords, and maintains the resource.

alert: A warning or report of an error in the form of an alert box, a sound from the computer's speaker, or both. See also **alert box**.

alert box: A box that appears on the screen to give a warning or to report an error message. Its appearance is usually accompanied by a sound warning such as a beep.

alias: (n.) An alternate name used to invoke or identify a command, a network host, a list of users or some other applicable entity. (v.) To provide an entity with an alternate name.

American Standard Code for Information Interchange: See **ASCII**.

Archie: A network service used for locating files that are publicly accessible by anonymous FTP.

ARPANET: A wide area network that linked government, academic and industrial installations around the world. Primarily connecting research sites, the ARPANET was developed in the 1960s by the Advanced Research Projects Agency of the U.S. Department of Defense.

ASCII: Acronym for American Standard Code for Information Interchange (pronounced "ASK-ee"). A standard that assigns a unique binary number to each text character and control character. ASCII code is used for representing text inside a computer and for transmitting text between computers or between a computer and a peripheral device.

asynchronous: Not synchronized by a mutual timing signal or clock. Compare **synchronous**.

asynchronous transmission: A method of data transmission in which the receiving and sending devices don't share a common timer, and no timing data is transmitted. Each information character is individually synchronized, usually by the use of start and stop bits. The time interval between characters isn't necessarily fixed. Compare **synchronous transmission**.

bandwidth: The range of transmission frequencies that a network can use. The greater the bandwidth, the greater the amount of information that can travel on the network at one time.

baseband: A transmission method in which a network uses its entire transmission frequency range to send a single communication or signal. Compare **broadband**.

baud: (1) A unit of data transmission speed: the number of discrete signal-state changes (signal events) per second. Often, but not always, equivalent to **bits per second**. Compare **bit rate**. (2) The maximum speed at which data can be sent down a channel, such as a telephone line; often confused with the actual speed at which the data is transmitted between two computers, measured in bits per second.

BBS: See **bulletin board system**.

bit: A contraction of **binary digit**. The smallest unit of information that a computer can hold. The value of a bit (1 or 0) represents a simple two-way choice, such as yes or no, on or off, positive or negative, something or nothing.

bit rate: The speed at which bits are transmitted, usually expressed as **bits per second**, or bps. Compare **baud**.

bits per second: See **bit rate**.

bridge: (1) A device that lets you connect two or more networking systems together. (2) A combination of hardware and software that connects two or more networks in an internet. Bridges are used to increase the number of devices and the distances covered in a network. See also **internet**.

broadband: A transmission method in which the network's range of transmission frequencies is divided into separate channels and each channel is used to send a different signal. Broadband transmission is often used to send signals of different kinds simultaneously, such as voice and data. Contrast with **baseband**.

bulletin board system (BBS): A computerized version of the bulletin boards frequently found in grocery stores—places to leave messages and to advertise things you want to buy or sell. One thing you get from a computerized bulletin board that you can't get from a cork board is free software.

bus topology: A layout scheme in which devices on a network are connected along the length of a main cable, or **bus**, rather than in a daisy chain or a loop.

byte: The number of bits used to represent a character. For personal computers, a byte is usually eight bits.

cable: An insulated bundle of wires with connectors on the ends. Examples are serial cables, disk drive cables and LocalTalk cables.

carrier: The background signal on a communication channel that is modified to carry information. Under RS-232-C rules, the carrier signal is equivalent to a continuous MARK (1) signal; a transition to 0 then represents a start bit.

CCITT: Abbreviation for **Consultative Committee on International Telegraphy and Telephony**; an international committee that sets standards and makes recommendations for international communication.

CIX: Abbreviation for **Commercial Internet Exchange**; an agreement among Internet service providers that allows them to account for commercial network traffic.

Clear To Send: An RS-232-C signal from a DCE to a DTE that is normally kept false until the DCE makes it true, indicating that all circuits are ready to transfer data. See also **Data Communication Equipment, Data Terminal Equipment**.

client: A computer that has access to services on a network. The computers that provide services are called **servers**. A user at a client may request file access, remote login, file transfer, printing or other available services from servers.

communications protocol: See **protocols**.

configuration: (1) A general-purpose computer term that can refer to the way you have your computer set up. (2) The total combination of hardware components—central processing unit, video display device, keyboard and peripheral devices—that make up a computer system. (3) The software settings that allow various hardware components of a computer system to communicate with one another.

configure: To change software or hardware actions by changing settings. Configurations can be set or reset in software or by manipulating hardware jumpers, switches or other elements.

connect time: The amount of time you spend connected to an information service.

data: Information, especially information used or operated on by a program. The smallest unit of information a computer can understand is a bit.

data bits: In the stream of bits being sent from your computer to a peripheral device or another computer, the bits that contain meaningful information; distinguished from bits used to indicate that a character is about to start, has stopped or is correct.

Data Carrier Detect (DCD): An RS-232-C signal from a DCE (such as a modem) to a DTE (such as a PC) indicating that a communication connection has been established. See also **Data Communication Equipment, Data Terminal Equipment**.

Data Communication Equipment (DCE): As defined by the RS-232-C standard, any device that transmits or receives information. Usually this device is a modem.

Data Set Ready (DSR): An RS-232-C signal from a DCE to a DTE indicating that the DCE has established a connection. See also **Data Communication Equipment, Data Terminal Equipment**.

Data Terminal Equipment (DTE): As defined by the RS-232-C standard, any device that generates or absorbs information, thus acting as an endpoint of a communication connection. A computer might serve as a DTE.

Data Terminal Ready (DTR): (1) One of the handshake lines in a data transmission interface. See also **hardware handshake**. (2) An RS-232-C signal from a DTE to a DCE indicating a readiness to transmit or receive data. See also **Data Communication Equipment, Data Terminal Equipment**.

default: A value, action or setting that a computer system assumes, unless the user gives an explicit instruction to the contrary. Default values prevent a program from stalling or crashing if no value is supplied by the user.

Defense Data Network (DDN): A single, wide area, packet-switching network that integrated the ARPANET research network and the MILNET defense network.

device: (1) A hardware component of a computer system, such as a video monitor, a disk drive or a printer. Also called a **peripheral device** because such equipment is often physically separate from, but attached to, the computer. (2) A part of the computer, or a piece of external equipment, that can transfer information. (3) Any piece of equipment that can be attached to a network—a computer, a printer, a file server, a print server or any other peripheral device.

dialog box: (1) A box that contains a message requesting more information from you. Sometimes the message warns you that you're asking your computer to do something it can't do or that you're about to destroy some of your information. In these cases, the message is often accompanied by a beep. (2) A box that a PC application displays to request information or to report that it is waiting for a process to complete.

download: To transfer files or information from one computer to another.

electronic mail: A network service that enables users to send and receive messages via computer.

Ethernet: A high-speed local area network that consists of a cable technology and a series of communication protocols. The hardware (cable) provides the physical link to connect systems together. The TCP/IP protocol allows different computers to exchange information over a network. The Ethernet specification was developed by Digital Equipment Corporation, Intel Corporation and Xerox Corporation. Ethernet is a registered trademark of Xerox Corporation.

Ethernet backbone: A network topology with separate AppleTalk networks interconnected to Ethernet gateways that are, in turn, connected to a single, continuous Ethernet cable.

Ethernet cable system: A system of high-performance coaxial cables widely used in the communications industry. Ethernet cables can be part of an AppleTalk network system.

even parity: The use of an extra bit set to 0 or 1 as necessary to make the total number of 1 bits an even number; used as a means of error checking in data transmission. Compare **MARK parity**, **odd parity**, **space parity**.

FAQ: Abbreviation for **Frequently Asked Question**; a list of frequently asked questions (and their answers). Most mailing lists and all network news newsgroups provide FAQ postings on a regular basis.

file: (1) Any named, ordered collection of information stored on a disk. Application programs and operating systems on disks are examples of files. You make a file when you create text or graphics, give the material a name and save it to disk; in this sense, **file** is synonymous with **document**. (2) For UNIX operating systems, an array of bytes; no other structure is implied by UNIX systems as they even treat devices like files.

file server: (1) A network device, usually consisting of a computer and one or more large capacity disks, on which network users can store files and applications in order to share them. (2) A specially equipped computer that allows network users to store and share information. (3) A combination of controller software and a mass-storage device that allows computer users to share common files and applications through a network.

file transfer protocol: A protocol that exchanges files with a host computer.

flame: A noxious and usually personal attack against the author of a network news article.

FTP: (n) (1) Abbreviation for **File Transfer Protocol**; a protocol that determines how files are transferred from one computer to another. (2) A software program that transfers files using FTP. (v) The act of transferring files using FTP.

full duplex: A four-wire communication circuit or protocol that allows two-way data transmission between two points at the same time. Compare **half duplex**.

full-duplex communication: A method of data transmission where two devices transmit data simultaneously. This method allows the receiving device to echo back each character of your message as it is received.

gateway: A device that connects networks that use different protocols. In effect, it translates between the protocols so that devices on the connected networks can exchange data.

Gopher: A menu-based means of exploring information resources.

half duplex: A two-wire communication circuit or protocol designed for data transmission in either direction but not both directions simultaneously. Compare **full duplex**.

half-duplex communication: A way of communicating between your computer and another computer or a peripheral device in which you can only send data or receive it at one time—not both. The other computer cannot echo back each character of your message as it is received.

handshaking: The exchange of status information between a **DCE** and a **DTE** used to control the transfer of data between them. The status information can be the state of a signal connecting the DCE and the DTE, or it can be in the form of a character transmitted with the rest of the data. See also **Data Carrier Detect, Data Set Ready, Data Terminal Ready, XOFF, XON**.

hardware handshake: A protocol that tells the computer to start or stop sending data by setting the DTR (Data Terminal Ready) line logic state. Also known as the Data Transfer Ready protocol. Compare **XON/XOFF**.

host computer: (1) A multi-user computer, such as a minicomputer or mainframe, that serves as a central processing unit for a number of terminals. (2) The computer that receives information from and sends data to terminals over telecommunication lines. The computer that is in control in a data communication network. The host computer may be a mainframe computer, minicomputer or microcomputer.

IAB: Abbreviation for **Internet Architecture Board**; the "council of elders" that makes decisions about Internet standards.

IETF: Abbreviation for **Internet Engineering Task Force**; a subgroup of the Internet Architecture Board that concerns itself with solving technical problems on the Internet.

internet: A network made up of two or more interconnected local area or wide area networks.

Internet: A worldwide, interconnected group of networks. Internally, the internet is composed of heterogeneous networks (such as ARPANET and CSNET) that use different message formats and protocols. Through the use of gateways that convert formats and protocols between networks, the Internet appears externally as a single network, with hosts on interconnected networks appearing as interconnected hosts.

internet address: (1) An address for a computer on a network. The internet address consists of a network number and a host number that is unique for that network. (2) The AppleTalk address and network number of a socket.

ISOC: Abbreviation for the **Internet Society**; an organization formed to support a world-wide information network, and the governing body of the Internet Architecture Board.

K: See **kilobyte**.

Kbit: See **kilobit**.

Kbyte: See **kilobyte**.

kilobit (Kbit): A unit of measurement, 1024 bits, commonly used in specifying the capacity of memory integrated circuits. Not to be confused with **kilobyte**.

kilobyte (K): A unit of measurement consisting of 1024 (2^{10}) bytes. Thus, 64K memory equals 65,536 bytes. The abbreviation **K** can also stand for the number 1024, in which case **Kbyte** or **KB** or is used for kilobyte. See also **megabyte**.

Knowbot: A knowledge robot; a software program that provides information retrieval.

LAN: See **local area network**.

local area network (LAN): A group of computers connected for the purpose of sharing resources. The computers on a local area network are typically joined by a single transmission cable and are located within a small area such as a single building or section of a building. Compare **wide area network**.

local system: The computer from which a user originates a network command. Compare **remote system**.

local system administration: Management of a single computer. This includes such functions as starting up and shutting down the system, adding and removing user accounts, and backing up and restoring data. Compare **network administration**.

login: To identify yourself to a system or network and start to use it. Usually logging on requires a password, depending on the system. Same as **log on**; opposite of **log off**.

login name: In UNIX systems, the name of a user's account. Used for identification purposes.

login prompt: The prompt (usually login: on UNIX systems) by which a system tells you it is ready to accept your login name.

log off: To indicate to a system or network that you have completed your work and are terminating interaction.

MARK parity: A method of error checking in data transmission in which the most significant bit of every byte is set to 1. The receiving device checks for errors by looking for this value on each character. Compare **even parity**, **odd parity**, **space parity**.

megabit (Mbit): A unit of measurement equal to 1,048,576 (2^{16}) bits, or 1024 kilobits, commonly used in specifying the capacity of memory ICs. Not to be confused with **megabyte**.

megabyte (MB): A unit of measurement equal to 1024 kilobytes, or 1,048,576 bytes. See also **kilobyte**.

modem: Short for **modulator/demodulator**; a peripheral device that links your computer to other computers and information services using the telephone lines.

modem command: An instruction to a computer system, usually typed from the keyboard, that directs a modem attached to the computer to perform some immediate action.

multi-user: (adj.) Characterizes a mode or ability of an operating system to support several people using the same computer at once.

multi-user system: An operating system, such as UNIX, that allows many users to access application software simultaneously.

name: The name presented to users of a network to identify a given network service.

naming protocol: A protocol used by AppleTalk to associate a name with the physical address of a network service.

network: A collection of interconnected, individually controlled computers, together with the hardware and software used to connect them. A network allows users to share data and peripheral devices, such as printers and storage media, to exchange electronic mail, and so on.

network administration: Management of the software and hardware that connects computers in a network. This includes such functions as assigning addresses to hosts, maintaining network data files across the network and setting up internetwork routing. Compare **local system administration**.

network administrator: The person who is responsible for setting up and maintaining the network.

network connection: A combination of hardware and software that lets you set up a particular implementation of the AppleTalk network system, such as LocalTalk or EtherTalk.

network device: A computer, printer, modem, terminal or any other physical entity connected to a network.

Network File System (NFS): A protocol suite developed and licensed by Sun Microsystems that allows different makes of computers running different operating systems to easily share files and disk storage.

network manager: The person responsible for maintaining and troubleshooting the network.

network number: A unique number to each network in an internetwork that has been assigned by a seed router.

network system: A family of network components that work together because they observe compatible methods of communication.

NFS: See **Network File System**.

NIC: Abbreviation for **Network Information Center**; an organization that's responsible for supplying information for any of the component networks that make up the Internet.

NOC: Abbreviation for **Network Operations Center**; an organization that's responsible for the day-to-day operation of the component networks that make up the Internet.

node: (1) A device that's attached to a network and communicates by means of the network. (2) Any network device that has an address on the network. (Some network devices, such as modems, may be connected to a network but not be a node themselves.)

node number: A number that distinguishes one node from all others on the network.

NREN: Abbreviation for **National Research and Education Network**; an effort to combine the networks operated by the U.S. government into a single high-speed network.

odd parity: The use of an extra bit in data transmission set to 0 or 1 as necessary to make the total number of 1 bits an odd number; used as a means of error checking. Compare **even parity**, **MARK parity**, **space parity**.

offline: (adj.) Not currently connected to or under the control of the computer. Used to refer to equipment such as printers and disk drives, information storage media such as disks and the information they contain. Compare **online**.

online: (adj.) Currently connected to and under the control of the computer. Used to refer to equipment such as printers and disk drives, information storage media such as disks and the information they contain. Compare **offline**.

OSI model: The Open Systems Interconnection (OSI) reference model for describing network **protocols**, devised by the International Standards Organization (ISO); divides protocols into seven layers to standardize and simplify protocol definitions.

packet: A unit of information that has been formatted for transmission on a network.

port: (n.) (1) A socket on the back panel of a computer where you plug in a cable for connection to a network or a peripheral device. (2) A connection between the central processor unit and main memory or a device (such as a terminal) for transferring data. (3) A unique number that identifies a particular Internet service. (v.) To move software from one hardware architecture to another.

PPP: Abbreviation of **Point to Point Protocol**; a protocol that enables a computer to communicate with other computers using TCP/IP over standard telephone lines and high-speed modems.

protocols: The rules that govern interaction on a network. Protocols determine where, when, how and in what format information is transmitted.

random-access memory (RAM): The part of the computer's memory that stores information temporarily while you're working on it. A computer with 512K RAM has 512 kilobytes of memory available to the user. Information in RAM can be referred to in an arbitrary or random order, hence the term random-access. (As an analogy, a book is a random-access storage device in that it can be opened and read at any point.) RAM can contain both application programs and your own information. Information in RAM is temporary, gone forever if you switch the power off without saving it on a disk or other storage medium. An exception is the battery RAM, which stores settings such as the time, and which is powered by a battery. (Technically, the read-only memory (ROM) is also random access, and what's called RAM should correctly be termed read-write memory.) Compare **read-only memory**.

read-only memory (ROM): Memory whose contents can be read but not changed; used for storing firmware. Information is placed into read-only memory once, during manufacture. It remains there permanently, even when the computer's power is turned off. Compare **random-access memory**.

remote: (adj.) At a distance. Unable to be connected directly using local wiring only, but requiring communications devices.

remote computer: A computer other than your own but in communication with yours through telephone lines, network wiring or other communication links. A remote computer can be at any distance from your computer, from right beside it to thousands of miles away.

remote site: A computer or network that is accessed through a long distance communications medium, such as telephone lines, network wiring, ISDN or a satellite.

remote system: On a network, any computer other than the local system.

RFC: Abbreviation for **Request for Comments**; a collection of papers that define the Internet standards and proposed standards.

server: A computer that provides a particular service across a network. The service may be file access, login access, file transfer, printing and so on. Computers from which users initiate the service are called **clients**.

service: A specialized function that a network provides to users, such as file sharing and electronic mail.

service provider: An organization that provides connections to the Internet.

signature: A text file, usually five lines or less, containing your identification and contact information that is added to your network news articles and e-mail messages.

SLIP: Abbreviation for **Serial Line Internet Protocol**; a protocol that enables a computer to communicate with other computers using TCP/IP over standard telephone lines and high-speed modems.

socket: On a network, a communication mechanism originally implemented on the BSD version of the UNIX operating system. Sockets are used as endpoints for sending and receiving data between computers.

space parity: A method of error checking in data transmission in which the most significant bit of every byte is set to 0. The receiving device checks for errors by looking for this value on each character. Compare **even parity**, **MARK parity**, **odd parity**.

standard: A set of specifications for designing hardware or software that is recognized by multiple vendors, an official standards organization or both.

synchronous: Able to perform two or more processes at the same time, such as sending and receiving data, by means of a mutual timing signal or clock. Compare **asynchronous**.

synchronous transmission: A transmission process that uses a clocking signal to ensure an integral number of unit (time) intervals between any two characters. Compare **asynchronous transmission**.

TCP/IP: Abbreviation for **Transmission Control Protocol/Internet Protocol**; a suite of networking protocols developed at the University of California for the U.S. Department of Defense.

TELNET: A terminal emulation protocol that enables you to login remotely to other computers on the Internet, using a command-line interface.

terminal: A keyboard and display screen through which users can access a **host computer**.

terminal emulation: Software that enables a personal computer to communicate with a **host computer** by transmitting in the form used by the host's terminals.

topology: The physical layout of a network.

traffic: Transmissions traveling across a network.

tty: A terminal; abbreviated from teletypewriter, which was the first terminal device used on UNIX operating systems.

USENET: a network of about 3 million users (mostly UNIX users) that communicate using the UNIX-to-UNIX Copy Protocol (UUCP).

WAIS: Abbreviation for **Wide-Area Information Server**; an Internet service for looking up specific information in Internet databases.

WAN: See **wide area network**.

wide area network: Computers and/or networks connected to each other using long distance communication methods, such as telephone lines and satellites. Compare with **local area network**.

World Wide Web (WWW): A hypertext-based Internet service used for browsing Internet resources.

XOFF: A special character (value $11) used for controlling the transfer of data between a **DTE** and a **DCE**. When one piece of equipment receives an XOFF character from the other, it stops transmitting characters until it receives an XON. See also **handshaking, XON**.

XON: A special character (value $13) used for controlling the transfer of data between a **DTE** and a **DCE**. See also **handshaking, XOFF**.

XON/XOFF: A communications protocol that tells the computer to start or stop sending data by sending the appropriate character: either an XON or an XOFF. Compare **hardware handshake**.

Bibliography

Benedikt, Michael, ed. *Cyberspace: First Steps*. Cambridge, Massachusetts: MIT Press, 1991.

Brand, Stewart. *The Media Lab: Inventing the Future at MIT*. New York: Viking, 1987.

Cerf, Vinton G. "Networks," *Scientific American*, vol. 265, no. 3, pp. 72–81. New York: Scientific American, September 1991.

Comer, Douglas E. *Internetworking with TCP/IP: Principles, Protocols, and Architecture, Volume I*. 2d ed. Englewood Cliffs, New Jersey: Prentice Hall, 1991.

Engelbart, Douglas C. "A Conceptual Framework for the Augmentation of Man's Intellect." In *Vistas in Information Handling*, edited by Howerton and Weeks. Washington, D.C.: Spartan Books, 1963.

Gibson, William. *Burning Chrome*. New York: Ace Books, 1986.

———. *Count Zero*. New York: Ace Books, 1986.

———. *Mona Lisa Overdrive*. New York: Bantam Books, 1988.

———. *Neuromancer*. New York: Ace Books, 1984.

Gore, Al. "Infrastructure for the Global Village," *Scientific American*, vol. 265, no. 3, pp. 150–153. New York: Scientific American, September 1991.

Greif, Irene, ed. *Computer-Supported Cooperative Work: A Book of Readings*. San Mateo, California: Morgan Kauffman Publishers, 1988.

Hiltz, Roxanne. *Online Communities: A Case Study of the Office of the Future.* Norwood, New Jersey: Ablex Press, 1984.

Kapor, Mitchell. "Civil Liberties in Cyberspace," *Scientific American*, vol. 265, no. 3, pp. 158–164. New York: Scientific American, September 1991.

Karraker, Roger. "Highways of the Mind," *Whole Earth Review*, no. 70, pp. 4–11. Sausalito, California: Point Foundation, Spring 1991.

Krol, Ed. *The Whole Internet User's Guide & Catalog.* Sebastopol, California: O'Reilly & Associates, 1992.

LaQuey, Tracy, and Jeanne C. Ryer. *The Internet Companion: A Beginner's Guide to Global Networking.* Reading, Massachusetts: Addison-Wesley, 1993.

Laurel, Brenda, ed. *The Art of Human-Computer Interface Design.* Reading, Massachusetts: Addison-Wesley, 1990.

Licklider, J.C.R., Robert Taylor, and E. Herbert. "The Computer as a Communication Device." In *International Science and Technology*, April 1978.

McLuhan, Marshall, and Bruce Powers. *The Global Village: New Science.* Toronto: University of Toronto Press, 1988.

McLuhan Marshall. *Understanding Media: The Extensions of Man.* New York: McGraw-Hill, 1965.

Quarterman, John S. *The Matrix: Computer Networks and Conferencing Systems Worldwide.* Burlington, Massachusetts: Digital Press, 1990.

Toffler, Alvin. *Powershift: Knowledge, Wealth, and Violence at the Edge of the 21st Century.* New York: Bantam Books, 1990.

Turoff, Murray, and Roxanne Hiltz. *The Network Nation: Human Communication via Computer.* Reading, Massachusetts: Addison-Wesley, 1978.

Index

Colophon

The PC Internet Tour Guide was produced on a Macintosh
Quadra 700 using PageMaker 5.0. Body text is set in Adobe
Palatino, sidebars are DTC Futura and Futura Bold and
heads are DTC Kabel. The cover art was produced on a
Macintosh Quadra 800 using Adobe Illustrator.

Page proofs were output to a LaserWriter IINT and final
film output was produced using an Agfa ProSet 9800.
Internet software was tested on a Gateway 486 PC-compatible using a Practical Peripherals 14400 FAX modem.

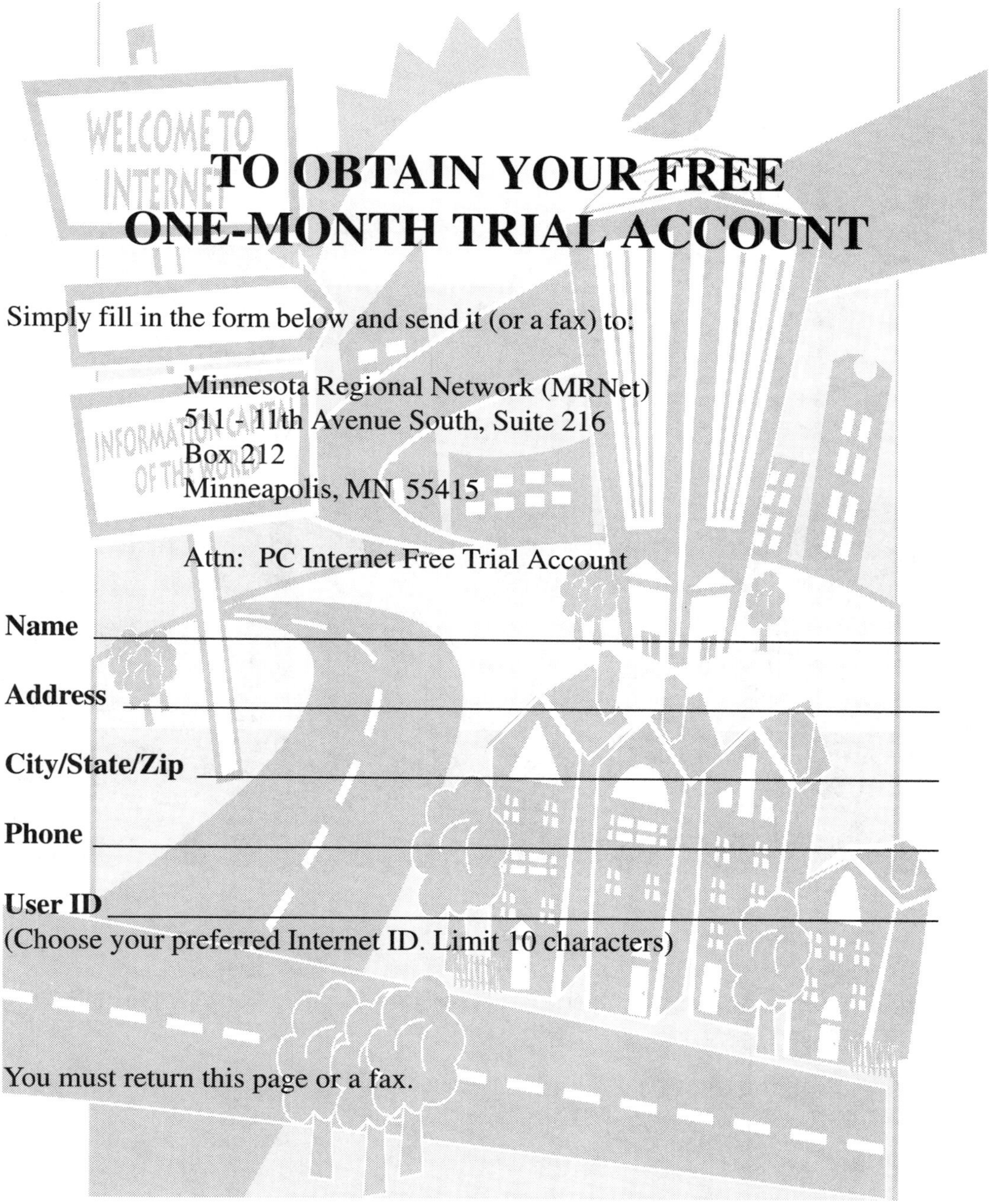

TO OBTAIN YOUR FREE
ONE-MONTH TRIAL ACCOUNT

Simply fill in the form below and send it (or a fax) to:

> Minnesota Regional Network (MRNet)
> 511 - 11th Avenue South, Suite 216
> Box 212
> Minneapolis, MN 55415
>
> Attn: PC Internet Free Trial Account

Name _____

Address _____

City/State/Zip _____

Phone _____

User ID _____
(Choose your preferred Internet ID. Limit 10 characters)

You must return this page or a fax.

From Ventana Press...

More Companions For Creative Computing

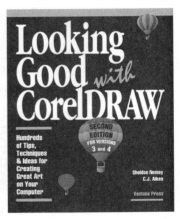

Available from bookstores or Ventana Press. Immediate shipment guaranteed. Your money returned if not satisfied. To order or for more information contact:

Ventana Press, P.O. Box 2468, Chapel Hill, NC 27515
919/942-0220   Fax 919/942-1140

Desktop Publishing With WordPerfect 6
$24.95
370 pages, illustrated
ISBN: 1-56604-049-3
The new graphics capabilities of WordPerfect 6.0 can save you thousands of dollars in design and typesetting costs. Includes invaluable design advice and annotated examples.

Desktop Publishing With Word for Windows, Second Edition
$21.95
328 pages, illustrated
ISBN: 1-56604-074-4
Desktop Publishing With Word for Windows is your key to creating attractive newsletters, brochures, ads, proposals and reports, correspondence and more.

Looking Good With CorelDRAW!, Second Edition
$27.95
328 pages, illustrated
ISBN: 1-56604-061-2
Guidelines and suggestions are given on how to best take advantage of CorelDRAW's powerful new desktop publishing features for Version 4.

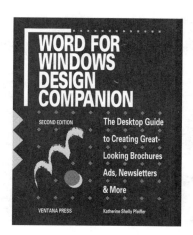

DOS, WordPerfect & Lotus Office Companion, Third Edition
$21.95
390 pages, illustrated
ISBN: 1-56604-048-5
The bible for business software users is now updated and expanded to include new versions of DOS (6.0), WordPerfect (6.0) and Lotus (2.4). This book will boost productivity for anyone who uses the most popular PC-compatible software packages!

Windows Shareware 500
$39.95
417 pages, illustrated
ISBN: 1-56604-045-0
This value-packed book/disk set introduces the world of afford-able software. Comes with 4 disks, including America Online membership disks and 10 hours of free online time.

Word for Windows Design Companion, Second Edition
$21.95
473 pages, illustrated
ISBN: 1-56604-075-2
Filled with innovative design advice and creative examples for getting the most from your Word investment. Covers Word for Windows through Version 6.

The Official America Online for Windows Membership Kit & Tour Guide
$34.95
402 pages, illustrated
ISBN: 1-56604-025-6
This book/disk set includes the AOL starter disk, 10 free hours of online time for new and current members, a free month's mem-bership plus your official AOL "tour guide."

WORK WONDERS WITH VENTANA VOODOO!

VOODOO NETWARE
$27.95
315 pages, illustrated
ISBN: 1-56604-077-9

Overcome network computing obstacles with insightful tips, tricks and shortcuts from *Voodoo NetWare*. This unique guide offers network managers an unparalleled collection of advice for troubleshooting, increasing user productivity and streamlining NetWare tasks. NetWare 4.0 users will find timely tips for a variety of commands and features.

VOODOO WINDOWS
$19.95
282 pages, illustrated
ISBN: 1-56604-005-1

A unique resource, *Voodoo Windows* bypasses the obscure technical information found in many Windows books to bring you an abundance of never-before-published tips, tricks and shortcuts for maximum Windows productivity. A one-of-a-kind reference for beginners and experienced users alike.

VOODOO OS/2

$24.95
288 pages, illustrated
ISBN: 1-56604-066-3
Optimize OS/2 with this unique collection of never-before-published tips and shortcuts from *Voodoo OS/2*! Whether multithreading or multitasking, you'll find a variety of productivity-enhancing ideas to help streamline tasks and save time.

VOODOO DOS, Second Edition

$21.95
277 pages, illustrated
ISBN: 1-56604-046-9
Updated for all versions of DOS through 6.0, *Voodoo DOS, Second Edition*, offers a wide range of time-saving techniques designed for all users. You'll find a wealth of help for customization; using the DOS editor; working with Shell and more! Learn to streamline time-consuming tasks and maximize your DOS productivity!

VOODOO MAC

$21.95
340 pages, illustrated
ISBN: 1-56604-028-0
Whether you're a power user or a beginner, *Voodoo Mac* has something for everyone! Computer veteran Kay Nelson has compiled hundreds of invaluable tips, tricks, hints and shortcuts that simplify your Macintosh tasks and save time, including disk and drive magic, font and printing tips, alias alchemy and more!

Special Offer: Buy all five books in the Ventana Press Voodoo™ Series Library and pay just $81.75, a 30% savings!

For faster service, order toll-free 800/743-5369 (U.S. Only).
Ventana Press, P.O. Box 2468, Chapel Hill, NC 27515 (919) 942-0220; Fax: (919) 942-1140

TO ORDER additional copies of *The PC Internet Tour Guide* or any Ventana Press title, please fill out this order form and return it to us for quick shipment.

	Quantity	Price		Total
Desktop Publishing With Word for Windows, Second Edition	_____	x $21.95	=	$_____
Desktop Publishing With WordPerfect 6	_____	x $24.95	=	$_____
DOS, WordPerfect & Lotus Office Companion, Third Edition	_____	x $21.95	=	$_____
Looking Good With CorelDRAW!, Second Edition	_____	x $27.95	=	$_____
The Official America Online for Windows Membership Kit & Tour Guide	_____	x $34.95	=	$_____
Voodoo DOS, Second Edition	_____	x $21.95	=	$_____
Voodoo Mac	_____	x $21.95	=	$_____
Voodoo NetWare	_____	x $27.95	=	$_____
Voodoo OS/2	_____	x $24.95	=	$_____
Voodoo Windows	_____	x $19.95	=	$_____
Windows, Word & Excel Office Companion	_____	x $21.95	=	$_____
Windows Shareware 500	_____	x $39.95	=	$_____
Word for Windows Design Companion, Second Edition	_____	x $21.95	=	$_____

Shipping: Please add $4.50/first book, $1.35/book thereafter; $8.25/book "two-day air," $2.25/book thereafter. For Canada, add $6.50/book.   = $_____

Send C.O.D. (add $4.50 to shipping charges)   = $_____

North Carolina residents add 6% sales tax   = $_____

                                              Total   = $_____

Name _____

Company _____

Address (No PO Box) _____

City_____ State_____ Zip_____

Daytime Telephone _____

___ Payment enclosed ___VISA ___MC Acc't # _____

Expiration Date_____ Interbank # _____

Signature _____

Please mail or fax to: **Ventana Press, PO Box 2468, Chapel Hill, NC 27515**
☎ **919/942-0220, FAX: 919/942-1140**
CAN'T WAIT? CALL TOLL-FREE ☎ 800/743-5369 (U.S. Only)!

Yes! I want to Stay Plugged In!
Send Me My Two Free Electronic Updates!

Navigating the strange and confusing highways and byways of the Internet can be a daunting proposition. New services spring up like fast food restaurants along the freeway. By sending in the card below, you'll receive two free updates via electronic mail and access to *The PC Internet Tour Guide* "Visitors Center." Your two free updates will feature the latest information about new Internet resources, file reviews, tips, tricks and pointers on finding and making the most of everything great on the Net.

The PC Internet Tour Guide electronic updates will be published and distributed on a quarterly basis. You'll receive the first two updates free of charge. After that, if you wish to continue receiving the updates, the yearly rate is only $25 for four issues. To subscribe now to a full year of updates (for a total of 6 issues), send a check for $25 (U.S. funds only) payable to Arts & Farces to: Arts & Farces, 2285 Stewart Avenue, Suite 1315, Saint Paul, MN 55116. For more information, send e-mail to: tour-guide-request@farces.com

For more details, see Appendix A. To receive your two free updates, fill out the card below (be sure to fill it out completely) and return it to:

> Ventana Press
> Attention: PC Internet Tour Guide
> PO Box 2468
> Chapel Hill, NC 27515

❏ **YES!** Please send me my two free editions of *The PC Internet Tour Guide* electronic update. Here's my e-mail address (in the standard format of username@domain.top-domain):

_____

❏ Please keep me up to date on future offers and information about other Internet and PC books and related materials.

Name _____

Organization or Company _____

Address _____

City _____ State _____ Zip _____

Ventana Press
Attention: PC Internet Tour Guide
PO Box 2468
Chapel Hill, NC 27515

Place
Stamp
Here

Ventana Press
Attention: PC Internet Tour Guide
PO Box 2468
Chapel Hill, NC 27515